BERWICK ON TWEED

COLDSTREAM

R·TILL

WOOLER

NORTHUMBERLAND

R·ALN

ALNWICK

ROTHBURY

R·REDE

R·N·TYNE

R·COQUET

KIELDER

HEXHAM

R·TYNE

R·S·TYNE

R·WEST ALLEN

R·EAST ALLEN

NEWCASTLE

Very best wishes

NORTHUMBERLAND
A Guide

Sacristy
Press

— STEPHEN PLATTEN —

Sacristy Press
PO Box 612, Durham, DH1 9HT

www.sacristy.co.uk

First published in 2022 by Sacristy Press, Durham

Sacristy Limited, registered in England & Wales, number 7565667

Printed and bound at Short Run Press Ltd, Exeter, UK

British Library Cataloguing-in-Publication Data
A catalogue record for the book is available from the British Library

ISBN 978-1-78959-231-3

This book is dedicated to Peter Burton,

in thanksgiving for all his work for the Shell Guide tradition.

CONTENTS

FOREWORD

by Ralph, Twelfth Duke of Northumberland

Northumberland offers much to the travelling visitor. The landscape stretches from heather-clad moorland in the west to long, sandy beaches on the east coast, with farms, forests and sparkling streams and lakes in between. Ancient castles reflect a violent and bloody past on the frontier between two nations at war for hundreds of years. Ruined abbeys stand as memorials to early Christianity and stand testimony to bloody violence at the hands of Viking raiders, vengeful armies and an acquisitive king. From Roman conquest to industrial innovation, Northumberland has a rich and colourful history, and has evolved a special culture in art, architecture, music and theatre, landscape and garden design, and in fine cuisine, much of which takes advantage of the fish and shellfish from its shores, meat and poultry from its farms and game from its woods and moors.

This wonderful new guidebook offers visitors a clear taste of every interesting place, leading them to well-known as well as obscure locations, and encouraging further investigation into the many gems that lie within this unusual and beautiful county.

PREFACE

Time was, perhaps a generation or so ago, when motorists would hurtle through Northumberland on their way to their Scottish holiday; Northumberland was little more than a gateway, glimpsed on the way to somewhere else. Times have changed and the county itself has become increasingly popular for holidays, and indeed there are now increasing numbers of "holiday lets", not to mention large numbers of second homes. This transformation is sufficient to make the writing of a new comprehensive guide a worthwhile initiative. But there are other reasons too for embarking on such a project. First of all, those who have either recently moved to Northumberland, or indeed who have lived here all their lives, are often interested in learning more about the remarkable and rich landscape within which they live. Second, the past fifty years have shown an extraordinary change in the landscape, the demography and the industry/living conditions within the county. The vast Kielder Water scheme, the decline of the coal, engineering and shipbuilding industries and the growth of tourism have each helped change the topography. Shifts in population and changes in industry and business have transformed the demography of the county.

The inspiration for this particular book lies with the former Shell County Guides, partly funded by the international oil company and then the brainchild of John Betjeman (later

knighted as the Poet Laureate) who edited them with the artist, John Piper.

Indeed, in describing this project, I have often referred to the embryonic work as "Not the Shell Guide to Northumberland". The earlier series began in 1934 with guides to Cornwall, Devon and Dorset. The guides had very much a character of their own. The remarkable Buildings of England series of county guides, begun after the Second World War by Sir Nikolaus Pevsner, contrasted with the Shell series inasmuch as they were focused on a far more technical architectural setting and with relatively little reference to those who had lived and worked in each county; they were straightforwardly factual but admittedly with some critical distance applied when it seemed vital to include this. Pevsner was, for example, quite a champion of modernism, alongside his extraordinary scholarship within architectural history. The Shell Guides were more quirky, and generally rooted in the present and past humanity of the locations they described.

The most recent and third edition of the Shell Guide to Northumberland was Thomas Sharp's 1969 guide, first published in 1937 with a second edition in 1954. Sharp was a town planner by profession, and indeed was the designer of the "model villages" built to house forestry workers as the enormous Kielder Forest developed. He brought to the task his own professional talents and skills. He was not frightened to write acerbically where he deemed it appropriate; he was particularly scornful of the impact of industry on the south-eastern corner of the county. Now, two generations on, it is time to review more sympathetically the contributions of the Industrial Revolution and the industries to which it gave birth. This present guide has attempted to achieve that without forsaking a proper critical eye in the process.

The three essays with which the book begins attempt to set the scene before the text embarks upon a gazetteer of the towns, villages, and other features of the county. The wealth of photographs is essential in any such book, and the principle established in the Shell Guides of using predominantly black and white images has been continued advisedly. As a medium, black and white photography is both an art form of its own and is particularly well adapted to providing images which bring out the contrasts between different aspects of both town and countryside, urban and rural.

The production of such a book does not spring forth *ex nihilo*! Many people have helped this book become a reality. Harland Walshaw, who took some photographs for the later Shell Guides, has played a seminal part in forming the author's approach; we are indeed fortunate to have his contribution, and that of Bill Boaden for digitizing his photographs; Harland was a friend and disciple of the multitalented Peter Burton to whom this book is dedicated. Peter was one of the key photographers for the Shell Guides, and also wrote his own follow-up to the series in the form of his *North Yorkshire—A Guide*, an excellent companion to the earlier books. Ian Hall, Michael Sadgrove, Peter Day,

Allan Brewes, Paul Kiddell and Angelo Hornak have also been very generous in their provision of excellent photographs. I am enormously grateful to Matthew Rice for the splendid end pages, but also for his enthusiasm more generally as I have worked on the book.

Lindsay Allason-Jones has kindly read the historical essay and the gazetteer entry for Newcastle, both as a professional archaeologist and as a resident of Tyneside for much of her life. Christopher Young offered some very useful information on Hadrian's Wall. John and Kitty Anderson of Kirkharle were both generous with their time and helpful suggestions about the project, far beyond their encyclopaedic knowledge of Capability Brown. John Brown-Swinburne read all the way through Thomas Sharp's 1969 Shell Guide, pointing out omissions and making suggestions for this book. Willy Brown-Swinburne was generous in showing us round Capheaton Hall and allowing us to take photographs. Tom Green, Philip Holland and John Carr-Ellison gave much to the book from their expert knowledge of the bird life of the county, and John was also a great encourager from the beginning. Tom Sample offered some fascinating information on Tyneside and Geoffrey Purves on Kirkwhelpington.

I am most grateful to the Northumberland Museums Service for allowing us free access to take photographs of Woodhorn Colliery, Monkseaton High School for the image of the school, and Jim Gibson for allowing us to use his images of the Berwick Barracks.

In the acknowledgments, I pay tribute and give thanks to a number of individuals and trust bodies who/which have contributed financially to this enterprise. It was Shell's sponsorship which made the earlier series possible, and those mentioned below have done the same thing for this book. I would also like to thank Sir Philip Mawer and Joe Kaines-Lang for facilitating the holding of these monies through the Berwick Barracks Heritage Trust, and Stuart Bankier, the treasurer. I am both honoured and very grateful to Ralph, His Grace, the Duke of Northumberland, for writing his most encouraging foreword.

Once again, my index supremo has been Kay Norman, and I could not have asked for more organized and jolly publishers in Natalie K. Watson and Richard Rutherford Hilton at Sacristy Press—enormous thanks to you all.

Without a doubt, however, I owe my greatest debt to Rosslie, my wife, who has supported me in countless publishing ventures, but in this case has accompanied me on any number of journeys across Northumberland. But, as if that were not enough, she has helped compile indices, an index card set of references, and then read through the entire text making crucial suggestions for improving the text. I cannot express my gratitude sufficiently.

— **Stephen Platten**

↓ Hedgehope

ACKNOWLEDGMENTS

The following have been very generous to make the publication of this book a reality, for which I offer my grateful thanks:

- Barbour Foundation
- Bishop of Newcastle
- Mr John Carr-Ellison
- Community Foundation for Tyne & Wear and Northumberland
- Lord Crewe Trustees
- Viscount Devonport
- Mr John Freeman
- Godman Trust
- Lord Hastings
- Mr Anthony Henfrey
- Sir Peter Marshall
- Sir Philip and Lady Mawer
- The Northumberland and Newcastle Society
- The Duke of Northumberland
- Viscount Ridley
- Sir Nigel Sherlock
- Lord Stevens
- Lord Vinson

LIST OF PHOTOGRAPHERS

Peter Burton (PB), Peter Day (PD), Ian Hall (IH), Angelo Hornak (AH), Kielder Water and Forrest Park, Stephen Platten (SP), Michael Sadgrove (MS), Harland Walshaw (HW), Allan Brewes, the Thomas Bewick Society, John Furnevel, Jim Gibson Photography, Paul Kiddell, Matthew Rice, David Taylor Photography, Monkseaton High School, Newcastle Cathedral, Newcastle City Library, Lady Waterford Trustees, Tate Images, Tate Britain.

All kindly contributed images.

LIST OF PHOTOGRAPHS

COLOUR PLATES

Cheviot Hills, Windy Gyle (MS)
ALNWICK Castle, Ducal Coach (SP)
ALNWICK Castle, Keep (SP)
BERWICK aerial view (Allan Brewes)
BERWICK Barracks, Riding the Bounds (Jim Gibson Photography)
BERWICK Lighthouse at the end of the pier (IH)
BERWICK hay harvest (SP)
BEWICK Old Bewick Church (SP)
BLANCHLAND Post Office (MS)
Breamish Valley (IH)
BYKER Wall (Lawsonrob/Wikipedia)
BYRNESS Church, Memorial Window To Those Lost In Building Catcleugh Dam (MS)
CHERRYBURN Thomas Bewick's Cottage (MS)
FARNE ISLANDS Puffins (Jonathan Cannon/Pixabay)
FORD Lady Waterford Hall, mural by Lady Waterford (Lady Waterford Trustees)
HALTWHISTLE water tank at the station (MS)
HEXHAM Tyne Green (MS)

Lindisfarne Gospels (State Library of South Australia)
LINDISFARNE St Aidan Statue (MS)
LINDISFARNE Castle (MS)
LINDISFARNE Priory, The Rainbow Arch (iStock/Gannet77)
NEWCASTLE Cathedral, spire and cityscape (Newcastle Cathedral)
NEWCASTLE Crown Spire (MS)
NEWCASTLE Grainger Market, Marks & Spencer Penny Bazaar (Newcastle City Library, Local Studies Collection)
J. M. W. Turner, NORHAM Castle (Tate Images, Tate Britain)
SCREMERSTON harvesting (SP)
Tyne Estuary, light tower at the end of South Pier (MS)
WALLINGTON Hall, mural in the central atrium (MS)
Mineworkers' banner for WEST SLEEKBURN (MS)
Model of Stephenson's Rocket (MS)
WYLAM Gantry and signal box (SP)
Hadrian's Wall, Sycamore Gap (Clementp.fr/ Wikimedia Commons)

↑ Northumberland landscape with Hadrian's Wall

THE LAND

Viewing England from above, and looking from south to north, reveals a powerful spine or backbone of high land, extending from the Peak District in Derbyshire, continuing through the Yorkshire Dales to Northumberland's Alston Moor and then, with the Cheviots, running up to the very southern tip of Scotland. Of course, this is not all one geological formation, but this northern end of the high land is a crucial part of what gives Northumberland its strong and robust character. The powerful landscapes owe their shape and panorama to the different geological patterns underlying this, England's northernmost county. So, if some areas of southern England are characterized by watercolours portraying soft green fields and thatched cottages, then Northumberland is "Cinemascope Country", breathing a healthy

↑ The Cheviots, Windy Gyle

→ Whinstone outcrop, **LINDISFARNE** Castle

air fuelled by a bracing climate and expansive large-scale scenery.

If we begin in the south, the massif of Alston Moor and the valleys of Allendale and the South Tyne effectively form the final expression of the Carboniferous outcropping of the Pennine chain of limestone, millstone grit and other associated sedimentary rocks. The incidence of lead and other metal ores is again consistent with the rock formations of the Pennines in Yorkshire and further south. The key break travelling north comes with the confluence of the North and South Tyne rivers, close to Hexham. The rich agricultural lands of the Tyne valleys form a natural gap between the two highland areas which form the northern extremity of this geological backbone. North of the Tyne Gap, however, we encounter the very different rock formations of the Cheviot Hills, which rise to a height of 816 m (2676 ft) in The Cheviot, 714 m (2343 ft) in Hedgehope and 619 m (2031 ft) at Windy Gyle—the northernmost peak, which straddles the border with Scotland. The Cheviots are hard igneous rocks, a remnant of an old volcano. In the eastern areas of Coquetdale and Redesdale, there are

also outcrops of Silurian deposits, still earlier in formation, and of the same age as the Lake District massif.

Moving further east there are sedimentary deposits of limestone, sandstone, and other associated strata. Prominent is the Fell Sandstone ridge forming a crescent shape starting from Berwick, making its way south through the Kyloe Hills and then curving round to the west, and finally northwards in the Simonside Hills which border on Coquetdale to the south of Rothbury. This pinkish sandstone provides unique character to the vernacular building material used throughout these parts of the county. The Cheviot foothills then slope down towards the coastal plain, and the landscape and its succession of river valleys have been further moulded and polished, most notably during the Ice Age. Melting glaciers brought down alluvial deposits adding to a flattish but uneven landscape in Milfield Plain. The plain itself was effectively the floor of a glacial lake. Corries were scoured out of the sides of the Cheviots. Erratics, formed of material foreign to these parts, were deposited by the ice. One of the most impressive is the enormous Kielder Stone. The Tyne valleys were also left with benching by the ice.

Older Carboniferous rocks are largely found within the foothills of the Cheviots. There are further Carboniferous limestone outcrops in the far north in the Scremerston coal and limestone measures; remains of limekilns are scattered across the county, even discernible on Lindisfarne—dramatic examples are clearly visible on the coast at Scremerston. More are visible around Alnwick and indeed all the way across to the Tyne Valley. The most productive coal measures were, of course, in the southeast triangle. It was these that helped Ashington to become the "largest pit village in the world"; the last surviving deep mine in the northeast of England at nearby Ellington closed in 2005 following a catastrophic flood within the pit. At Ellington, the seams were up to 3.5 m thick, with the deepest being 800 m below sea level. At one time, the workings extended 15 miles out under the sea. So, "bringing coals to Newcastle", as the old expression runs, indicates how dependent Victorian Britain became on the "black gold" mined at such enormous human cost in this south-eastern triangle of the county.

Another unique intrusive rock is the dolerite Great Whin Sill which makes its mark in prominences across Northumberland. The eastern extremity of the sill manifests itself in the twenty-eight islands which make up the Farnes. On a clear day, they sit rather ominously just off the coast, looking for all the world like enemy submarines emerging from the North Sea waters. Their *truly* ominous nature has, of course, been most obviously experienced in the numerous wrecks and disasters around the islands. The most famous one, doubtless, was the wrecking of the *Forfarshire*, which occasioned the valorous rescue of some of the crew by Grace Darling, the daughter of the lighthouse man at Longstone. On the coast, outcrops of the sill add drama to the scenery as the bases to three perfectly sited castles on Lindisfarne, at Bamburgh and at Dunstanburgh. The basalt-like columns forming the low cliffs at Howick are also impressive and offer a more detailed picture of the crystalline formation of the

↗ Sandstone, **BERWICK** old bridge
→ Sandstone, St Bartholomew, **NEWBIGGIN-BY-THE-SEA**

dolerite rock. Again, across the county, there are outcrops of this immensely hard rock. At various points, the Romans also took advantage of this when constructing Hadrian's remarkable 115-km-long Wall.

Alongside these varied rock formations and deposits, the county's rivers, running off the Cheviot watershed, are also key contributors to the overall character of the landscape. The most northerly is the Tweed, some 97 miles in length, most of its course being in Scotland, but with its estuary in Berwick. Moving south, the tiny Waren Burn issues into the sea at Budle Bay; although only an eleven-mile stream in total, its mouth supported a significant port at Waren Mill in the Middle Ages. The Aln too meets the sea at what was once the prosperous port of Alnmouth. Telford had constructed a toll road all the way from Hexham to Alnmouth for the transport of lime and other goods, and Alnmouth only ceased to be a significant port following the great storm of 1806, when the course of its estuary was radically changed. The Coquet, some 40 miles in length, winds its way down from the great army ranges of Redesdale past Rothbury and empties into the sea at the former staithe port and, more recently, impressive marina at Amble. Some of the most attractive scenery of mid-Northumberland is within upper Coquetdale. Only a little further south, the Blyth and Wansbeck enter the sea. Closer to the coast, they have lost some of their character through the industrialization of the landscape. Even here, however, higher up both valleys are attractive towns including Felton, Morpeth, and Mitford.

Finally, there is the mighty Tyne, captured mythically in David Wynne's dramatic sculpture of the "Tyne River God" set at the entrance to Newcastle's twentieth-century Civic Centre. The Tyne is 73 miles in length, and it changes its face throughout its "dual course", for its origins lie in the confluence of two rivers, the North and South Tynes. The North Tyne's waters are now harvested in the vast Kielder Water scheme (the largest artificial lake of northern Europe), bringing plentiful supplies of water to the cities and towns of north-east England and generating electrical power. All this is placed amidst the largest planted forest of northern Europe within wide areas of surrounding moorland. The River Rede and Redesdale again run through pretty, wild country, set as they are between Kielder Forest and the military ranges; it was this valley that was first used to harvest water in the county, with Catcleugh Reservoir having been completed as early as 1905. The South Tyne and the River Allen spring again in moorland areas, this time in the Carboniferous landscape of the North Pennines. Stunning scenery opens up all along the course of these rivers and later, towards Newcastle, the Tyne became a powerhouse of industry. From Wylam onwards, the combination of coal with the enterprise of remarkable Victorian engineers transformed the lower Tyne Valley—glassworks, mills and foundries all jostled with one another along its banks, and perhaps most famously in William Armstrong's great Elswick Works. The riverside is now transformed as one arrives at Newcastle and Gateshead, with so many of the industrial buildings having disappeared, including Lord Armstrong's vast works at Elswick and Scotswood. Further downstream were shipyards, ferries to mainland Europe, and

↑ **NEWCASTLE** Civic Centre, David Wynne, "Tyne River God"

↑ **BERWICK** aerial view

important port facilities at the former Tyne Commission Quay; even here modern enterprise has opened up the riverside to new industries, including tourism. Finally, the commanding ruins of Tynemouth Priory, together with both northern and southern piers, herald the river's emergence into the North Sea.

Northumberland remains a rich farming county. Traditionally the fertile pastures of the Tyne Valley have focused on dairy. The equally rich agricultural land of the coastal plain, with the land skirting the Cheviots to the north and east, remains productive arable territory. Farms tend

to be large, and Northumberland Estates (land relating to the Percys) owns c.100,000 acres—the majority of which is farmland, although there has been diversification. Some landowners have diversified by installing substantial windfarms and solar power generation. The area around Berwick and immediately to the south is among the most highly productive wheat and barley country in the UK, and there are substantial maltings in Berwick itself. Elsewhere in this part of the county, wheat and other cereal crops predominate. The hill country is largely given over to sheep farming, with mostly Cheviot and

Swaledale but with Blackface often represented. Livestock farming of cattle is another key contributor to the agricultural economy.

The coast of Northumberland is shaped by its bordering onto the lowland plain, largely formed of sedimentary rock. It is rarely craggy except where the Great Whin Sill intrudes, for example from Dunstanburgh to Howick, or where limestone and sandstones outcrop. So the coast from Marshall Meadows north of Berwick, and then south beyond Scremerston, sports some modest cliffs of different sandstone and limestone outcrops, with former limekilns still visible on Cocklawburn Beach. Magnesian Limestone cliffs make a momentary appearance at Tynemouth. But a great deal of the coast is skirted with dunes offering their own unique habitat for birds, insects, rodents and various kinds of grasses. A long stretch of dune country extends from Cocklawburn, past Goswick, and then down to and including Lindisfarne. This continues further towards Budle Bay and then takes up again at Bamburgh running down to Seahouses and on to Beadnell. It picks up yet again from Alnmouth to Amble and then continues in a glorious sweep along Druridge Bay. Patches of similar scenery appear once more south of Blyth and towards Seaton Sluice. Industry has left its marks and sea coal remains a common feature of the beaches; in places industry has had sufficient impact to require remedial measures. At Newbiggin, for example, half a million tonnes of sand have been imported from Skegness in Lincolnshire to restore the beach. Elsewhere, new industries have sprung forth in the wind farms just off the coast to the south of Blyth.

The landscape has, of course, also set the scene for communication in this frontier county. The courses of the old drovers' roads can still be traced clearly in both upper Alndale and Coquetdale. Predictably, these fairly challenging arteries were used both positively and negatively. Salters' Road speaks for its own utility, but all were also used for the passage of sheep, cattle and other commodities. However, their comparative isolation made for dangerous journeys on account of the violent outlaw behaviour of the Border Reivers. These roads often followed earlier trackways whose origins are lost in the mists of time. Then, although the Roman conquest powerfully marked out the edge of the Empire with Hadrian's Wall, still the conquerors built a more northerly network of roads. In this debatable land between the Tyne-Solway fortifications and the less developed barrier of the Antonine Wall from Forth to Clyde, a road network was established across what was often an uninviting landscape. Dere Street carried the legionaries over the present-day border through Jedburgh. On its way, at Bremenium, next to present-day Rochester, another highway branched due east, across the Cheviot divide, to join up with another north–south artery, known now as Devil's Causeway, at Alavna, that is, Low Learchild. Devil's Causeway carried people and materials from Corbridge to modern day Tweedmouth, almost certainly terminating at a Tweedside port there where military supplies could be transferred from small ships to continue their journey using land transport and making their way to the fort at Trimontium next to modern-day Melrose. These ships would have been coasters bringing materials from the main port/fort of Arbeia (South Shields).

Much more recently, geology posed a challenge to Field Marshal Wade, when building his "Military Road" from 1751–8, parallel with Hadrian's Wall. This had been occasioned by the shock received by the government in the 1745 Jacobite rebellion. Just a little later, at the turn of the nineteenth century, Telford rose to the challenge of the same landscape as he built his road from Hexham across to Alnmouth, and, at the same time, improved other highways. He had, for example, seen the Morpeth-Wooler-Coldstream road as the obvious link between Newcastle and Edinburgh. In pursuit of this aim, he constructed some of the earliest diversions around villages—what we would now call bypasses.

Only a few years later, Northumberland became the birthplace of railways. Again, land and landscape played a significant part. First, the need to transport both coal and lime necessitated wagonways and then later railways to move ore and associated products. Then commerce, in the form of "the great railway race" to build new, and often competing lines, had also to face the challenge of the land. The High Level Bridge in Newcastle and the Royal Border Bridge over the Tweed are outstanding examples of engineering meeting these challenges. Numerous other engineering feats (some now no longer used)—cuttings, tunnels, and viaducts—were a product of this extraordinary revolution. The little station at Wylam is one of the oldest in Britain still in continuous use, having been opened in the 1840s as part of this great enterprise.

All that we have described offers a wide variety of habitats, some of which remain unique or unusual in the flora and fauna which they support. Then, the night skies—both in the Ingram Valley and throughout the Kielder Forest—are some of the darkest of English skies, free of the light pollution inherent in urban landscapes. Kielder is a fascinating environment in itself, made more unusual by human intervention both in afforestation and the harvesting of water. Much of the original moorland covering Redesdale and the North Tyne Valley was spread in almost pampas-like fashion with *Molinia caerulea*, a hardy moorland grass. The development of the great forest, which took over from the grassland, dates back to the Great War, when timber shortages began to rear their heads. This resulted in the creation of the Forestry Commission in 1919. Land prices were low, particularly in remote areas—also land holdings were often large which made government acquisition of land that much simpler. It was an Australian, Roy Robinson, who was the visionary entrepreneur who took forward the work of the Commission, and who notably focused on Kielder; indeed, he was ennobled later as Baron Robinson of Kielder Forest. Without a doubt, as the largest single area of forestry in England, this has manifested one of the key changes in the county's landscape in the twentieth century. The forest has predictably been an excellent habitat for roe deer, especially in younger parts of the forest. In the battle for the survival of the red squirrel against the incursion of the North American grey squirrel, the relative remoteness of Kielder has been important; control of grey squirrels, however, remains important in buffer

zones. Amongst birds, who thrive in coniferous settings, is the crossbill nesting high in the trees, and also, black grouse. Here, as within so much of the high land in Northumberland, is a common home for birds of prey, including peregrines, buzzard, goshawk, kestrel, merlin and sparrowhawk.

The significance of Kielder has increased with the construction of the dam and reservoir, which is the largest in terms of water capacity in England; ironically, the water requirements have dropped considerably since the scheme was completed. The lake has, however, transformed the scenery, softening the impact of the vast forest to some degree. In the 1970s, you could still follow the course of the former Borders Railway all the way through to Deadwater and Riccarton Junction; now much

of the course is submerged, with the only clear survival being that of the substantial Kielder Viaduct. Alongside water supply and electricity generation, the reservoir has also offered new habitats and plentiful leisure possibilities for the Northeast. Moorland and forest extend west—well beyond Kielder and across to the moorland and forest of east Cumbria at Eskdalemuir and Spadeadam Forest, the location of the former rocket-launching site, just north of the village of Gilsland, a village shared by Cumbria and Northumberland.

Flora in other parts of Northumberland include the rich agricultural crops already mentioned. Agriculture has continued to develop in much the same way as in other parts of England, with landscapes transformed in past generations by outbreaks of "yellow fever" in the popular

planting of the cash crop of oilseed rape. Moving from the moorland and forest scenery strikes a remarkable contrast as one moves south down the North Tyne Valley to the lower pastures of the Tyne Gap. The presence of fertile land gave birth to arable farming alongside dairy and livestock. One by-product of arable farming was the construction of "gingangs" both in the Tyne Valley and also further north, in the rich pastures of lower Coquetdale. The gingang was generally a circular (sometimes polygonal or square) building with a slate or stone tiled roof. It was either attached to, or adjacent to, a barn. It was used as a threshing shed. A horse would walk (gang) round a central spindle which worked the thresher and consequently emptied the wheat ears into the gin.

Moving to the animal world, Northumberland has its share of unusual species. In the north, close to the Borders, and around Hethpool and Kilham, feral or wild goats are fairly easily spotted in the valleys running into the Cheviots. More remarkable still, however, is the unique Chillingham herd of wild cattle, immortalized in Thomas Bewick's celebrated engraving. The herd lives in a park of some 300 acres on the slopes of Fell Sandstone uplands. It is a closed herd and entirely inbred, requiring immense care in the sporadic outbreaks of foot and mouth disease. The cattle are white with partially red

↙ **KIELDER** paddleboarder

↓ Gingang in southern Northumberland

ears, and a bull acts as "king" of the herd. Once the bull becomes too old or weak, he will be fought by a younger beast who will take over his role. The herd appears to derive directly from mediaeval cattle, perhaps of a feral kind. Fortunately, in recent years, numbers have risen to about a hundred. The late Dowager Countess of Tankerville worked tirelessly for the survival of the herd, and it now falls within the care of the Chillingham Wild Cattle Association.

As we have already seen, the coast brings its own unique interest. Craster, through the Robson family, boasts of the world's best kippers, and direct experience suggests that they are accurate in their claim! The little harbour at Craster still has a tiny fleet of fishing boats. Fishing has declined in Northumberland, as indeed it has throughout the United Kingdom. The fishing harbour formerly on the northern edge of Berwick is now no more than an archae-ological site. Seahouses retains a small fishing fleet and has diversified into fishing trips for vis-itors—it also performs an important role in pro-viding regular boating trips to the Farnes. The coast has continued its role in providing facili-ties for holidaymakers. Tastes have, of course, changed and the attractive seaside buildings at Spittal and Newbiggin now have a slightly dated feel. Along the coast, however, there is much activity, with Seahouses continuing to provide the best in traditional English holiday fayre.

And so to bird life. Alongside the redshanks, eiders (only on tidal water) and curlews are seen on the rivers, but it is the coast which offers the vast profusion of birds for which the county has become famous. The estuary of the Tweed at Berwick and the early river course running up toward Norham form together the habitat for a remarkable bevy of mute swans, some eiders in the tidal waters, sandpipers and oystercatchers aplenty. Whooper swans from Iceland winter here, and their red necks are signs of them feeding on the mineral waters back in their Iceland habitat. In agricultural areas, game birds including pheasants and partridges are not only common but are bred for the open shooting season; red and black grouse, ring ouzels, golden plovers and curlews are seen in moorland areas across the county. Pink-footed geese, greylag geese and pale-bellied Brent geese winter in Northumberland, and the pink-footed and greylag geese fly across noisily in the autumn in great squadrons! Rather amazingly, kittiwakes enjoy nesting on the taller buildings in Newcastle. While focusing on flying fauna, however, one should not forget the provision by another Robson family who founded the amazing honey farm at Horncliffe. The Robsons have hundreds of hives scattered over north Northumberland and the Borders. Every con-ceivable product of the apiary is available at the farm, from candles to polish and from soap to honey; a fascinating transport and agricultural museum is an integral part of the farm.

Then moving south with the bird popula-tion, Budle Bay offers a remarkable viewpoint for waders—especially at low tide, of course. The Farnes are a sanctuary and a trip in a boat from Seahouses offers a rich harvest of sightings for bird lovers—always wear a hat, however: Arctic terns can be savage in their attacks on the human hairline. Puffins are here in abundance, and the National Trust, which is the guardian of the islands, has effectively made the puffin

↑ **ALSTON** signposts

the logo for the Farnes. Guillemots, razorbills, Sandwich and roseate tern habitats are also important on the Farnes. Coquet Island, an outcrop of limestone off the coast at Amble, is managed by the RSPB and is another sanctuary for bird life, as indeed are the dunes coming south from Goswick to Lindisfarne. Druridge Bay and even the coastal strip much further south, which includes the former coalfield, continues the same dune habitat.

This brief essay has merely scratched the surface of the richness of this panoramic county. Our intention has been to illustrate how the nature of the land itself has been so crucial in forming the character and life of the county. Other volumes noted in the bibliography will carry the enthusiastic individual into greater detail and knowledge of this remarkable environment. It forms a dramatic set of vertebrae holding together the most northerly part of the powerful backbone of England. Now it may be appropriate to ask, how has human habitation and a continuously unfolding history built upon that foundation?

↑ Hadrian's Wall

↓ **CAWFIELDS** fortlet

THE STORY

Known history begins to unfold very early on in Northumberland—the land itself would have appeared as a rugged and mixed rocky *tabula rasa*, but this apparently clean slate also offered rich soils for agriculture and cultivation early on. So far, the evidence suggests that human habitation began here as the Ice Age retreated, that is at the beginning of the Mesolithic Period, the Middle Stone Age. This *was* then real hunter-gatherer country, and simple flint tools have been found throughout the county. The earliest evidence for human *settlement* in the area, and some of the earliest within the country as a whole, has been excavated in Howick and dated to 9–10000 BC. It was, however, in the New Stone Age, the Neolithic period, that something of a revolution occurred. Agriculture developed and more sophisticated tools have been found in Coquetdale and the Breamish and Till Valleys, and although the evidence remains limited, there are signs of settlement at Yeavering and Thirlings. Burial places are clearer—notably long cairns—of which there are examples in Kielder and Bellshiel Law in the Otterburn ranges.

From 2000 BC onwards, there are clear signs of the further development of social structure with land areas divided up for farming. Around Milfield was a grouping of henges, thought to be spiritual centres. Today Maelmin, at Milfield, has a helpful reconstruction of a typical henge set as the focus of an area where much evidence of such ritualistic practice has been discovered. Another puzzling but well-scattered survival is the plethora of "cup and ring" marked rocks, most frequently cut into Fell Sandstone. Dod Law near Doddington sees them in particular profusion, but they are also scattered elsewhere; the "Ringses" are part of this. There remains much uncertainty as to the meaning of these carvings—one assumption is that they are associated with ritual of some sort. Early standing stones are found in the south of the county, for example at Ingoe and Matfen. Stone circles are rarer; the fascinating "ear-shaped" stones at Duddo have been dated to c.4000 BC. In the Neolithic period, stone cairns were used for burials, as can be seen near Chew Green, also on the edge of the ranges nearer to Alwinton, whilst examples of Bronze Age cist burials can be found at Blawearie, northeast of Eglingham. The settlements of the living during the Bronze Age remain visible across the Cheviots.

It is from the turn of the next millennium, c.1000 BC, that we see the growth in the number of hill forts. These are numerous, with smaller examples up the Ingram Valley, and at Harehope, Hepburn and Ros Castle near Bewick; the impressive earthworks on the double summit of Yeavering Bell, however, cover almost fourteen acres. Signs of circular stone houses of this same period can be detected in the lee of ramparts near Ingram and at Hesleyhurst, south of Rothbury. Crop marks indicate many Iron Age

homesteads along the coastal plain, and in the North Tynedale and Redesdale Valleys. All this evidence reminds us of significant activity well before the Romans arrived with their legions.

The Roman conquest in the first century AD, while not exactly a *Blitzkrieg*, was nevertheless accomplished with some expedition; by AD 79, we know that Agricola had reached the Tay. At the beginning of the second century, however, something appears to have disturbed the calm sufficiently to alarm the Emperor, Hadrian. His visit to Britain, in 122, occasioned the start of the construction of a frontier barrier from the Tyne to the Solway—some 76 miles or 122 km. Images of Hadrian's Wall striding across the often rough terrain of southern Northumberland and northern Cumbria are startling reminders of the extraordinary scope and massive nature of this piece of second-century civil engineering. Hadrian's first plans were relatively simple, intended to swiftly take forward this linear evidence of the might of Rome. The wall itself was to be of stone (except initially that stretch which crosses Cumbria, as we now know it, which was to be of turf) about 3 m thick and faced with dressed, coursed sandstone and (much less frequently) whinstone. Mortar, sometimes just clay, was used to bond the stones together. On the north side, there was a level tract 6 m wide, in some cases containing stake pits or *lilia*, and

← **CHESTERS** hypocaust   ↑ **CHESTERS** Roman sculpture

dividing the curtain wall from a V-shaped ditch, again 6 m wide and 3 m deep. The height of the wall is uncertain, although it has been calculated to have been c.4.6 m rising to about 6 m where there was a parapet. The wall was the basis for patrols rather than a defensive platform. At the end of every Roman mile was a milecastle (something between a gateway and tiny fort), and evidence of a number of these can be seen at Cawfields and Housesteads; two turrets were placed between each set of milecastles; good examples are found at Denton and Brunton.

A few years on, however, there was a significant change in policy: new forts were to be built some 6 to 9 miles apart to supplement those on the Stanegate to the south—in Northumberland these were at Benwell, Rudchester, Haltonchesters, Chesters, Great Chesters and Housesteads. The other significant new element was the construction of the Vallum. This large earthwork consisted of a flat-bottomed ditch, with a level berm on either side of it and continuous upcast banks. A new eastern extension was also built to Wallsend. Much later still the fort at Carrawburgh was constructed, and the early fort at Carvoran, at the junction of the Stanegate and Maiden's Way roads, was rebuilt in stone.

In AD 136, Hadrian died and was succeeded by Antoninus Pius, who wished to expand the Roman Empire into Scotland. In AD 139, Antoninus rebuilt the bases at Corbridge and High Rochester before conducting campaigns in Scotland and constructing the Antonine Wall, as the new frontier between the Forth and the Clyde. Antoninus died in AD 161, and then the frontier retreated to the southern wall. Although Hadrian's Wall was refurbished, it was still breached in about AD 180, when local tribes "crossed the wall" and did "much damage, killing a general and the troops he had with him"; peace was swiftly restored. But, at the start

of the third century, Septimus Severus, faced with more rebellion, attempted to invade to the north, rebuilding Hadrian's Wall to a narrower gauge, but this venture failed. Throughout the centuries, there were constant refurbishments, yet civilian life in places like Corbridge thrived. Instability increased in the fourth century, and eventually the sack of Rome and further problems in mainland Europe led to the withdrawal of all troops to Rome, in AD 411. Doubtless, this would not have been a first choice posting for all Roman foot soldiers, as W. H. Auden's amusing lines suggest:

Over the heather the wet wind blows,
    I've lice in my tunic and a cold in my nose.
The rain comes pattering out of the sky,
    I'm a Wall soldier, I don't know why.
The mist creeps over the hard grey stone,
    My girl's in Tungria; I sleep alone.
Aulus goes hanging around her place,
    I don't like his manners, I don't like his face.
Piso's a Christian, he worships a fish;
    There'd be no kissing if he had his wish.
She gave me a ring but I diced it away;
    I want my girl and I want my pay.
When I'm a veteran with only one eye
    I shall do nothing but look at the sky.

Apart from the Wall itself there are, of course, other remnants of the Roman occupation, and some of the forts and roads surface in this book (see the gazetteer). Dere Street and Devil's Causeway are relatively easily traceable on a map, and there are impressive fragments of structures at High Rochester and the old Roman town at Corbridge. It is remarkable that there

↑ Heavenfield

is also clear evidence of the Roman occupation on both the east and west sides of modern Newcastle—the relatively recent presentation of Segedunum, to the east of the city, is a positive outcome from the recent decline of certain industries.

The next unique element in the history of the county comes from the re-evangelization of England in the seventh century. This would eventually result in the kingdom of Northumbria becoming one of the key crucibles

← **HEXHAM** Abbey, the worn night stair
↑ **HEXHAM** Abbey, crossing ceiling

of European Christian civilization and culture. The seventh and eighth centuries were tumultuous but concluded with the uniting of the two Northumbrian kingdoms, the southern kingdom of Deira and the northern, Bernicia. In 616, Edwin had been installed as king of these two united sub-kingdoms by Raedwald of East Anglia (thought to have been the king

↑ **HEXHAM** Abbey, Frith stool

whose remains were discovered in the ship burial at Sutton Hoo). Edwin was defeated and slain at the Battle of Hatfield Chase by Penda and Cadwallon, after which the two kingdoms were again sundered. Oswald succeeded him and thence defeated Cadwallon at Heavenfield, reuniting the kingdoms. The surviving material culture from this period is very thin. A modern large wooden cross and a nearby chapel mark the assumed location of the Battle of Heavenfield, near the village of Wall. The outline of Edwin's palace at Yeavering was discovered through aerial photography and later was the subject of an excavation under Brian Hope-Taylor. The recently converted Edwin brought Paulinus (later Bishop of York) to Northumbria, beginning re-Christianization following the Roman tradition. Oswald was also a Christian, and he persuaded the monks on Iona, this time from the Irish tradition, to send missionaries south. The second and successful missionary, who also became counsellor to the king, was Aidan. Aidan is revered at his shrine in Bamburgh Church, and also commemorated by a statue in Holy Island churchyard. Bamburgh was Oswald's capital, although no evidence of his palace can be seen; it is likely to have been under the same site now occupied by the castle. One material survival which has recently received greater prominence is the collection of remains from the Bowl Hole early mediaeval cemetery some 300 m south of the castle. These skeletons, first discovered in 1816–17, are thought to be the remains of members of the royal court of Northumbria. The skeletons have now been reburied in an ossuary in the crypt beneath the east end of Bamburgh Church.

Aidan set up his monastery on Lindisfarne and later became the first bishop there. The holy Cuthbert, whose shrine is in Durham Cathedral, followed Aidan later in the seventh century. Cuthbert's mortal remains travelled far, after his death, as monks from Lindisfarne sought to escape the pillaging of Danish invaders. From this tiny kernel, alongside the work and witness of the monastery at Jarrow/Wearmouth, issued riches which marked the growth of culture in this northern kingdom. The remarkable Lindisfarne Gospels, for example, might well be claimed as the oldest surviving, most spectacular book produced in England. Cuthbert's pectoral cross and other artefacts are yet more examples of the richness born of the kingdom of Northumbria. In 2018, the Codex Amiatinus, another product of the period, was brought from Rome for the first time in well over 1,000 years for an exhibition, *Anglo-Saxon Kingdoms*, in the British Library.

Interestingly, the Danish invaders did not settle in Northumbria, as is clear from the paucity of Danish place names, in contrast to such names in Yorkshire, Lincolnshire and Norfolk. Nonetheless, this did not mean that the Northumbrians lived in peace—far from it! The scattered battle sites across the county are evidence of the continued hostility between the Scots and the Northumbrian English. Halidon Hill, Homildon Hill and Otterburn (commemorated in the *Ballad of Chevy Chase*) are just a sprinkling of the battlegrounds discovered in almost any traversal of Northumberland. It

↓ **BAMBURGH** Church, crypt to the east

was the Battle of Carham, however, in 1018, which helped establish the beginnings of a border between the two kingdoms and indeed appears to have irrevocably secured Lothian as part of Scotland. The continuing hostilities, alongside the presence of the Border Reivers, families of outlaws who were frequently dangerously violent and under the control of neither kingdom, help to explain the extraordinary number of tower houses, pele towers and bastles (fortified farmhouses) across the county. Some of these eventually became quite grand and were incorporated into larger manor houses or even mansions. At least four—at Elsdon, Embleton, Alnham and Shilbottle—were, for some centuries, used as vicarages. Halton Castle is one fine example of a pele tower becoming first a fifteenth-century manor house, and then later a seventeenth-/eighteenth-century country mansion. In Haltwhistle, there is a rare example of an urban pele tower which was later absorbed into a hostelry. Crawley Tower near the village of Powburn, in contrast, is a maintained ruin.

Proximity to the border also made Northumberland a realm of castles. Both by their position and feeling of presence, Alnwick and Bamburgh are arguably two of the most splendid fortresses in Britain, alongside the royal castle at Windsor. Alnwick's location on the bluff above the Aln indicates why it was built *there*, as a defensive stronghold; something similar could be said of Bamburgh, set high up on the coast on a prominence provided by an outcrop of the Great Whin Sill. Newcastle and Berwick castles, despite the Philistine manner in which they were despoiled in the Victorian "railway race", still stand as sentinels above Tyne and Tweed respectively. Other castles are often tower houses which were rebuilt as private residences but licensed by the then monarch to include defensive crenellation; Langley, Haughton and Bellister are just three such examples.

Threats from the north led to the construction of significant defensive structures in Berwick, for over four centuries. King Edward I built substantial defensive walls from 1313 onwards. Remnants of these walls to the north of the town are still clearly visible. Elsewhere, to the east, and along the Tweed estuary, they are now buried beneath the later walls built in

about the threat of Mary, Queen of Scots. Elizabeth's rebuilding of Berwick's defences was the largest single infrastructure project of her reign. This time the north perimeter walls were constructed closer to the heart of the town and an octagonal watch tower was added to spy out possible incursions from over the border. The walls, which are similar to those around Lucca in Italy, remain impressive and offer a great vantage point from which to see the town and indeed beyond.

With the imprisonment, and later the execution of Mary, the military threat receded, and the walls were never fully completed to the original plans. For just over a century, the Borders became less of an uncertain land. Furthermore, with the accession of James VI of Scotland as James I of England, even the wildness of the Reivers was tamed, as governments began to work in unison. This was not to last, however, for the 1715 Jacobite rebellion lit again the torches of war; the British government was seriously unhorsed by the lack of security which it revealed. Their immediate response was to start building the first purpose-built infantry barracks in England, in 1717. Thus came into being the Ravensdowne Barracks in Berwick, designed initially by Nicholas Hawksmoor. The first troops marched in, in 1721, and the barracks remained in use all the way through to 1963, having by then been the depot for the King's Own Scottish Borderers for the best part of a century. History, however, tells that this was not the last to be heard of the Jacobites. The 1745 rebellion occasioned still further nervousness from central government. This provoked another remarkable civil engineering

Tudor times. Alarmed by the Franco-Scottish alliance, Henry VIII built new bastions at Lord's Mount at the northeast corner of the town. Queen Elizabeth I remained concerned

← **BERWICK** Watch Tower

↑ **BERWICK** Bridges

achievement, this time in the south of the county, with Field Marshal Wade's construction of the Military Road along the route of Hadrian's Wall.

In many ways, it was the eighteenth century that heralded the greatest revolution in modern times. There were several contributors to this. The enclosures, which had been proceeding from the sixteenth century onwards, came to something of a climax with the Inclosure Act of 1773; widespread abuse of this Act by landowners exacerbated its impact on the landscape. The impact of the enclosures, as it gathered further pace, was to remove common land and bring it into private ownership. Predictably this changed the landscape profoundly, with walls, hedgerows and individual fields replacing the previously open countryside. At the same time, the last remnants of the common strip-farming of the ancient "open field system" were brought to an end. Across the county, as indeed elsewhere in England, clear evidence of this survives, with the broad furrows indicating where the "strip lynchets" were previously farmed. Sometimes these are even found in higher and more remote places, where land might now look to be rather infertile. Rather incongruously, the golf links at Magdalene Fields, to the northeast of Berwick

29

↑ **CAPHEATON** Hall, south front

town centre, require the player to ascend and descend many of these ridges and furrows along certain parts of the course! The enclosures in Northumberland were often the work of large landowners, which may partly account for the long stretches of straight road in the county.

As with much of England, both prosperity and fashion changed the architectural landscape of the county during the eighteenth century, with the building of substantial country houses, often in Palladian or semi-Palladian style. Two of the most remarkable are Vanbrugh's Seaton

↑ **SEATON DELAVAL** detail of columns
→ **SEATON DELAVAL** rusticated columns

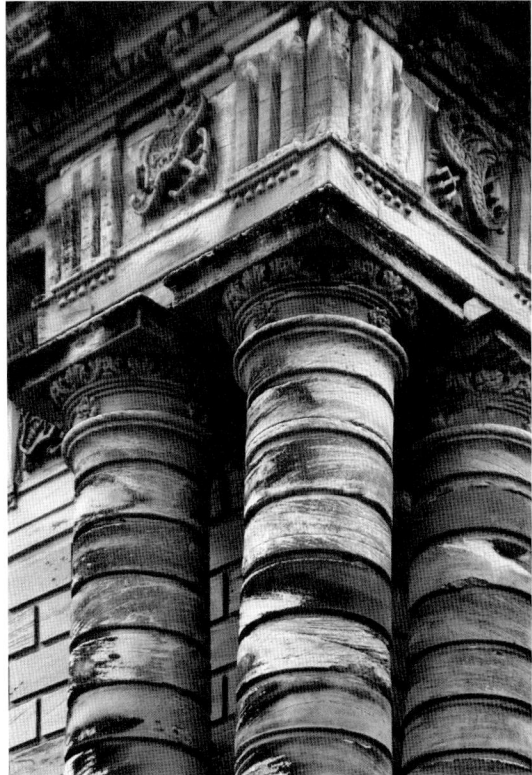

Delaval Hall for the Hastings family, built in English Baroque (rooted in the Palladian fashion introduced by Inigo Jones), and then the remodelling of Wallington Hall for the Blacketts. Across Northumberland lesser piles also emerged, often through the enlargement of former farmhouses or by expanding bastles and tower houses; at Belsay you can see each stage as the family built afresh on a new plot. Both the Agrarian and Industrial Revolutions produced the flowering of a new gentry, many of whom then made their mark by constructing impressive new mansions, in the Classical style, representing their new status within society.

That part of the county which experienced the most radical changes from the Industrial Revolution was, however, the south-eastern triangle moving north from the estuary of the River Tyne. The discovery of large coal reserves in this part of the county, together with the presence of good port facilities on the river, and on the coast northwards toward Blyth, meant the burgeoning of new industries, which resulted in a very different pattern from that heretofore. Pit villages, often with poor housing, together with a gradual but more general urbanization, to a large degree replaced the former rural industry and farming. The late eighteenth century saw the coal and lead industries flourish with their concomitant contributions to prosperity, but also their contribution to dire working conditions underground, with frequent loss of life in the mines. These changes accelerated still further as the nineteenth century saw greater expansion of industry. In the late 1840s, for example, the Duke of Portland granted the fledgling Ashington Coal Company rights to land, to begin mining for coal in a rural part of the coastal plain, on the banks of the Wansbeck and close to Ashington Farm, just above the hamlet of Sheepwash. From this sprang a great complex of five collieries at Linton, Lynemouth, Woodhorn, Ellington and Ashington itself; the main pit in Ashington sprawled over a large expanse to the north of the town, now replaced

↑ **BELSAY** Hall

by a trading estate, but with a very useful trail which traces the earlier buildings and the processes which they performed. Just 2 miles to the east, the former Woodhorn Colliery has been partially preserved and a good modern museum added. Including some of the "Pitman Painters'" work, the museum gives a good idea of what this complex looked and felt like at the height of production in the late nineteenth and early twentieth centuries. Woodhorn Colliery closed in 1981, and Ashington pit finally ceased its work in 1988.

Evidence survives throughout of multifarious industrial activity. At Lemington, on the Tyne, the large brick-built cone, looking rather like a cross between a cooling tower and a pottery kiln, is a lone survivor of similar structures from the large glassworks there. Not far away, and again associated with the glass industry, Joseph Swan invented the incandescent light bulb which would be manufactured in Benwell. Next door again, running from Newburgh to Wylam on the north bank of the river, is the course of the old wagonway, which passes George Stephenson's birthplace. This is just one reminder of the beginnings of the worldwide railway revolution, which began in this county. We shall later meet some of the other key personalities who, along with Stephenson and his son Robert, set the railways on their way across the world. The workshop in which the *Rocket* was built still stands in the "Stephenson Quarter" just behind Newcastle Central Station, now having adopted the unlikely guise of a night club. The railways were in some ways direct products of the needs of both lime and coal industries for moving their materials. Early examples also existed in

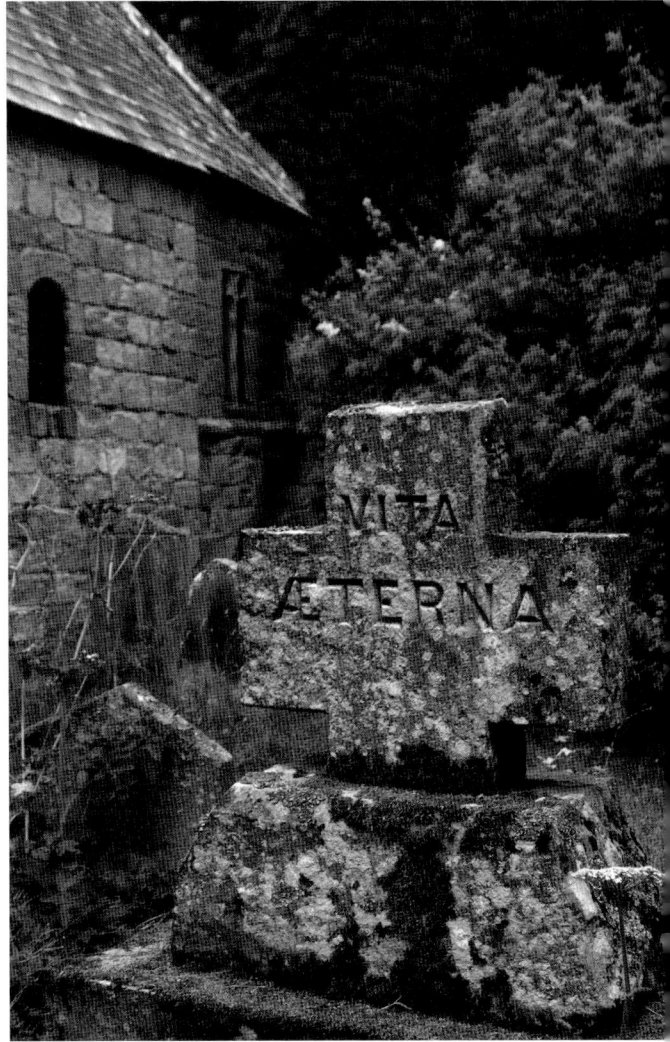

↑ **BEWICK** headstone

the far north at Scremerston, where the courses of former wagonways and pithead railway links can still be traced.

On the Tyne itself, of course, there developed shipbuilding, *Swan, Hunter and Wigham Richardson* having been the key players. Swan Hunter, with its bright blue and yellow cranes, finally closed in 2006, and there is little now to see of the former shipyards, which built and

launched the RMS *Mauretania* and the last HMS *Ark Royal*. Further along the north bank of the river at Elswick, William Armstrong developed his remarkable engineering works which expanded into Scotswood. Eventually, in the twentieth century, this became the great tank factory, of which there is now virtually no sign.

 The eighteenth and nineteenth centuries, then, changed the face of Southeast Northumberland, and it became almost fashionable to pour scorn on the impact of industry. A generation further on, however, there have been significant changes in attitude. Some industrial landscapes have their own aesthetic merit and industrial archaeology, and a proper sense of history has meant that now, where there is good evidence of earlier industry, artefacts have been preserved and been given helpful interpretation. Such industry was to make Britain the first nation into the Industrial Revolution. It also brought Britain forward to being a premier world power and the focus of a vast empire. The beginning in decline reaches back to the Great Depression of the 1920s and 1930s. Once again, the Northeast of England gave a sharp pointer toward this, when from Jarrow (albeit south of the Tyne) in 1936, victims of the depression made their way on the so-called "Jarrow March" to Westminster, calling for action following the failure of Palmer's Shipyard.

 The growth of industry from the eighteenth century onwards also brought something of a religious revolution. The established Church of England was slow to respond to these changes and not always effective at communicating its message to the increasing numbers of urban poor. Nonconformity, and notably Methodism, was more effective, and there remain numerous chapels across Northumberland, especially founded by the Primitive Methodist movement; ultimately some of these chapels had short lives. West Ancroft Chapel (Allerdean), for example, was opened in 1816 and closed sometime in the twentieth century. Presbyterianism also had its influence, especially in the north of the county near to the Scottish border. There was also growth in the Roman Catholic community when people looking for work came for jobs in the expanding coal industry.

 As elsewhere in Britain, the Church of England woke up eventually to urbanization and in Newcastle and North Tyneside some good Victorian churches were designed by John Dobson—notably St Thomas' in Barras Bridge in Newcastle and, not far away, Jesmond Parish Church. R. J. Johnson, Benjamin Green, and Hicks and Charlewood—all local architects— also produced some noble church buildings. Across Northumberland there are, of course, some very fine mediaeval buildings, including St Nicholas' Cathedral in Newcastle, Hexham Abbey, St Andrew's Corbridge and St Aidan's Bamburgh. From the nineteenth century, two outstanding churches are A. W. N. Pugin's Roman Catholic Cathedral of St Mary and John Loughborough Pearson's St George's in Cullercoats.

 The twentieth and twenty-first centuries have added their own contributions to the Northumberland skyline. The cityscape of Newcastle, and particularly on the waterside, has been hugely transformed. Both universities in the city have also contributed well, and St James' Park football ground makes a powerful statement, as does the Civic Centre. The Byker

↑ Spittal Prom

↓ Tweedmouth Signal Box

Wall and the housing development it encloses is a major contribution to the built environment. The Tyneside Metro has been a seminal addition not only to urban architecture, but also to the local infrastructure. Of the two new towns, Killingworth has shown greater imagination with its central lake and with some very good industrial architecture; sadly, insufficient care has been lavished on it and already some of the buildings of the late 1960s and 1970s have vanished. Undoubtedly within the rural landscape, the major contribution has been both the afforestation and then the reservoir at Kielder.

At lightning speed, we have travelled through both three millennia of time and through the entire county of Northumberland, touching on the impact of history on the county's character and inheritance. Perhaps what contributes most powerfully is the variety of serious human challenges it has faced. Alongside the vagaries of climate, which cannot be ignored with a county

with such a long seaboard and such rugged landscapes, have come the factors relating to this being frontier land, a land that has known conflict throughout its history. Responding to this history of conflict has not only moulded the landscape, but also contributed to the character of its people. What sort of people and culture has it begotten?

THE PEOPLE

In his excellent history of Northeast England, *The Northumbrians*, Dan Jackson writes early on: "Indeed, it was centuries of conflict with the Scots that really set the Northumbrians apart from the rest of England, which had long since beaten its swords into ploughshares." Here, undoubtedly, he captures something which is essential to the *culture* of the locality and the county. When we speak of *culture*, of course, we mean the people, both individually and collectively. One could amplify Jackson's reflection, for as well as with the Scots, the Northumbrians had, much earlier on, been at war with Mercia and with Gwynedd. Also there had been the continued raids by the Danes and, earliest of all within the compass we have covered, they had been subjugated—or partially so—by the Romans. This, alongside the rugged landscape,

↓ **BERWICK** Pilot Inn, used by fishermen

the North Sea frontier and often a not entirely friendly climate, made the Northumbrians formidable adversaries and powerful survivors, toughened by the world in which they were set. This may also account, to at least some degree, for their resilience and creativity. Both land and history helped mould the people, from whom emerged Northumbrian culture. This resilience, then, is also reflected in the twenty-first-century landscape which we encounter as we travel across the county.

Elements of that fighting spirit are there in the literature. Both the Border Ballads and Sir Walter Scott's *Minstrelsy of the Scottish Borders* convey something of this. So, *The Battle of Chevy Chase*, describing the carnage at the Battle of Otterburn, probably first appeared as early as the fifteenth century. Later, the sixteenth-century Scottish ballad, *The Flowers of the Forest*, tells the tale of the Battle of Flodden (1513) in the form of a lament. In the nineteenth century, John Mackay Wilson's *Tales of the Borders* captured some of this romantic swashbuckling past. The stories of the Reivers add spice to all this. The numerous defensive buildings, described in the earlier essay and in the gazetteer, are clear evidence of this tumultuous history. Still later, Sir Henry Newbolt, writing in 1905, captured it thus in his *The Old and Bold*:

> When England sets her banner forth,
> and bids her armour shine
> She'll not forget the famous North,
> the lads of moor and Tyne.

Of course, even the dialect brings its own fascination. *Larn Yersel Geordie* is but one of a number of books picking up something of the local patois. When first staying at Alnmouth, a young lad asked if I wanted to be part of an adventure that evening: "Why, yer gan the boout tha neet?" Which being translated meant: "Are you up for going out in the boat tonight?" Northumberland has also done better than most counties in preserving its own minstrelsy, its own folk melodies. Most famous of all is doubtless *Blaydon Races*, which captures some of the urban landscape in its lines:

> Ah went to Blaydon Races,
> 'twas on the ninth of Joon
> In eighteen hundred an' sixty-two,
> on a summer's afternoon
> Ah tyuk the bus frae Balmbra's,
> an' she wis heavy laden
> Away we went alang Collingwood Street,
> that's on the road to Blaydon.

Later on, the Scotswood Road and Armstrong's factory both make appearances. Then too, local characters join the scene, so for example, in the ballad of the broken-hearted keel-man lamenting his unrequited love for *Cushie Butterfield*:

> She's a big lass, she's a Bonny lass
> And she likes her beer
> And they call her Cushie Butterfield
> And I wish she were here.

Of course, many of us, from all over England, may well know of keel-men, from singing a traditional Northumbrian song which "went nationwide", that is, *The Keel Row*:

↑ **HEXHAM** Smeaton Bridge

As I went through Sandgate,
> through Sandgate, through Sandgate

As I went through Sandgate, I heard a lassie sing:

Oh weel may the keel row,
> the keel row, the keel row

Oh weel may the keel row, that my laddie's in.

Then, finally, and made more famous in the late twentieth century through a television series, is the song, *When the boat comes in*. This time the earliest version originated in the Farne Islands and picks up the fishing communities of the Northumberland coast:

> Dance to your daddie, my little laddie
> Dance to your daddie, my little man
> Thou shalt have a fishy on a little dishy
> Thou shall have a fishy when the boat comes in.

Alongside the folk songs came also the Northumbrian pipes. Northumbrian small pipes are "bellows blown" in contrast with Scottish pipes which are blown by the mouth. Visitors to Wallington Hall, even in the early twenty-first century, might have heard Patricia Jennings, the last surviving daughter of Sir Charles Trevelyan, playing the small pipes in the glassed-in courtyard at the heart of the Hall.

Already, then, we have something of the feel of the county, which the visitor will encounter in terms of its written and musical culture. The visual arts too have an important place. J. M. W. Turner painted several landscapes in Northumberland. Perhaps two of his most famous pictures are of Norham Castle. On his first visit there in 1797, he painted a watercolour which became renowned very early on in his career. He later made at least three other visits there and, on one occasion, the friend accompanying him watched him bow in the direction of the castle. Asking him why he did so, Turner replied: "This was the place that set me on the path to become an artist." In modern parlance, that was the place that "put him on the map". In 1845, Turner painted a dramatic oil of Norham at sunrise, now in his late, "almost" Impressionist phase, for which he became particularly noted. At the same period, Thomas Bewick was born at Cherryburn, near Ovingham. Bewick went on to become the most celebrated of all English wood engravers, with a skill that has never been surpassed. His illustrations of birds and quadrupeds helped to change our view of the natural world. *The History of Birds* entranced the heroine in *Jane Eyre*, and the Bewick's swan, newly discovered in 1843, was named after the artist. He considered his masterpiece to be the engraving *The Wild Bull of Chillingham*, a work of art described by Simon

↓ **BERWICK** shelter, later painted by L. S. Lowry

Schama as "perhaps the greatest icon of British natural history". Bewick also produced book plates and tail pieces. His art is wedded to his home county, particularly his tail pieces, vivid and often comical vignettes of Northumbrian country life. Wordsworth wrote:

> O now that the genius of Bewick were mine,
> And the skill that he heartned on
> the banks of the Tyne!

Then, working just a little later, James William Carmichael, who was born in Ouseburn in Newcastle in 1800, became a noted marine painter, often capturing the seascapes which he would have first encountered on both the Tyne and the Northumbrian coast.

Artistic genius was, however, not new to the county. Reverting some twelve centuries takes one to the earlier "golden age" of Northumbrian art with the remarkable *Lindisfarne Gospels*. These remind us of the legacy of the monastic life in the county of Northumberland, at the time of the Kingdom of Northumbria. This also encompassed the life of Lindisfarne Priory, which, alongside the work of Bede and the Wearmouth-Jarrow monks, became a crucible of culture exerting an influence well beyond that island and throughout Europe. The twelfth century also saw a veritable explosion of monastic life across England, and Northumberland enjoyed its own part within this flowering. The later Benedictine monastery at Lindisfarne, which succeeded what were doubtless the wooden buildings of Aidan and Cuthbert's day, was part of this flowering, but there is much evidence elsewhere. Brinkburn Priory, near Rothbury,

was an Augustinian foundation. Hexham too became an Augustinian house in the twelfth century, although Wilfrid's original monastery there had been Benedictine. At Alnwick, the fine gatehouse of the Premonstratensian abbey stands nobly within the park, by the Eglingham Road, and, further into the park, are the extensive remains of the Carmelite priory at Hulne; there are also remains of a monastic lazar house (leprosy hospital), on the road out of Alnwick toward Berwick-upon-Tweed. At Morpeth, there is the scant surviving evidence of the Cistercian monastery of Newminster Abbey. At Bamburgh, standing tall in a domestic garden, is the corner of the church of a former Dominican friary. Blanchland is unique as a village constructed from the extant remains of another Premonstratensian abbey. In Newcastle itself are the very considerable remains of the Dominican friary, and there were once a further six foundations, all of friars of several different congregations. At Berwick, in mediaeval times, there were upwards of a dozen religious houses, but virtually no evidence above ground has survived of any of them; happily, in a recent housing development close to the Elizabethan walls, a cross has been included in the landscaping to mark the place of a former Carmelite monastery. As with elsewhere in England, these religious houses helped to mould the culture. The dissolution of the monasteries had, of course, a revolutionary impact, with the disappearance of religious houses from the landscape. There have been some post-Reformation Roman Catholic foundations, there are Anglican Franciscan friars at Alnmouth, and there is a small, largely lay foundation in the

↑ Stephenson poster, Locomotion

presence of the Northumbria Community at Felton in mid-Northumberland.

Without a doubt, of all the revolutions to arrive in the county, in the modern period, it was the Industrial Revolution which had the greatest impact. The presence of large-scale coal measures, close to the coast and the River Tyne, offered prime conditions for the development of heavy industry. Alongside this too was the emergence locally of some extraordinarily gifted engineers. It is no exaggeration to say that the "birth of railways" worldwide began here. Indeed, it was George Stephenson's rail gauge of four feet eight and a half inches (1.43 m) which would become the "standard gauge", and which continues to be used by a majority of railways worldwide. Undoubtedly the two key figures were George and Robert Stephenson—father and son. George was born at Wylam on the Tyne, and the tiny cottage where he spent his early childhood survives, alongside the course of the former Newburgh wagonway. George's father was fireman at Wylam Colliery and earning a pitiful wage with which to support his family. George himself was something of an autodidact but he eventually found his way to

↑ **WYLAM** Station

night school, having been illiterate until the age of eighteen. Largely due to issues with the health of the family, he moved the family to West Moor, just next to the village of Killingworth. There, he became the brakeman at the Killingworth wagonway, for which he would design his first locomotive, which he named *Blucher*. George also designed a miners' safety lamp, exactly concurrently with Humphrey Davy.

Realizing the need for education, from his own experience, he sent Robert, his son, to a private school so that he should speak "standard English" rather than the local dialect which he himself still spoke. Amongst other things, George and Robert together designed *Locomotion No. 1* for the Stockton and Darlington Railway and then the *Rocket* for the Liverpool and Manchester Railway. Robert also branched out into civil engineering, designing both the pioneering road/rail High Level Bridge in Newcastle and the monumental Royal Border Bridge over the Tweed at Berwick. But the Stephensons were not alone in railway innovation in the county, for William Hedley, the resident engineer at Wylam Colliery, was the designer of the famous *Puffing Billy*, for use

↑ **NEWCASTLE** St James' Park

in that colliery; this was itself an influence on George Stephenson as a designer and engineer.

As if this were not enough, two other remarkable innovators sprang from the county. The engineer, William Armstrong, was the son of a wealthy corn merchant who later became Mayor of Newcastle. Young Armstrong was sent to the Royal Grammar School and then Bishop Auckland Grammar School; his father had decided his son should become a lawyer and had him articled to a solicitor. William soon had other ideas, however, having been attracted to engineering. He went on to pioneer hydroelectricity, hydraulics, and then also modern artillery; shipbuilding came later with a partner, James Whitworth. Armstrong's impact was enormous, and the Elswick Works became colossal, extending for three-quarters of a mile along the Tyne, later developing into the vast tank factory which continued in existence into the early twenty-first century. Later, Armstrong would buy the Cragside Estate near Rothbury and transform a rather bleak and rocky valley into a blaze of colour in the summer. His house, designed by the prominent early "Arts and Crafts" architect, Norman Shaw,

↑ **HEXHAM** former Forum cinema

↓ **HEXHAM** The Grapes

was the first house in the world to be powered by hydroelectric power and boasting a hydraulic lift between floors. Armstrong's trademark, both literally and metaphorically, is stamped all over the county.

The next celebrity to step into the witness box is one Charles Parsons. Parsons came from a landed family. He was the son of an earl and of Anglo-Irish parentage. After gaining mathematics degrees at both Trinity College, Dublin and St John's, Cambridge (where he gained a first), he went to work for William Armstrong in his Elswick Works on the Tyne. It was Parsons who developed the steam turbine which revolutionized shipping. He set up his own company, which would then later build power stations, developing the sophisticated switchgear needed for the transmission of electric power. Parsons is buried at Kirkwhelpington, alongside his wife, Katharine, who was also a talented engineer, and who, with their daughter, set up the Women's Engineering Society.

Joseph Swan, born in Pallion on the Wear in County Durham, came to work in Newcastle. At exactly the same time as Thomas Edison, in New York, he pioneered the incandescent light bulb and set up his factory on the Tyne, joining forces with Edison to form the Ediswan electrical manufacturing company, which survived into the third quarter of the twentieth century. Other significant developments had an important impact on the landscape as we see it today. So, George Culley was an agriculturalist, at first becoming a specialist in cattle breeding—his "Wooler herd" became famous enough for people to visit his farms to understand better how to improve their own herds.

Later, following in the footsteps of "Turnip Townshend", and at the same time as "Coke of Norfolk", he developed new agricultural methods, including patterns of crop rotation, eventually helping to transform agriculture across the world.

On the urban landscape, two of the key figures were Richard Grainger and John Dobson. Grainger, rather after the pattern of George Stephenson, took hold of his own life early on. So, having been educated at a charity school, and the son of a Quayside porter, he became a most successful builder and visionary who transformed the face of central Newcastle, leaving as his legacy what we now know as Grainger Town, perhaps the most attractively planned nineteenth-century city centre in Britain. Alongside him worked John Dobson, an architect who built some of the key buildings in Grainger Town, but who also contributed much to the face of nineteenth-century Northumberland. The traveller will stumble on countless buildings of high quality which grew from Dobson's drawing office and architectural practice.

Interestingly, many buildings in Northumberland include pantiled roofs. This is largely because coasters sailing from the Netherlands to the Tyne would use pantiles as ballast. Thrifty builders soon began to use the pantile to produce interesting roofscapes. Often the pantiling will cease a metre or so above the gutter, giving way to slate or stone, so that rainwater is carried more efficiently away.

Thus far we have not mentioned sport and leisure. Northumberland has its own fair share of both. The attractive dune lands along the

↑ Tyneside, Baltic Gallery

coast have been used for golf links all the way from Berwick and Goswick in the north down to the Tyne in the south. The links were also much used as locations for Miners' Picnics, which, standing alongside the annual Miners' Galas, brought together the mining communities across the region. Often such occasions were also used as opportunities for the trade unions to gather their members. Then, perhaps best known of all, in the realm of football, Newcastle's St James' Park stadium is a key building within the cityscape; the local rivalry with Sunderland has become legend. Local football stars have included Jackie Milburn, Bobby Charlton, Jackie Charlton, Bobby Robson and Alan Shearer.

Alongside all this, the various towns and villages are still peppered with working men's clubs, a direct by-product of the mining and shipbuilding industries. Although those industries are now largely lost, Northumberland and Newcastle have not lost their energy for enjoying themselves. Night clubs, cinemas, the Sage Music Centre across the river in Gateshead and galleries still thrive and bear witness to the continuing cultural life. The "Lit and Phil", the

Newcastle Literary and Philosophical Society, with its vast library (the largest independent library in the UK outside London) and with its varied programme of lectures and other activities, was a pioneer. Similarly, other "Lit and Phils" were spawned throughout the county. Northumberland's attractiveness through its landscape is just the tip—not of an iceberg, but rather of one of the founding cultural cradles of western Europe.

↓ **BLYTH** beach huts

GAZETTEER

Please note that inclusion in this gazetteer does not imply public access.

ACKLINGTON

Memories of two world wars at the former Acklington aerodrome, then swallowed up first by opencast coal working and now by a penal institution. St John the Divine Church is simple but handsome Early English by James Deacon (1860). The neighbouring former vicarage is an attractive study in country Gothick.

ACOMB

Former lead-mining village with little but one single street. There are, however, some dated houses from the seventeenth and eighteenth centuries. Acomb House is a five-bay house of 1737 with an east wing of 1925. The mill is late eighteenth century, although the miller's house is dated 1728. Travelling north through the village takes one to an interesting gated, unfenced road which eventually meets the main road at Heavenfield (*qv* Wall).

St John Lee, half a mile south of Acomb, has Dobson's attractive church (1818) dedicated to St John of Beverley. There is an uninscribed Roman altar which has been converted into a sundial. The Hermitage, 800 m southeast, is the legendary site of the seventh-century hermitage of St John of Beverley. There has been a house here since the late fifteenth century although the present building is largely mid-eighteenth century. There is a ferryman's cottage, Boatacres, on the riverbank to the southeast.

ALLENDALE TOWN

The Allen and South Tyne Dales are yet another stunning part of the county, effectively part of the North Pennines but sharing the wildness of terrain seen both around the Roman Wall and further north in the Simonside and Cheviot Hills. Allendale Town is both the entry point and tiny "capital" of Allendale. Grouped around the Market Square and high above the river, it

↓ **ALLENHEADS** lead washing plant

↑ **ALLENDALE TOWN** workshops

is attractive and a good centre for walking and visiting the surrounding country. St Cuthbert's Church is a slightly gaunt piece of nineteenth-century Gothick but set in a picturesque corner of the square. The 1842 sundial on the south wall claims Allendale Town as the centre of Britain! The former Trustee Savings Bank is a handsome building of 1873 still retaining its railings. The Golden Lion and the King's Head form a good backdrop to the town centre. The town bridge is of 1825 with a corn mill immediately next to it. The Allen Smelt Mill has been saved through heritage funding and hosts a brewery and other small businesses. In the eighteenth century, the curate here was much caught up into the 1715 uprising and later turned King's Evidence. On New Year's Eve, there is a great bonfire with fancy-dressed men carrying pans of blazing tar on their heads.

Wooley, 1 mile to the southwest, includes an intriguing group of buildings next to the farm. They are grouped around a triangular yard in a defensive manner and have recently been restored.

Sinderhope to the south is surrounded by remains of lead mines and with a Jubilee Primitive Methodist Chapel of 1860 as one approaches from the north—now a private dwelling.

Spartylea, 2 miles south of Sinderhope, sports more signs of the former lead mining industry notably at Sipton and Long Drag, including here a powder house for the lead mines. St Peter's Church, just south and next to a former corn mill, is picturesquely situated with a churchyard entirely overrun by rabbits. The church, a preaching box of 1825 and given Gothic character in 1893, has been well converted for wider community use.

ALLENHEADS

As its eponymous name suggests, it lies at the head of eastern Allendale and is the former nerve centre of lead mining with much of interest to be discovered. Both the horse track (a spiral shaft) and the miners' entrance to the former key Gin Hill Shaft of the Beaumont Mine are perfectly preserved and there is good interpretative material. The Beaumont family lived in Allenheads Hall (1847) at the heart of the village. The crucial figure here was the mining engineer and director, Thomas Sopwith, a friend of William (later Lord) Armstrong (himself an engineer); he was also father of Tommy Sopwith, the early aviation pioneer. There are very impressive remains of the washing floor for the ore and the bouse teams, in which the bouse or raw newly mined ore was stacked. These consist of fourteen apsidal

↑ **ALLENHEADS** pony tunnel entrance

ALLERDEAN

Scattered around are the scant remains of former coal mines. Half a mile north and east of the Berwick Road are the footings and spoil tip of the former Blackhill Colliery, opened in 1942 and the focus of an orchestrated but unsuccessful campaign in 1959 to block its closure. For a brief time thereafter, the nearby Allerdean drift mine was resuscitated. At Unthank and elsewhere, evidence points to earlier mining. Former Primitive Methodist Chapel (1902) at crossroads. Shoresdean, the site of a nineteenth-century colliery, is a small loop of houses built in the mid-twentieth century to house those working in local collieries.

One mile south-south-west, on the left at Ancroft Northmoor, chapel and manse. Chapel founded 1845 for English Presbyterian Congregation.

bays with stepped walls—again, as with the Gin Hill Shaft there is helpful interpretation. Hopefully, further conservation will allow the site to be still better understood. The Beaumonts with Thomas Sopwith created a model village with a school of 1849 and rows of miners' houses. A former pub, closed many years ago and with its carriage arch still visible, is now the heritage centre. The Allenheads Inn next door has a seventeenth-century fireplace but otherwise is largely eighteenth century. At Dirt Pot, 1 mile north, was a lead-smelting mill. Fluorspar has been mined here more recently.

To the northwest, the road leads westwards over Alston Moor with stupendous views in all directions—if the weather is clear, you can see both the Simonside Hills and Cheviot Hills to the north.

↓ West Ancroft chapel, **ALLERDEAN**

ALNHAM

Remotely placed near the source of the Aln at the southern end of Salters' Road, one of the ancient drovers' roads over the Borders. The former vicarage was a vicar's pele, and the churchyard is normally kept in trim by a small flock of sheep. St Michael's Church is a stunning example of unfussy Romanesque with a fine broad single-chamfered chancel arch. The north aisle was demolished, but the arcading is well set into the north wall. The church with its simple bellcote was rescued from desuetude in 1870 and then stunningly refurbished in 2020.

A clear green mound southeast of the church is the site of the former castle, probably razed to the ground by the Scotts of Teviotdale c.1532. A report of 1586 notes: " ... the faire strong Tower ... was strongly ... vaulted over ... the Gates and Dores be all of strong Iron Barres ... the house is now ruinous in some decay, by reason the Farmer useth to carry his sheep up the stares and to lay them in the Chambers which rotteth the vaults ... " The lumps and bumps of a lost village are clearly visible nearby.

On a hill to the southeast of Ewartly Shank is High Knowes, a camp from the Iron Age period. Also near Ewartly Shank is a memorial to two farmers who, while making their way back from Rothbury market in 1962, were tragically lost in a terrible blizzard.

ALNMOUTH

In 1806, a great tempest caused the estuary of the Aln to shift 200 metres north, isolating much of the old town and leading to a decline in its importance as a port. A Telford Road had been built to link with Hexham and bring lime and other commodities for export. On Church Hill, south of the estuary, a cross marks the site of St Waleric, the former cruciform, Romanesque Saxon church. Indeed, Alnmouth appears originally to have been part of the neighbouring village of Lesbury; it was called St Waleric. St John the Baptist (1876), the present church, is simple Gothic with a western tower and spire.

Prominent on the cliff is the Franciscan friary, built originally for the Scholefield family (shipping merchants) as Lint Close by W. H. Knowles. The Duchess's Bridge over which one enters is noble (1864), with its four arches. To the north of the bridge the river inscribes broad meanders that would grace any

↓ **ALNMOUTH** tank traps

↑ **ALNMOUTH** view over Aln estuary

geography textbook. Alnmouth Bay has splendid vistas down to Coquet Island (off the coast at Amble). The mediaeval plan of the village survives with some pleasant buildings, some of them converted granaries. On the bank of the pre-1806 estuary is a guano shed standing alone.

Sparse remnants of a former artillery battery built for Algernon Percy, fourth Duke of Northumberland, (manned by the Percy Artillery Volunteers until the Second World War) are hidden in the cliffs just north of the town golf course—from 1906—mid-1930s Battery Hostel, at the foot of Bracken Hill, catered for trippers from Tyneside. Beacon Hill Camp earthwork is just to the north. High Buston House is a mile and a half southwest. Alnmouth makes a delightfully picturesque tableau from the train.

ALNWICK

Entering Alnwick from the north leaves one in no shadow of doubt as to why the ducal castle of the Percy family was built where it was! Its position is stunning, with the River Aln acting as a natural moat, and the fortress itself spreading proudly across the bluff on which it is set. Then, John Adam's Gothick 1773 Lion Bridge over which one now travels, with the determined lion facing you—its tail assertively horizontal—completes the tableau, with all finally crowned by the gatehouse

53

and barbican and its apotropaic figures aloft. Entering from the south, one is confronted with the equally uncompromising Hotspur Gate (or Bondgate Tower), the last remnant of the former town walls. This is Ducal Northumberland.

An attractive introduction to the town is the walk from the Lion Bridge along the river path eastwards to the 1766 Denwick Bridge by Robert Mylne. Turning right at the end of the bridge, the road rises past the remarkably restored and redeveloped Castle Garden and then up to the Tenantry Column, a 25 m-high Doric column by David Stephenson, sometimes referred to as the Farmers' Folly: the apocryphal story says that the 1816 column, commissioned by the Duke's tenants in gratitude for a 25 per cent rent reduction, was followed by him announcing a significant rent increase since clearly the farmers could easily afford it. The Tuscan "Peace Column", in Swansfield Park, prematurely commemorates the peace of 1814 and is actually set on the remains of a small oval hill fort.

The mediaeval fortress is set within the eighteenth-century park designed by the Northumbrian landscape genius, Lancelot "Capability" Brown from Kirkharle. Brown was also commissioned to refashion the grounds of the Duke's Thameside London residence at Syon Park, at the same time. Returning to Alnwick, a motte and bailey castle was the first fortification here, although this had already been walled in stone by 1157. The castle's plan is a stretched triangle

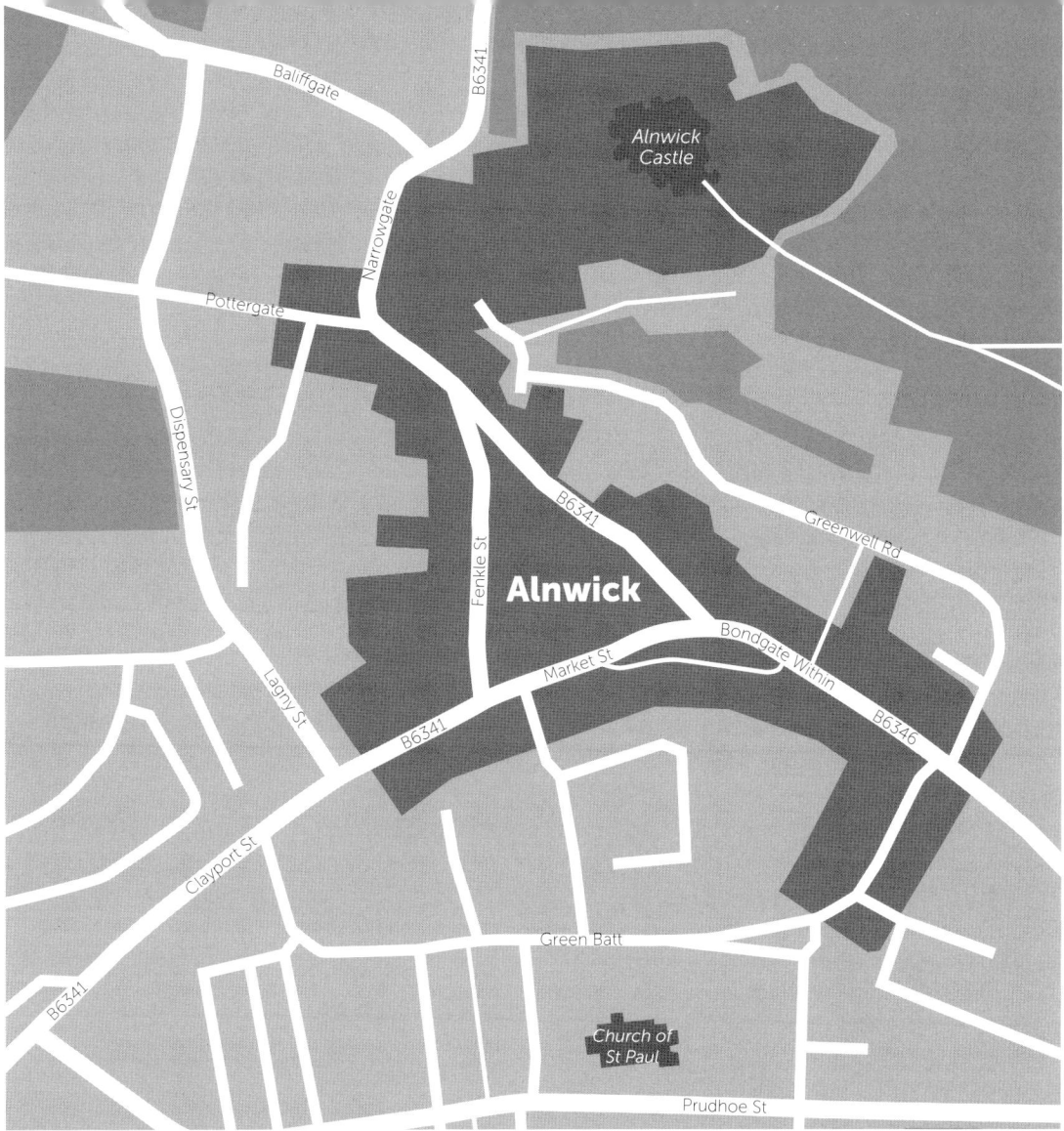

Baliffgate

B6341

Alnwick
Castle

Narrowgate

Pottergate

Dispensary St

Fenkle St

B6341

Greenwell Rd

Alnwick

Bondgate Within

Lagny St

Market St

B6341

B6346

Clayport St

Green Batt

B6341

Church of
St Paul

Prudhoe St

along the bluff with its short side facing Bailiffgate. With a central shell keep and a bailey either side, the twelfth-century plan is not dissimilar to Windsor. It was in 1309 that the castle was bought by Henry de Percy and the 700-year association with the Percys began; thereafter both the "Percy Lion" and the "Percy Crescent" would be familiar symbols attached to buildings and much else too. This is the town of

Shakespeare's Hotspur; the swash-buckling son of the first Earl was killed at the Battle of Shrewsbury, fighting against the King. To commemorate 700 years of the Percys in Alnwick, a statue of Hotspur was placed in Pottergate in 2009; the sculptor, Keith Maddison, captures Hotspur with his visor open—this was the cause of his death, lifting his visor to get a better view, through which a spear passed and killed him.

Anthony Bek, the brutal Bishop of Durham, briefly held the inheritance of the castle in trust for the de Vescy family, the previous owners, and he handled the sale. Having developed the castle, Percy's son, also Henry, built the impressive barbican we see today. Interestingly, no Percy made Alnwick his home from the later Middle Ages until the mid-eighteenth century. The fourth Lord, however, was given an earldom. Eleven Earls of Northumberland followed, after which there was no male heir; Lady Elizabeth Seymour inherited the seat and her husband, Sir Hugh Smithson, took on and continued the family name—he became the first Duke of Northumberland in 1750. The present Duke, Ralph Percy, is the twelfth in succession.

It was the first Duke who rescued the castle from a ruinous state and both James Paine and Robert Adam, inspired by Horace Walpole, produced a remarkable Strawberry Hill Gothick castle/mansion. This inspired more Strawberry Hill, locally—at Hulne Priory in the Home Park, Craster, Fowberry Tower and Ford Castle.

With the fourth Duke, it was once again all change. Why the next shift in thought? Amongst other things, the present Duke notes that Sir Walter Scott had commented on the castle's lack of grandeur and proposed that a high tower be added as a central feature. Anthony Salvin, a noted Victorian architect who had completed substantial restoration at Norwich Cathedral and elsewhere and who had designed the amazing Harlaxton House in Lincolnshire, was the Duke's choice to aggrandize the castle. Having selected Salvin, known for his Gothick work elsewhere, perversely the Duke insisted that he work in a Classical style, running directly counter to the architect's advice. This renovation, which cost £250,000, a vast sum at that time, effectively swept away all Adam's Gothick work, save the breakfast room! The Prudhoe Tower, following Scott's suggestion, is entirely Salvin's, and certainly Salvin's work helped further enhance the profile of the castle as we see it today. There are now regular excellent tours and the castle's use as a film location adds further fascination. A brief description of the castle may encourage all readers to join a tour.

We have already encountered the Gatehouse and Barbican. The soldiers on the crenellations probably date to the eighteenth century, but doubtless replaced earlier figures designed to frighten away prospective marauders. The gate is vaulted and in earlier days there would have been a ditch and drawbridge. Once inside the western bailey, the mediaeval curtain wall (dated variously because of rebuilds) is revealed. The Abbot's Tower is in the northwest corner and Salvin's Falconer Tower to the east. There is a broad mid-eighteenth-century Gun Terrace. Immediately to the right of the gateway are first Avener's Tower, then the Clock Tower—further on embedded in a range of buildings is the D-shaped Auditor's/Beefstand Tower. The Middle Gateway dates to the fourteenth century, and here the battlement soldiers are weathered figures from that same period. To the south is Salvin's Garden Gate— the Record Tower lies at the extreme east end of the castle bailey, with the Constable's Tower and Postern Tower next along to the northwest. There is a further fine gateway into the keep. The Inner Court is largely Salvin's 1854 creation—this swept away most of Adam's work including his splendid staircase. Salvin's chapel is rib-vaulted, and

to the north is the library which now functions as the family's main living room. It is in this part of the castle that the nineteenth-century Italian influence is most obvious. An anteroom leads from the library to the grand staircase where there is an interesting transition from Gothick to Italianate. The other side of the anteroom connects to the main state rooms—beyond is Salvin's vast vaulted kitchen.

Leaving the castle by the Barbican, directly ahead is the imposing Bailiffgate, tree-lined with good eighteenth-/nineteenth-century houses on either side. On the left and set back is the former vicarage, designed c.1840 by the Duchess —good and capacious Victorian. Continuing straight ahead leads into the Home Park, where one encounters fine unspoilt parkland, and also agricultural land—further excitements are dotted around: so, in 1776 the first Duchess died, and the Duke, who was inconsolable, commissioned Brizlee Tower to be built in Hulne Park in her memory. At 24 m high, with its Gothick detail, it is a landmark rising above the surrounding woodland. Moor Lodge near the Forest Lodge entrance is another eruption of Gothick. Park Farm, 1 mile northwest of Forest Lodge, is the home farm; the 1832 farmhouse is impressively pedimented. Almost 2 miles northwest of the castle lies Hulne Priory within its eponymous Park; the stone wall along the Eglingham Road extends some 4 miles, before thereafter running cross country. Hulne Priory is of great interest, as it is almost certainly the earliest foundation of the Carmelite friars in England. The monastery is contained within a curtain wall with a plain gatehouse to the south. In the eighteenth century, Gothick gateways were added. The church is in fairly good condition with the divided nave and chancel. There is a small courtyard at the end of the east walk of the cloister; the sacristy is interesting, and the outline of the buildings is clear. A Gothick summer house was built within the curtilage in 1778, as part of the improvement plans of Robert Adam and Capability Brown. There is a large tower of 1486 built by Sir Henry Percy.

After retracing one's steps to the Eglingham Road and turning hard left, just over the Canongate Bridge, the impressive fourteenth-century gatehouse, the only remnant of the Premonstratensian Alnwick Abbey, comes into view. The abbey was founded in 1147 by the de Vescy family (owners of the castle before the Percys)—the footings of the nave arcading have been traced into the meadow; it was probably the most significant house of this order in northern England.

St Michael's, the ancient parish church on the left at the top of the hill, is a magnificent example of late Gothic; externally it is entirely Perpendicular. In 1464, Henry VI granted tolls to make and repair the church. Gothick added in the eighteenth century was again swept away in Salvin's nineteenth-century restoration. Wide-aisled with five bays, the chancel has three chapels; the tower is over the western bay of the south aisle. The west window of the north aisle is all that is visible of the pre-Perpendicular rebuild. Internally one can discover some reused Norman stonework. The Hotspur capital carries the Percy Crescent. Some fragments of fifteenth-century stained glass, but otherwise good Victorian. Interesting tablets and two sculptures under the tower including Henry VI. The interior breathes its own majesty.

St Paul's Church of 1846 (originally a second Anglican parish church but now Roman Catholic) is again by Salvin and at the Duke's expense—good Victorian Decorated Gothick; there is a monument to the third Duke. Stained glass by the Scottish Pre-Raphaelite William Dyce made in Munich by Ainmuller. Several other church buildings in the town.

On the left-hand side of the road north, after the Lion Bridge, lie the reconstructed remains of St Leonard's Hospital, a lazar house built by the de Vescys c.1200—the ruins were only rediscovered as late as 1845 through ploughing. A little further on and near to the roundabout is Malcolm's Cross, commemorating the death of Malcolm of Scotland during the siege of Alnwick in 1093.

The town itself is bustling, with a market at its centre, enclosed on one side by the arcaded Northumberland Hall. Built in 1826, and now housing small shops, it rather dwarfs the smaller 1731 Town Hall with its modest square tower, underneath which runs a passage from Fenkle Street to the Market Place. The curving Bondgate Within, with its attractive cobbled terracing, has a collection of good vernacular buildings. The White Swan Hotel, a former coaching inn on the Great North Road, has the amazing Olympic Room, salvaged from *Titanic*'s sister ship, the *Olympic*, before she was broken up in Jarrow. In Walkergate are the ruins of the 1449 St Mary's Chantry—originally it was probably a priest's house and then a school. Pottergate Tower is 1868 by Henry Bell having replaced a mediaeval gateway; it is strong and a real landmark.

One cannot leave Alnwick without remarking on the monumental former railway terminus by William Bell. It was on the branch from the main line at Alnmouth to Alnwick and was also the final stop on that line which went to Cornhill-on-Tweed, confusingly called Coldstream, 2 miles further on and over the border. One cannot but surmise that the Duke was instrumental in the building of such a grand edifice, which now houses the largest second-hand bookshop in northern England! The Aln Valley Railway is gradually reopening the former branch line to Alnmouth with the eventual hope of linking again with the main line; the new station is on the edge of the Lionheart Business Park just to the south of the town.

Heiferlaw Tower, 3 miles north, was built as a lookout tower for Alnwick Abbey, and by the Percy Arms on the southern and eastern sides, it can be dated precisely as being erected between 1470 and 1489. Second-World-War control room in the woods just to the north.

ALSTON

In Cumbria—just, but ecclesiastically still in the Diocese of Newcastle—the vast majority of Allendale and South Tynedale is in Northumberland. Alston is not immediately welcoming in its location—set within vast areas of moorland to the east and to the south, it bears the scars of tough weather and tough industry. The centre is spoilt by a surfeit of parked motor vehicles, but behind these obtrusions lie some pleasant buildings with a focus in the frequently rebuilt 1765 Market or Butter Cross. Alston has the distinction of being the highest market town in England, with the smallest state secondary school.

The Town Hall, Library and Savings Bank (one structure, and built in 1857) is by A. B. Higham of Newcastle, who designed other buildings including churches in this part of the county. The former Barclays Bank has an attractive semi-circular porch. St Augustine's Church, originally by Smeaton (of Coldstream Bridge and Eddystone Lighthouse fame) and built in 1770 but demolished and rebuilt in 1870 by G. D. Oliver, is a fairly gaunt building. There are some good monuments, and the interior is well lit. The churchyard is part circular and was open to the Market Place, but there is now just a gap for access. The Friends' Meeting House is of 1732 and after a period of disuse was refurbished in 1996. There are a number of bastle houses and some good cottages within the town. High Mill, north of the Market Square, was equipped with machinery in 1767, which was restored to working order in 1992.

The Nenthead Level is intriguing. An adit (rather like the entry

↓ **ALSTON** shop by market cross

into a drift mine) was driven underground towards Nenthead to drain the lead mines there. Begun in 1776, work continued until 1842 with work resuming from 1897 to 1904, but never completed. Nonetheless, it did drain much ground, and pleasure boats carried the intrepid into the inner darkness. The Alston end is now blocked and lost in a builder's yard. The mining was much developed by the Quaker-owned London Lead Company which expanded production from 1836 onwards.

Alston Station, just north of the town centre and in the valley, is now the southern terminus of the South Tynedale Railway, a narrow-gauge line which at present extends 5 miles north to Slaggyford; there are active plans to reopen the line throughout the entire route of the former branch, thus terminating at Haltwhistle.

ALWINTON

This really is the last village in Coquetdale; The Rose and Thistle, the pub's name, points to the nearness of the border between the two nations. St Michael's Church is off-centre from the village, placed south of the confluence of the Rivers Coquet and Alwin, and set into the hillside, such that the twelfth-century chancel rises high above the nave. There is a crypt beneath which has not been opened for a century. The mediaeval chancel was altered in the fourteenth century, but the rest of the building is Victorian (1851) by Pickering, except for part of the north aisle, the east and north walls, and the west wall. Clennell family tablets and two rustic carved table tombs in the north aisle. Occasionally a nineteenth-century horse-drawn bier has been kept on display in the church. Just north of the tiny village centre is Clennell Street, a mediaeval drovers' road across the border running north-northwest to Hownam. There is a hill fort near Gallow Law. Further afield on the border, at the summit of Windy Gyle (619 m/2031 ft), one

of the highest peaks in the Cheviots, is Russell's Cairn, probably Bronze Age; later it was associated with the murder of Lord Francis Russell on a day of truce in 1585. Cock Law (1 mile east-northeast) is a possible alternative scene of the crime.

Some ten miles west-northwest up the Coquet Valley are both Kemylpethe and Chew Green. Kemylpethe is a deserted village in extremely remote countryside; there are earthen banks but also the remains of a stone-built chapel—a small sandstone cross was found nearby in 1889. Kemylpethe had been a trysting place for border disputes as early as the mid-thirteenth century, and there are still references to it as late as 1550.

Chew Green includes the most significant visible evidence of Roman earthworks in Britain. On a clear day, it helps to continue for about half a mile and view the site from a distance. By now, one is in the army training area, and so information must be sought as to whether there is test firing in operation—there are warning flags and telephone numbers with which to check. Dere Street, the Roman road across the border heading for Jedburgh, is relatively easily identified, running to the east of a small fort defended by an inner rampart and three defensive ditches. To the west-southwest are ditches almost certainly defining a square fort, and then a long and narrow temporary camp. Superimposed on all these is a large square camp, the earliest feature of the site. There is a further camp just north of here and over the present Scottish border. At

↑ **AMBLE** Marina

Thirlmoor, a summit of some 558 m, are three massive burial cairns from either the late Neolithic or early Bronze Age periods.

AMBLE

Amble's raison d'être was as a staithe port serving the coalfield including local pits—before that it had been nothing more than a hamlet. In the nineteenth century, the harbour was improved with long breakwaters designed by John Rennie, but a dock was never constructed—only staithes. A small fishing industry has survived even during a period of significant depression and the collapse of the local economy. Imaginative investment and the work of a development agency has transformed the town. Queen Street has interesting shops on both sides throughout its length—a town square has been created around the

Gothic tower-style war memorial. The building of the marina in 1987 and the more recent construction of attractive quayside housing on the river, and the "harbour village", have given the entire town an utterly different feel. St Cuthbert's Church (1870) has a good Jacobean-style vicarage of 1876. In a building on the north side of the High Street, there is a fragment of a fifteenth-century window.

Hauxley, bordering to the south, has evidence of Mesolithic and Iron Age settlements with an early Bronze Age cemetery. In the nineteenth century, there was briefly a horse-racing course between here and Amble. There was significant opencast mining here in the 1970s with the vast "Big Geordie" dragline becoming virtually a tourist attraction.

ANCROFT

Five miles southwest of Berwick, the tower of St Anne's Church is a favourite subject for pictorial calendars. There is a pele, built in the late thirteenth century over the west end of the nave. The interior is plain but improved of late by the replacement of "lavatory glass" in the window with good quality plain glass. The rebuild, which included the pele, blocked the twelfth-century Romanesque southwest door, the door frame of which is still plainly visible. There is part of a mediaeval cross which had formed a slab grave cover in the ground floor room at the foot of the tower; it was transported from Durham in more recent times. Ancroft had a troubled past—a musket ball in the nearby field is a sign of why the pele was built in these dangerous borderlands! Across the main road are humps and bumps concealing buildings buried to quell the plague. The village recovered and by the end of the eighteenth century, it was noted for clog making, and notably for the Royal Navy. A short verse relates:

The cobblers of Ancroft
    were famous
Famed throughout all the land
Their boots were worn by everyone
The poor, the gentry and grand.
They supplied boots and
    shoes to the navy
Nelson, he was heard to say
Give thanks to the
    cobblers of Ancroft
Their duty they have done the day.

Movingly one can discover a headstone just west of the tower

↓ **ANCROFT** Church

with the name of Mary Catherine Smith and other religious sisters from north-eastern France, who had been given sanctuary from the French Revolution at Haggerston Castle by the recusant Sir Carnaby Haggerston. The remaining sisters would eventually move to a house at Scorton in North Yorkshire.

↓ **ANCROFT** Sisters' headstone

The Just Shall be in Everlasting Rememberance Psalm IIIV 7 To the Memory of Mary Catherine Smith deceasd the 20th of Jany 1799 in whom were Joind Virtue & Religion to Prudence & afability of Manners by which She gaind Universal Esteem & was Superiour of the Religious Community who by the Bounty of SIR CARNABY HAGGERSTON Bart were receivd & lodged at his Castle during 12 Years after the French Revolution of which Community are also here interrd Mary Castell Helen Chadwick Elizabeth Jackson Helen Hool, Elizabeth Blundell Elizabeth Hagan, Jane Philips Elizabeth Smith, Monica Hagan.

May they Rest in Peace

ASHINGTON

"The largest pit village in the world" (as it came to be known) and a nursery for footballers: the Charlton brothers and Jackie Milburn (of whom there is a statue in the main street) all hailed from here. In the early nineteenth century, there was virtually nothing here bar Ashington Farm, three-quarters of a mile southwest of the present town centre. The landscape was transformed by the Ashington Coal Company in the mid-nineteenth century—the first 300 houses were built between 1855 and 1878 and the classical "rows" of coal mining towns have survived here in large part. First Row has cottages of good brick with their painted stone lintels and sills. It has been less tampered with than many of the other rows; originally behind each row was a tramway system for the removal of rubbish and waste from ash closets.

The colliery, which closed in 1988, covered a vast space immediately to the north of the town. All evidence of its existence is gone except for a very good heritage trail, in the midst of a business park, explaining the placing of different elements within the colliery and describing something of how the industry operated. Ashington has not been well served by architects

↓ **ASHINGTON** farm

and town planners. The lack of height and variation of rooflines casts a deadening effect on the townscape. Still more sadly, some of the more interesting buildings have been lost. Methodist Central Hall, formerly on Woodhorn Road, had panache with an Art Deco use of tiling; the Grand Hotel which formerly stood on the south-eastern corner of the town centre on North Seaton Road was good late-nineteenth-century Gothic with a rotunda on the corner and good gabling. The Elephant (formerly the North Seaton Hotel) on Newbiggin Road survives and is of similar style. The former Cooperative Arcade (1924) was originally an open arcade on the ground floor; good terracotta tiling survives as does the grand imperial staircase inside

with its bronze handrails, but the building would benefit from careful conservation.

Holy Sepulchre parish church, its dedication doubtless taken from the former mediaeval chapel of that name at Sheepwash (1887–96), is a good five-bay Perpendicular-style building by W. S. Hicks; it has a western narthex. Sadly, the north-east tower was never built, since the Ashington Coal Company was fearful that its bells would wake its night-time shift workers! Good former vicarage next door with an Arts and Crafts flavour.

Wansbeck General Hospital by Powell and Moya is a distinguished piece of modern building (1991).

The Ashington area repays a visit despite the paucity of architectural merit. It remains a crucial

reminder of the coal industry and of the industry's key contribution in both world wars. Just to the north-west of the town was the First World War Ashington Landing Field, part of the Home Defence Squadron; it is still identifiable from a large wood planted in a + pattern, which was the ground symbol used by pilots to locate the grass landing strip! The town has spawned two distinguished opera singers, Sheila Armstrong and Janice Cairns, and then also, in the visual arts, the "Pitmen Painters", now immortalized in the play of that name (*qv* Woodhorn).

Stakeford, due south, takes its name from the former river crossing marked by stakes, the remains of which can still be seen when the dam is opened downriver. Sheepwash, a hamlet three-quarters of a mile west again, takes its name from its place on the River Wansbeck where sheep were dipped; the mediaeval church of the Holy Sepulchre is completely lost, but the extensive Old Rectory, with an interesting interior, survives; there is a spectacular ceiling with much ornament. Little remains on the northern bank of a former mediaeval bridge just west of the present road bridge.

Pegswood, 3 miles west of Ashington, is an ancient farming settlement, radically transformed by the coal industry when the first shaft was sunk in 1873 (the colliery closed in 1969). There are some good older houses in the main street—much of the colliery housing has been demolished for newer housing development. North Farm is an impressive eighteenth-century house, with East Farm a smaller house. Cookswell House at the western end of the village (1768) is brick with stone lintels and a good door surround. The Bothal Roundabout boasts the locally dubbed Robin of Pegswood, a bronze figure with an adjacent steel girder. Stephenson railway viaduct a mile southwest, and footings of fifteenth-century Lady Chapel 1 mile south.

BACKWORTH

Backworth Manor was noted in 1292 as belonging to Tynemouth Priory. West Backworth is a deserted medieval village. A Roman hoard was found here in 1812. Replacing a seventeenth-century house, Backworth Hall was built by William Newton for R. W. Grey (1778–80). The five-bay south front has a pediment and is of high quality—it now houses the Miners' Welfare Hall, with the spacious grounds converted into a golf course. Duke's Cottages, on Front Street, have been attractively restored with rear courtyards.

BAMBURGH

The north Northumbrian coastal horizon is dominated from both southern and northern perspectives by the twin fortresses of Lindisfarne and Bamburgh, with Bamburgh being perhaps the most impressive castle profile in Britain and often acting as an emblem for Northumberland. Bamburgh's origins reach back into the Celtic period of "British" civilization. Later it became the capital successively of Bernicia and then the united kingdom of Northumbria. In 1816–17, evidence of this was made

↓ **BAMBURGH** Castle

↑ **BAMBURGH** Church

↓ **BAMBURGH** Grace Darling tomb

manifest, when a storm revealed skeletons from a seventh-/eighth-century cemetery. Two hundred years later, these have undergone further research, and the crypt of St Aidan's Church now forms a fascinating ossuary. Evidence from their decayed teeth suggests that these people had lived sumptuously as members of the royal court!

The castle, whose present appearance now owes most to the eighteenth and nineteenth centuries (Salvin), nonetheless stands on the site of the eighth-century royal palace of Edwin and Oswald. Lord Crewe, Bishop of Durham, bought the ruins in 1704 and, in 1757, Dr Sharp began the restoration. In the late nineteenth century, the Crewe Trustees sold the castle to Lord Armstrong, the Tyneside industrial magnate and engineer, who made further major changes between 1894 and 1904.

St Aidan's Church is an equal treasury of both beauty and interest. Aidan himself is believed to have died in the first church, leaning against a wooden Y-shaped post which now forms part of the ceiling of the tower. A modern shrine to Aidan, designed by Donald Buttress, was dedicated in 2013 and stands on the north side of the entrance to the chancel. The church is broad and spacious and full of architectural interest, dating back in its present form to the early thirteenth century. In the north aisle lies the recumbent effigy of Grace Darling, the heroic rescuer, in 1838, of survivors from the crippled vessel, *Forfarshire*. Her grave is near the western edge of the churchyard. There is a good modern museum dedicated to her memory west of the main road and opposite the churchyard.

Further north along the road and on the left by Friary Farm is the remaining fragment of the northeast corner of the church of the former Dominican friary of 1265. The village is attractively set around a triangular green with some fine houses. Its attractiveness leaves it open to siege by vast numbers of tourists in busy seasons!

BARDON MILL

Dominated by the pottery which is a converted water-powered woollen mill. Converted originally to make sanitary ware (something of a Tyneside speciality!) and now mainly garden ware, it still uses "Newcastle downdraft kilns". Fine Tudor-style stationmaster's house. Other bastle houses nearby.

BARRASFORD

Elwood House—late eighteenth-century three-bay house similar to the house at Great Swinburne. Romano-British settlement 400 m northwest of Barrasford Park.

Wonderful survival of a small rural railway station!

Across the North Tyne is the splendid profile of Haughton Castle standing high above the river. Its origins are in a thirteenth-century first-floor hall/tower house not dissimilar to that recently excavated at Edlingham—the hall doorway survives. There had also been a gateway and curtain wall now lost; the last two centuries have seen much remodelling including work by Dobson from 1845. Interesting furnishings including large Jacobean overmantels imported from a house in Newcastle. Salvin built a further embattled wing to the west in 1876. The chapel is a solitary ruin in the park 150 m southeast of the castle—it was partially demolished c.1816 when the village of Haughton was cleared and the park enclosed.

Gunnerton, 2 miles northwest, includes St Christopher's Church (1899), built by the Revd J. C. Hawes who was curate here and later became a Roman Catholic, building churches in Australia. Later still he lived as a hermit on Cat Island in the Bahamas! Some Arts and Crafts work in the gallery and a plastered interior with bare stone exposed in places.

BAVINGTON HALL

Just to the west of Little Bavington stands the late-seventeenth-century Shafto family's Bavington Hall. It was extended and remodelled by Admiral Delaval c.1720. Within a foreground of pleasant, wooded gardens and much topiary stands the seven-bayed two-and-a-half-storey house. It includes a heavy-arched doorway with a surround by Gibbs. There are good interiors including a fine staircase. An eighteenth-century gazebo survives in the grounds, alongside the fragments of a grotto, a brick pedestal, whose statue has been lost—and an eye-catcher a little to the southwest looking like a miniature castle.

Great Bavington village is no more, except for earthworks, although in 1377, the Poll Tax registered thirty-seven adults here. The present hamlet comprises a few houses by Mire Farm. Bare bedrock forms the surface of the main street. Presbyterian church built in 1725.

BEADNELL

A tiny fishing port boasting the only west-facing harbour on England's east coast. Historic limekilns by the harbour (1798) by Richard Pringle for John Wood of Beadnell Hall; the Hall is early eighteenth-century with Gothick additions. St Ebba's Chapel stood on rocks northeast of the harbour—only earthworks and masonry survive. The eighteenth-century Parish Church of St Ebba has an eccentric octagonal screen at the base of the spire. Annstead Farm, 1 mile north, has a pedimented centre with blank Venetian windows.

Tughall, 4 miles to the southwest, has the remains of an early-Norman chapel which stood at the centre of the former village finally abandoned in the nineteenth century. The chapel was the possession of the Augustinian Nostell Priory in West Yorkshire, although later the Premonstratensian Alnwick Abbey collected most of the tithes; legend tells of the chapel being built at one of the resting places of St Cuthbert's body, in its great pilgrimage after his death. Tughall Hall just to the east is a modest but handsome twentieth-century remodelling of an eighteenth-century house. Lord Beveridge, author of the report giving birth to the welfare state, who was briefly MP for Berwick-upon-Tweed, lived here. Next door is the former airfield, built as a satellite to the nearby training base at Milfield.

BEDLINGTON

More widely known for its eponymous lamb-like terriers, it was formerly capital of Bedlingtonshire, part of the County Palatine of Durham (Detached).

Despite being absorbed into the coalfield, there are signs of its historic origins. The long and broad Front Street boasts an eighteenth-century market cross in the form of an obelisk. Some pantiled houses have survived. The King's Arms is of classical design—five bays. There are some curiosities: the early rolling mill at the former ironworks made the rails for the Stockton and Darlington Railway; a memorial to Daniel Gooch who laid the Atlantic cables (1865–89); a memorial in the

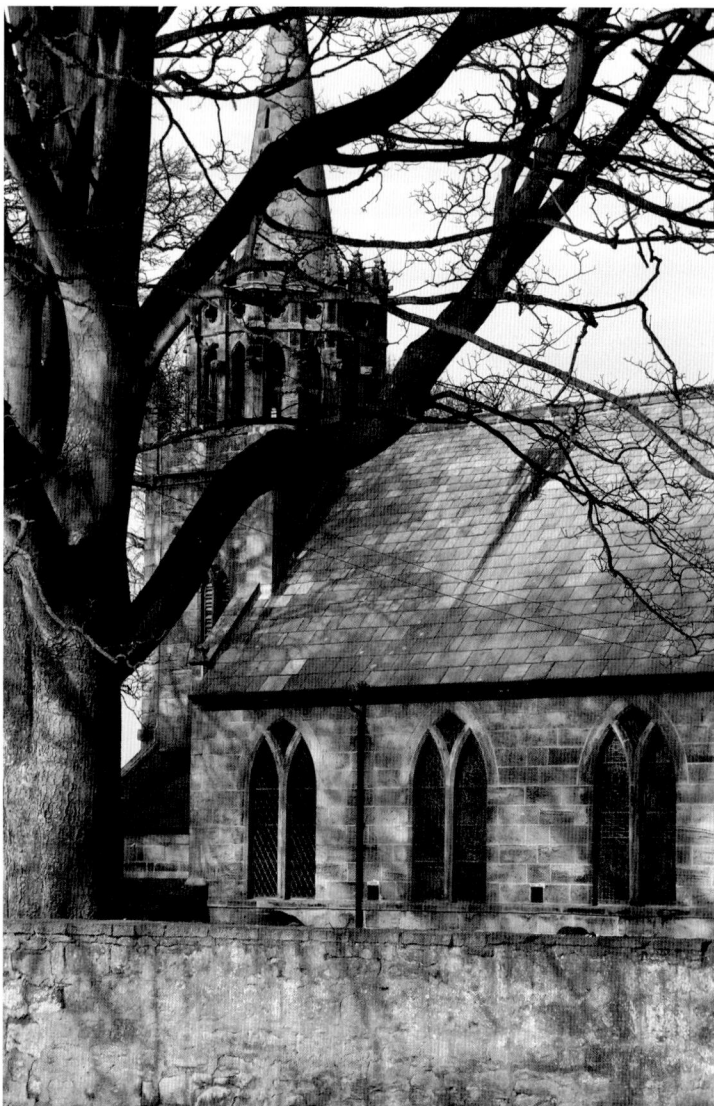

↑ **BEADNELL** church spire

church titled "Watson's Wake", to a man who climbed the church tower in his sleep and fell to his death when someone woke him; finally a headstone in the churchyard with the rhyme: *Poems and epitaphs are but stuff—here lies Robert Barras, that's enough.* St Cuthbert's Church has a twelfth-century nave, but in the mid-eighteenth century the nave was turned at a right angle—all rebuilt in the nineteenth century in Romanesque style, including the west tower. The chancel arch is an unusual piece of Norman.

St Peter's Church at West Sleekburn (1845), 3 miles northeast, is Transitional style with an apse—the nave aisles were never completed so the arcades were eccentrically bricked up.

BELFORD

Still styled a town, Belford was the last coaching stop before Berwick-upon-Tweed, as the abiding presence of *The Bluebell* suggests. The tollhouse survives. The 1983 bypass makes it feel something of a backwater in contrast to the buzzing scene heretofore. The church was rebuilt with some style by Dobson in 1828, with tall lancets on either side. Elements of the mediaeval building have survived somewhat randomly, including the interestingly chamfered, dog-toothed Norman chancel arch. Compact Belford Hall (1754–6) by James Paine welcomes those approaching from the south; there is something of a treasury of mansions and lost houses in the vicinity. Easington Grange, just a mile and a half northeast, boasts a handsome eighteenth-century farmhouse.

Adderstone Hall, 2 miles southeast, is a five-bay mansion with a porte-cochère by William Burn (1819). Near Warenford, 1 mile southwest, stood Twizell House, another fine mansion (demolished 1950s) of the ubiquitous and recusant Selby family—a lodge gate points to former glory. Four miles south, on the Great North Road, are two monumental gate pillars, originally the main gateway to Bellshill House, built for John Pratt in 1790, later bought by another Selby, and again demolished after the Second World War. Notable granaries close by to another of Benjamin Green's fine Tudor-style railway stations, sadly disused at the time of writing. For St Cuthbert's Cave, see Holburn (*qv*).

BELLINGHAM

The old Shell Guide to Northumberland put it well when it described Bellingham as the "'capital' of North Tyne country and Redesdale"—to that we would now perforce add Kielder and all that means. Although there is not a profusion of architectural merit in this tiny market town, nonetheless it is an attractive centre with some nice shopfronts and some old houses by the river.

The station which was on the Border Counties Railway survives as offices, and the Heritage Centre is in the former goods yard, with disused railway carriages serving as a restaurant; the railway went through remarkably remote countryside as it tracked north via Deadwater and then Riccarton Junction.

St Cuthbert's Church is eccentric because of its development over the centuries. Much of it is thirteenth century with lancets, and there is a long south transept which originally had a western aisle. In 1609, there was a substantial remodelling which resulted in both nave and transept being vaulted in stone, along with twenty-two chamfered transverse arches; a Tudor south door was added. The seventeenth-century roof is unique to the county with alternate strips of single and double stone slabs. Some interesting memorials including the "Long Pack" gravestone associated with a local legend. St Ignatius' Roman Catholic Church is by Ignatius Bonomi (1839).

A good bridge here by John Green with single-storey tollhouse. Some rows of cottages and some spoil heaps on the hillside tell of the former Hareshaw Ironworks, opened in 1838 and closing just ten years later; upriver are the remains of the ironworks dam, once some 6 m high. At Riding Wood, a mile and a half northwest, there is an Iron Age and then later Romano-British homestead. Bastle at The Riding half a mile southeast. Arts and Crafts lychgate to the cemetery by Robert Mauchlen.

Hesleyside, 2 miles west-north-west, is the historic home of the Charltons; an eighteenth-century courtyard house but with evidence of a 1632 loggia. The front with the carriage arch is 1847 by Ignatius Bonomi. There are some fine interior features including an imperial stair and Ionic and Corinthian columned screens. Two miles east-southeast of Bellingham is Redesmouth, where the Rede

↑ **BELLINGHAM** station

confluences with the North Tyne, and the Rede was bridged attractively in the early nineteenth century with two segmental arches. Another Romano-British settlement, a third of a mile north. The recovered locomotive from the Tay Bridge disaster was renovated here.

BELSAY

The hill fort at Bantam Hill indicates the longevity of Belsay in terms of human settlement. In the fourteenth century, the castle was built at the foot of the hill by the de Middleton family. Sir Charles Monck, a scion of the Middleton family, abandoned the castle in

1807, following his honeymoon in Germany and Greece, and he then built the magnificent Grecian mansion, which was rescued by English Heritage, sometime after the Middleton family had left the house in 1962.

The castle, somewhat hidden in the grounds of the Hall, remains impressive. Its history, both architecturally and indeed more generally, is to a degree unknown. The Middletons had lived here since 1270, and the tower which formed the basis of the castle was built a hundred years later. The house was then altered in 1614 to become a manor. It is built to an

L-shaped plan with a tower enclosing three large rooms each on top of the other—the lowest of these has a tunnel vault and was used as a kitchen. The hall has a large fireplace with fifteenth-century decoration. The castle has a romantic appearance with fine masonry of a honey-coloured sandstone. Most splendid of all is the roof with its four rounded barbizans.

Belsay Hall was built between 1807 and 1817. There is a certain austerity in its composition which is emphasized internally by the lack of furnishings. Monck appears to have designed the house himself, albeit with a powerful influence

from Sir William Gell, a noted antiquary of the time. The six-by-seven-bayed building is exactly 100 feet square (about 30 metres). The severity of the design is increased by the windows being cut without mouldings. The atrium-like hall has light from a clerestory. The fluted Ionic columns are paired with Doric columns above. There are coffered ceilings throughout and large vaulted cellars. The octagonal lantern on the stables reflects the "Tower of the Winds" in Athens.

The grounds are fashioned using eighteenth-/nineteenth-century garden design. They are romantic and picturesque, and the existence of the castle adds to this intriguing atmosphere. There are ornate bridges across the Coal Burn. There is a mediaeval village cross 250 m east of the castle.

The old village was cleared from the southwest of the castle, and the cottages in the new village are Italianate in feel, especially in the wide-arcaded ground floor. Wood House (1836) is the former inn, and the old school is dated 1829.

Swinstead lies 400 m north-northeast of the Hall and was built in 1750 for Thomas, the brother of Sir William Middleton. Harnham Hall is 2 miles northwest of Belsay. It includes a sixteenth-century tower at the back, and the rest of the house, of a similar date, was much altered in the seventeenth and eighteenth centuries. The dragon on the ceiling in the main room represents the Babington family who lived here from 1660–77. Dame Katherine Babington, a fierce dissenter, plotted with the village blacksmith to expel the vicar of Bolam from his pulpit during a church service; on account of this she was excommunicated and refused burial in consecrated ground—she was buried in a tomb hollowed out of the rock in the garden below the house. The tiny village snuggles next door with some good houses.

↑ **BELSAY** Castle

BELTINGHAM

Good Tudor/very late Perpendicular church rather over-restored in 1884. Nonetheless, there is fine fenestration, and the Tudor style has survived—there are rustic carvings in the easternmost windows—northwest chancel window by Kempe. Former southeast doorway has what is probably a pre-Conquest cross slab in the recess. Plain thirteenth-century cross in the churchyard and outside the west end of the nave is a Roman altar. Beltingham House next door is a handsome three-bay eighteenth-century house; White Heather Cottage on the other side of the church is older but remodelled in the eighteenth century. A little further away, the fine ashlar Old Vicarage (1845) has a curved centre bow. In the north-western corner of the churchyard is a remarkable yew tree thought to be c.1,000 years old.

Willimoteswick, 1 mile west, is a fortified manor of the Ridleys set on a still older site; it seems to have replaced an H-plan tower house. Much rebuilding in 1900 in Tudor style using mouldings from the earlier structure. The gatehouse to the northeast is almost complete.

BERWICK-UPON-TWEED

Nikolaus Pevsner described Berwick-upon-Tweed as "one of the most exciting towns in England . . . with hardly any irritating buildings anywhere". Saving the 1960s Cooperative Building, this remains true, although some "Berwickers" would dispute its English status. Nor would they see it as Scottish— Berwick's tempestuous history saw the town changing hands many times between the Scots and English in the Middle Ages. It has been part of England now for over 500 years but remains anomalous: it causes the national boundary to deviate from the Tweed so that it may be included in England. This nodal location lay at the heart of its strategic importance to both nations.

It also explains its great interest, characterized most powerfully by the only complete set of Elizabethan walls surviving. The double threat from Scotland and France provoked the building of these ramparts. In

74

↑ **BERWICK** Royal Border Bridge

↓ **BERWICK** Cowport

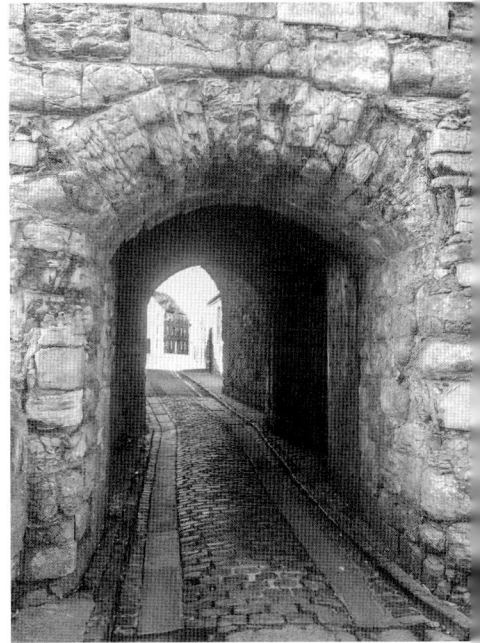

1568, with Mary Queen of Scots no longer a threat, the construction ceased, although some work continued with the Cowport not being completed until the 1590s. Sir Richard Lee used an Italianate pattern which he had pioneered in Portsmouth; Berwick's ramparts thus have clear resonances of those in Lucca in Italy! On the south and along the Quay, the walls follow the line of Edward I's fortifications but on the northern side they are closer to the town centre—Edward's earlier foundations are still visible from Northumberland Avenue, later topped by an Elizabethan watch tower. The walls are a mile and a half in length and 7 m high. They were the most expensive infrastructure project in Elizabeth's reign. Meg's Mount, a bastion high above the Tweed, is a great vantage point looking down toward the castle ruins. (Just below it on Bank Hill stands a curious gabled building, a former public convenience, said to be the earliest in England!) The Brass, Cumberland and Windmill Bastions are impressive, as is Coxon's Tower. The latter stands close to the Saluting Platform overlooking the Tweed Estuary, equipped with one former Crimean cannon to remind everyone of the original function of

the platform. There are four gates piercing the walls, with Cowport leading out to Magdalene Fields where the golf links now occupy clearly marked strip lynchets, evidence of the old "open field" system of strip farming.

Just inside Cowport are the parish church and barracks. The barracks are remarkable, the first purpose-built infantry barracks in England. Based on an original design of Nicholas Hawksmoor, the plans were sadly mauled by a military engineer in the interests of saving money for the Ordnance Department. Opened in 1720, they were a reaction to the "Fifteen" when troops supporting James, the "Old Pretender", pushed as far south as the "English" Midlands. Built to accommodate 600 soldiers, the elevations are clearly in Hawksmoor's style. They eventually became the home "depot" of the King's Own Scottish Borderers and its predecessor regiment for close on a century. They now include the regimental museum, alongside the town museum and that of the fortifications. A fragment of the Burrell Collection is housed in the town museum.

Holy Trinity Church across the Parade is equally intriguing,

as one of very few churches completed during the Cromwellian Commonwealth period. Replacing a crumbling mediaeval predecessor, it was designed by John Young of Blackfriars in London and finished in 1652. The money had been assigned during the reign of Charles I, but the final initiative came

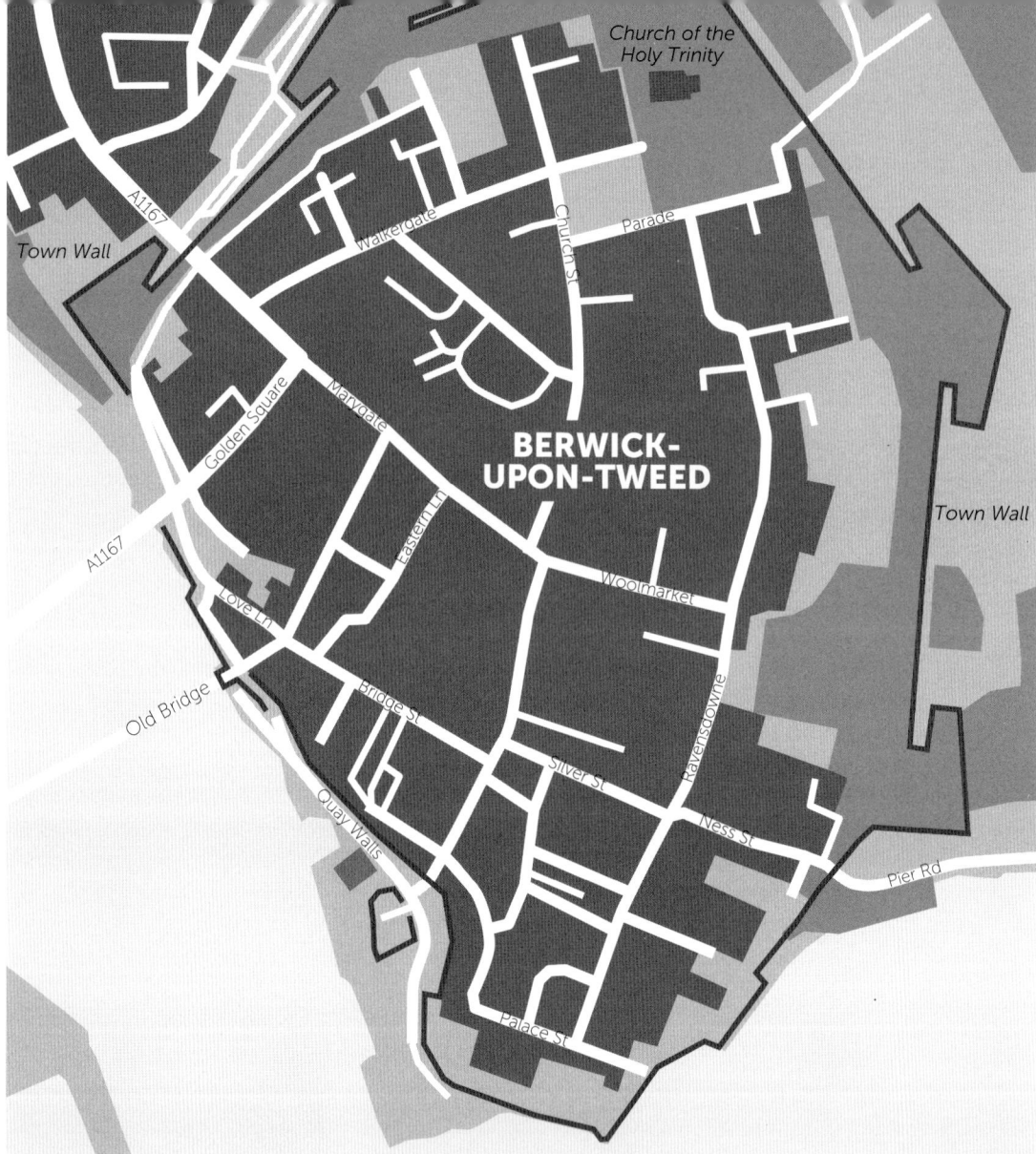

Church of the Holy Trinity

Town Wall

A1167

Walkergate

Church St

Parade

Golden Square

Marygate

BERWICK-UPON-TWEED

A1167

Eastern Ln

Town Wall

Love Ln

Woolmarket

Old Bridge

Bridge St

Ravensdowne

Silver St

Ness St

Quay Walls

Pier Rd

Palace St

from one of Cromwell's generals, George Fenwicke, then Governor of Berwick. It is a strange mixture of Gothic and Classical. Originally it had Venetian windows throughout. The proposed tower was vetoed by Cromwell himself, who passed through Berwick on his way to the Battle of Dunbar. There is a west gallery and an unusual chapel on the north side, now a choir room enclosed by a screen. The reredos is an understated early work of Sir Edwin Lutyens. St Andrew's Presbyterian Church, next door, has a tall spire springing from a dwarf tower. One cannot help but think that the flamboyance of the building was meant to compete with its next-door neighbour. The 1872 Masonic Hall has some curious detail. Around the corner in Wallace Green are the former council offices, originally the gaol, in castellated Tudor.

The best way to see the town is to return to the ramparts and proceed anti-clockwise to the Scotsgate which gives a splendid panoramic view down Marygate. The focus is the Town Hall, built 1754–61. A well-known image of this view is that by L. S. Lowry, who holidayed regularly in Berwick—there is a good, illustrated Lowry trail in Berwick and Tweedmouth (*qv*). Looking north from here, the gentle curve of Castlegate opens up views of some good vernacular buildings. The vista down Marygate is equally attractive. Happily, the hideous gap left by the former bus station was closed some years ago with some slightly pastiche but effective infill. Sadly, the south side was permanently scarred, when the new bridge was driven into the main thoroughfare, dismembering the streetscape. A brief diversion toward the Royal Tweed Bridge brings one to the former Corporation Academy (1798) on the north-western corner of the bridge—simple and well preserved, it now serves as a hostelry. Behind it on Bankhill is the former

chapel of the Presbyterian Church of England of 1836—plain but neat.

The Town Hall is a great centrepiece—Tuscan columns, tall tower of four stages (Lowry's painting heightened it still further!), a strong portico, and with an attractive undercroft at the rear. The town gaol is preserved on the top floor in its original state; below is a pleasant large airy meeting hall with a stucco figure of *Justice blindfolded* in a rococo cartouche.

Hide Hill's gentle curve includes some attractive buildings. On the left as one descends is the grand Art Deco facade of a former cinema. Next comes the King's Arms Hotel rather in the tradition of a Georgian country house, and then the former Corn Exchange, later becoming swimming baths and now residential. The Queen's Head Hotel and other buildings are good vernacular and Sandgate takes one under

the quay walls via the Shoregate and out onto the quay. Returning to Sandgate and turning right into Palace Street, the narrow road opens up into a hidden quarter with the feel of a sleepy French town, and a green at its centre.

Moving on and turning left, Palace Green takes one past the early-eighteenth-century former Military Governor's House—noble but slightly tired in feel. The gardens in front, on the site of a former Carmelite priory, now host an imaginative modern development which honours the former religious foundation in the design of its garden. Palace Street East begins with the corner house, No. 10 boasting a hint of Arts and Crafts, then No. 4 is very pretty with its coat of arms and painted wrought-iron balconies. More interesting houses in The Avenue (ironically sporting no trees) and then the former

↓ **BERWICK** Governor's Gardens

↑ **BERWICK** Spittal, Wilson effigies

Grammar School (1754), now residences for young people in need. Fragments of old Berwick in the web of ginnels—Weddells Lane, Oil Mill Lane, Foul Ford.

Berwick's three bridges are further jewels in the crown. The seventeenth-century bridge, clothed in a beautiful soft-tinted red sandstone, is a study in balance and perspective rising beautifully to the main arch for river traffic, close to the northern shore. Begun in 1611, and replacing a wooden structure, it was completed in 1626. Next comes the unapologetically modernist concrete road bridge opened by the Prince of Wales in 1928—its prospect has been much improved with good lighting and street furniture. It is an impressive span of about a third of a mile—it was the longest concrete span in Britain when it was completed. Then comes Robert Stephenson's amazing Royal Border Bridge opened by Queen Victoria in 1850. Carrying the London–Edinburgh main line over myriad arches, it has the feel of a Roman aqueduct.

Following the riverside path on the Walls to the east, and passing the old quay, Quay Walls opens to an attractive quadrant of houses, some former granaries and otherwise Georgian town houses, including the former Custom House. Wellington Terrace follows with three more austerely grand Georgian-style properties, one a former manse. On the corner here is the Old Whaling House. Behind these is the pedimented mid-eighteenth-century Main Guard, moved here from Marygate in 1815.

Returning up Palace Street East, a walk up Ravensdowne passes several fine late-Georgian villas—immediately behind these is the old Powder Magazine and the powerfully positioned early-nineteenth-century

Lion House, keeping its watch down the coast as far as Lindisfarne and Longstone lighthouse. A detour here brings one through Ness Gate onto Pier Road, past the former whaling factory later converted into maltings, and now residential; the pier stands at the end with its attractive red and white lighthouse. Further up Ravensdowne and hidden behind an arch is the modest Roman Catholic Church of St Mary and St Cuthbert, built appropriately in the year of Catholic Emancipation, 1829.

Finally, making one's way up Castlegate, one passes the "Greenes", modest housing built for the fishermen who plied from the stone jetty near Magdalene Fields. The station, at the top of Castlegate, is of 1924–7 replacing a piece of Victorian Philistinism. Its predecessor occasioned the demolition of much of the mediaeval castle! The platforms stand within the former Great Hall where Edward I confirmed the ill-fated John Balliol as King of Scotland. The castle had admittedly been abandoned by 1611 and was thereafter used as a quarry for building stone. Fragments of the drawbridge survive in Castle Vale Park. The splendid twelfth-century Constable Tower remains, as does the amazing "White" Wall protecting the castle all the way down to the river embankment and concluding with the Water Tower, reconstructed in 1540. Castle Hills House, a flamboyant villa further along the river, was built c.1810 for the Askew family. Along Castle Terrace is a patch of open land, beneath which are the foundations of a mediaeval church. Here is the only evidence for the former village of Bondington which was at least as old as Berwick; it had a nunnery on its north boundary next to the modern bypass.

Across the river lie Tweedmouth and Spittal. Tweedmouth is still a working port through Tweed Dock. The old town is attractive with its back alleys and eighteenth-century St Bartholomew's Church, in whose churchyard is the impressive headstone of John Mackay Wilson, collector of "Tales from the Borders". Sadly, the Royal Tweed Bridge sundered the town in 1928. A viaduct and track bed survive from a quirky zigzag railway which connected Tweed Dock and its maltings with the main line. Tweedmouth was very briefly the terminus of the Newcastle and Berwick Railway and also, as Tweedmouth Junction, the eastern end of the Tweedmouth–St Boswells branch line; at the bridge over Northumberland Road, the track branched westwards and the former course can still be traced in places. The crumbling remnants of the substantial locomotive depot were demolished in 2020, but happily the 1961 signal box remains—a rare example of good "contemporary" 1960s architecture. Just one stone gatepost stands, as a reminder of the once grand station and its adjacent hotel.

Spittal's name derives from a former lazar house (leprosy hospital) which stood at the gateway to the village on the approach from Tweedmouth. It has for long been an industrial hub and still boasts two printing works. Some good Art Deco buildings on the sweeping promenade in this most northerly English seaside resort.

Ord (now East Ord), 1 mile southwest of Berwick, is pleasantly grouped around the village green. Ord House, built originally for the Osborne family in 1789, is of five bays; it now forms the centre of a holiday park. The St Boswells branch of the North Eastern Railway passed through the village.

BIDDLESTONE

Remote and high above Upper Coquetdale, Biddlestone is approached from the west on a poorly maintained gated road, but it is worth persevering. Biddlestone Hall was the ancient home of the ubiquitous Northumberland Selby family. The house is no more, but the recusant Roman Catholic chapel (1820), built on to a fourteenth-century tower, survives, and falls under the care of the Historic Chapels Trust. The vaulted ground floor of the tower was retained and the chapel itself is in a severe Greek Revival style; mediaeval masonry remains to the eaves level on the north side. The stencilling on the walls has been lost. 100 m southeast of the chapel within the unattractive plantation lie the Biddlestones; one is an uncut stone and the other the base of a mediaeval cross. Beyond the plantation, across the road and in the corner of the field, is a tiny cemetery of the Selbys.

Two miles west is Clennell Hall, the origins of which lie in a late-fourteenth-century tower. The present house is sixteenth and seventeenth century, with interesting windows and a fine fireplace; much of the building was added in 1897. Nearby there are the contours of a hill fort on Clennell Hill.

BIRTLEY

An isolated village, high up behind Chipchase. St Giles' Church has retained its completely plain Norman chancel arch despite all restorations—there is also a blocked sixteenth-century doorway in the northern nave wall. Fascinatingly, on the north wall of the chancel is a very early (dated 700) and crude cross of the Lindisfarne type with crossbars at the end of the arms; it is marked with the letters ORPE. There is a ruinous tower in the former vicarage garden, probably late sixteenth century.

BLANCHLAND

The unique appearance of this beautiful village results from the transformation of the former Premonstratensian monastery by the Lord Crewe Trustees in the eighteenth century. The village is grouped around The Square which was effectively the outer court of the former abbey. The central focus to the square is a Pant of 1897 commemorating the Queen's Diamond Jubilee. The fifteenth-century crenellated monastic gatehouse acts as one entrance into the square and opposite is the Lord Crewe Arms, which again is an amalgam of former monastic buildings, and at the north end of which is a further embattled tower which may have been the Abbot's Lodge. The inn has been the haunt of celebrated personalities including W. H. Auden, Christopher Isherwood,

↑ **BLANCHLAND** Lord Crewe Arms

Philip Larkin, Benjamin Britten and Peter Pears. The houses in the square are eighteenth and nineteenth century. Gowland's Cottage has within a good fifteenth-century beamed ceiling—it was part of the east claustral range. On the lane to the west is the former police house quaintly adorned by two new blue lamps. Almost next door is a former mill. To the south an attractive two arched bridge. The former school of 1860 is thought to be by S. S. Teulon.

St Mary's Church was raised from the ruins of the monastic church by the Trustees. In the present

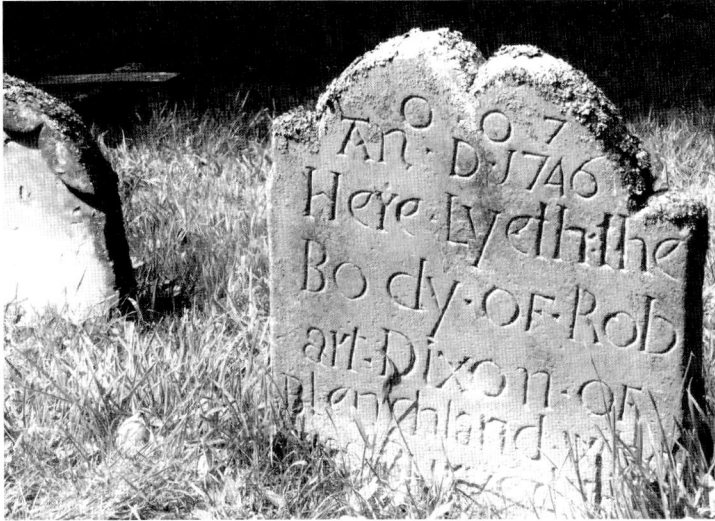

↑ **BLANCHLAND** headstone

L-shaped building, the monastic chancel, crossing and north transept survive. The chancel retains a thirteenth-century feel with its Early English lancets. The wall bounding the Lord Crewe Arms' garden is the south wall of the long but narrow monastic nave. There is a strong thirteenth-century tower with a fourteenth-century belfry stage. There is a good thirteenth-century cross in the churchyard.

The Derwent Reservoir, only a mile and a half east-northeast, was begun in 1960 and finally opened in 1967. It provides water for South Tyneside and lower Wearside and is connected by a sophisticated "water grid" with the vast Kielder scheme (*qv*), to the north-northwest and almost bordering Scotland. There is sailing and windsurfing on the lake, and there is also a hydroelectric plant as part of the wider scheme.

BLYTH

Not a paradise of modern architecture but a product of the thriving coal industry in the nineteenth and early twentieth centuries. The 1813 map shows two shipbuilding yards,

but it was the railways, alongside coal, that brought industrial development. Many of the worthwhile buildings even from this modern period have been lost. Tweed House and the former National School are interesting, as are the Harbour Commissioners' Offices of 1913—the panels of Dutch glazed tiles come from the SS *Walmer Castle*. The 1896 police station towers above the streetscape and is an estimable structure with plenty of carved decoration. The first of all English railways was laid here in the early seventeenth century, carrying coal from the Bebside Pit to the river using horse-drawn locomotion, along wooden rails.

St Cuthbert's is a good late nineteenth-century building by W. S. Hicks, similar to his excellent work in Shilbottle. St Mary's was also extended by Hicks just a little later (1902) and again includes good work.

Blyth Battery is a fascinating survival from the First World War. The

→ **BLYTH** Battery

↑ **BLYTH** beach huts

bombardment of Hartlepool in 1916 prompted a wider coastal defence plan and the artillery station was built at that time. The battery was recommissioned in the Second World War, and new facilities built slightly to the north including flat-roofed structures housing powerful artillery.

BOLAM

Only the park, hall and church survive from a village of "200 slated houses around the green". Bolam Hall stands on the site of the former castle and was built for Robert Horsley, who died in 1809. The large and most beautiful Bolam Lake, designed by Dobson, was originally in the grounds, and the Hall was probably also designed by Dobson. Iron Age fort to the north. The church of St Andrew has a strong Saxon tower and a Norman nave—the quoins of the nave are also Saxon. A fine interior indicating a fairly complicated history in the development of the building—dogtooth decoration in the doorway. Mid-fourteenth-century effigy of a knight minus much of his legs. Tiny window in south aisle shows where a bomb, jettisoned from a German aeroplane, entered the church without exploding! Old Vicarage nestling attractively next to the church.

Poind and his Man is a Bronze Age barrow with a standing stone, on moorland to the west—Poind is still here, but a second stone migrated to Wallington. Devil's Causeway, the Roman road to Berwick, is just to the northwest. Large red brick Gallowhill by Septimus Oswald 1 mile southeast.

BOTHAL

Bothal was the main centre of the extensive Welbeck estates in Northumberland—the Portland family name still occurs on buildings and roads in the area. The castle remains a private residence of the family. It is built on

↑ **BOLAM** Church

a spur overlooking the Wansbeck. Originating as a tower house, the castle was given to William Rufus in 1095 by Guy de Balliol. Balliol's daughter married William Bertram, Baron of Mitford. Robert Bertram gained his licence to crenellate in 1343. Originally, as well as the prominent gatehouse, there were several other square towers. The gatehouse was restored in 1831 as a separate residence, with a western wing added in 1858 and extended

in 1909. In the west face of the nineteenth-century stable range is included masonry from the Yethouse Court.

St Andrew's Church dates back to the twelfth century, and indeed the nave walls may be older. The chancel is thirteenth century and, a century later, the south chapel was extended into a full south aisle. The Perpendicular work came with the building of the Holgate Chantry in 1398. The east end of the chancel was rebuilt in 1887 with a triplet of lancets. There is a curious triple bell tower, fragments of fourteenth-century glass and a magnificent sixteenth-century alabaster table tomb with effigies of Ralph, Lord Ogle (1516).

BOULMER

The Fishing Boat Inn, formerly a centre of smuggling in Northumberland, still preserves its local feel. The inn, still prominent in the village, lay at the heart of the smuggling activity, with its landlord, Isaac Addison. On one occasion, Addison and his fellow smugglers came into conflict with the *Blackboy*, a royal cutter. Addison shot one of the king's men, but he was acquitted since the cutter had not raised its colours before firing on the smugglers' lugger! The hostelry has not been suburbanized, nor indeed has this almost primitively attractive fishing hamlet with boats still moored on the shingle beach.

There is an independent lifeboat service. The eerie presence of the RAF base with its revolving radar dishes, where nine-tenths of the action is underground, does not impinge overmuch; the radar base tracks movements from North Cape and down towards southern Europe, even to Gibraltar. The tracks of the former runways of the Second World War base can still be seen as one drives down the perimeter road, now part of the public highway.

→ **BRANXTON** Flodden
Field memorial

BRANTON and BRANDON

Both hamlets lie to the west of the Wooler–Coldstream Road either side of the River Breamish. Branton to the south is grouped around the farm. Some of the former farm buildings have been well converted into holiday accommodation, workshops and at one point a pottery. The very plain former Presbyterian church of 1781 has now been put to business/residential use.

Crossing the fast-flowing Breamish to Brandon is least perilous using the rebuilt footbridge. The rocky riverbed through which runs what passes for a ford is only for heavy farm vehicles. The farm is effectively the village, with a neat row of cottages, incorporating an erstwhile forge and a handsome late-eighteenth-century farmhouse; one of the buildings in the farmyard is inscribed RL ALLGOOD 1831. To the west of the village, south of the road is the abandoned churchyard. Research suggests the church was thirteenth century on

Saxon foundations, with nave and chancel and a narrower sanctuary which had a south chapel of similar proportions.

BRANXTON

Celebrated as the site of the Battle of Flodden (1513), 400 m to the southwest on Branxton Hill—sometimes referred to as the Battle of Branxton Moor. Flodden Hill is nearby, almost directly south, and is where the Scots set up camp. The pitched battle, the bloodiest of all between the Scots and the English, claimed at least 15,000 lives in one day. James IV of Scotland died in the battle alongside the cream of the Scottish aristocracy—the King was laid in state in Branxton Church. It followed significant plunder by the Scots with Norham and Etal Castles suffering serious damage. In 1910, the Berwickshire Naturalists Club set up a memorial on Piper's Hill. There is a good eco-museum stretching out across a wide area interpreting the battle. Within the

village there was a curious "concrete menagerie" in one of the gardens close to the playing field, but in 2021, it was transported to a new home in the grounds of Ayton Castle, over the border to the west of Eyemouth.

St Paul's Church is neo-Romanesque of 1849 with a thirteenth-century chancel arch and a seventeenth-century altar rail.

Pallinsburn House, 1 mile northeast, named after the eponymous stream, is an "all-sorts" house with roots going back at least to an eccentric eighteenth-century mansion sporting pagoda-like columns, then rebuilt and remodelled in the twentieth century, c.1930, in Jacobean style. The two projecting wings on the north side have kept their nineteenth-century façade. The interiors are quite beautiful and there is a fine garden.

Just a mile east-southeast is the King's Stone, a prehistoric monolith, or trysting stone, of c.2500 BC, some 2.5 m high. Probably a site for ancient tribal gatherings. The name is derived from Scott's *Marmion*, in which poem he places the site where King James IV of Scotland was slain, although the Battle of Flodden was some three-quarters of a mile south.

Crookham, 2 miles east, was the site of a late border affray between the English and Scots in 1678. Plain but distinguished Arts-and-Crafts-style Presbyterian church of 1932.

BUDLE

The coastal route opens up to a panorama from either direction. Budle Bay is about a mile square and was already a grain port developed by Henry III in the thirteenth century. Later silting put paid to the port, although Waren Mill still exported grain in the late eighteenth century. The mill was rebuilt successively in 1780, 1819 and 1835. It closed finally in 1980 and after lying desolate has been redeveloped as "Manhattan-style apartments", to use the estate agents' most unlikely imagery.

The bay is a paradise for birdwatchers and forms part of Lindisfarne National Nature Reserve; purple sandpipers (best seen around the rocky headland to Bamburgh—notably in the winter), Brent and barnacle geese, shelduck, grey plover, spotted redshanks and bar-tailed godwit are all seen here. There are useful laybys available for watchers with very good interpretative material for those who are not expert ornithologists. Eel grass, mud and saltmarsh (especially valuable for absorbing CO_2) are a key to the ecosystem here. Summer and winter are undoubtedly the best seasons for birds at Budle; it is visited both by birds from the Arctic and by shore birds. Budle Hall is of delicate pink ashlar from 1810.

On the hill, Outchester (or Spindlestone) Ducket appears for all the world as a former windmill, some 22 m high of coursed stone, but it was built as a dovecote—the Scots version is "doocot", hence Ducket. Hereabouts there are whispers of ancient Rome: Outchester points to the nearby Roman camp of Ulterius, but the Latinized Glororum close to—now with its holiday park—most likely comes from reference to a medi-aeval fort overlooking Bamburgh.

It is a corruption of "Glower o'er 'em", meaning overlooking the old capital.

BYRNESS

Largely a Forestry Commission village built in the 1950s, and designed by Thomas Sharp, who also designed Kielder village; Sharp wrote the earlier Shell Guide to Northumberland. An industrial retraining village had been established here in the 1930s, but that was closed at the outbreak of the Second World War—before that the village had expanded to house workers on the reservoir. At Cottonshopeburnfoot, a little further south, is the Three Kings, a "four-poster" stone circle, probably from the early part of the second millennium BC; here too, the Forestry Drive to Kielder branches westwards—much care needs to be taken if using this fairly rough road. The tiny Church of St Francis of Assisi was built in 1796 and paid for by Mr Louis Dutens, the vicar of Elsdon, who had been the first to establish a permanent modern village here, at that time. There is a window commemorating those who died in the building of the nearby Catcleugh Reservoir. (See colour illustration.)

The reservoir was constructed between 1884 and 1905 to supply Tyneside with water; it is just short of 2 miles long and links with the Whittle Dene reservoir near Stamfordham. It is now designated as a Local Wildlife Site, and the surrounding area a Site of Special Scientific Interest (SSSI).

BYWELL

There is a counter intuitive "southern" feel to this estate village with its castle, hall and two splendid churches—the white fences and manicured fields of the Allendale estates contribute to its character. It is very picturesque, and beautifully situated alongside the river, although the actual village disappeared halfway through the nineteenth century in the landscaping which has made Bywell as it is now.

Bywell Hall, which is open for tours regularly, was built as a grand villa by James Paine for William Fenwick. The south front has a central pediment amidst three wide bays. The pediment rests on giant Ionic columns. Bywell Castle is a large rectangular gatehouse tower and was built in the seventeenth century for Ralph Neville, the second Earl of Westmorland. Now roofless, the shell remains intact; fireplaces also survive. Some remaining curtain-walling was built into the nineteenth-century Bywell Castle House.

The two churches are remarkable and only yards apart. St Andrew's, now in the care of the Churches Conservation Trust, has a first-rate Saxon tower; inside the tower arch is low, and the upper parts are assumed to be c.1000, but the base is almost certainly earlier. The rest of the church was rebuilt three times in the nineteenth century, but all has been done with impeccable taste including very high-quality wooden furnishings. There are early arches preserved in the chancel and south transept. At the east end of the church are some fine cross slabs and Saxon masonry

survives in the nave walls. The Old Vicarage to the north of St Andrew's has late-seventeenth-century work. The high southwest garden wall is known as the "Spite Wall", as it was built to screen the house from the view of the Hall; when the village was moved, the vicar remained determined to stay put!

St Peter's is equally fine and remains the parish church. The north wall and west parts of the narrow Early English chancel are now assumed to be part of a large Saxon church. It could even have been the building in which Bishop Egbert of Lindisfarne was consecrated in the year 802. In the north wall of the nave, Saxon features remain, with their round arches cut into the large rectangular stone blocks; there are elements corresponding to the unique

seventh-century Saxon church at Escomb in County Durham. The Saxon church here was very large and at least the size of the building at Monkwearmouth—it may well have been monastic in origin, explaining the two ancient churches in such close proximity—St Andrew's would have been the parish church. Again, there was heavy restoration by Benjamin Ferrey and others in the nineteenth century. More survives, however, than in St Andrew's, including the fourteenth century nave and the north chapel, and here also are a series of Victorian stained-glass windows dedicated to the Wailes family, and probably executed by William Wailes, a family member and esteemed stained-glass artist. There is a heavily restored chantry chapel in the southeast of the church. The tower has a

↗ **CAPHEATON** Hall, east front
→ **CAPHEATON** Hall, glasshouse

↑ **BYWELL** scratch sundial

pitched roof as was once the case at Longhoughton and Corbridge. On the outside of the south wall a rare "scratch sundial" survives.

To the east of St Andrew's, the village cross remains with its thirteenth-century shaft and a seventeenth-century ball finial.

CAMBO

Set perfectly on a ridge just to the north of Wallington, this undoubted estate village of 1740 is placed between the woodlands of the Wansbeck Vale and the tougher country to the east and looking north toward the Harwood Forest. The former post office is an ancient bastle. Daniel Garrett may have designed the cottages for the Wallington Estate, and Sir Charles Trevelyan remodelled them and added another floor. At the west end of the southernmost row of cottages, the Two Queens, closed not by changes in twenty-first-century drinking patterns, but much earlier, in 1846, when Sir Walter Trevelyan had it closed as part of his campaign against liquor traffic.

The 1842 Holy Trinity Church is unpretentious, but to square it with the dignity of Wallington a Perpendicular tower was added in 1884. Nice barrel ceilings and eight mediaeval "sepulchral slabs" from an earlier chapel (two in the vestry and six in the tower).

One mile north at Hartington is Herterton House. The remarkable gardens of this sixteenth-century farmhouse were landscaped from 1976 onwards by Frank and Marjorie Lawley and include topiary, physic, and flower gardens.

CAPHEATON

One of the most interesting houses in the county, the estate fell to the Swinburnes in the thirteenth century, previously having been owned by a branch of the ubiquitous Fenwick clan. The hall is the first "non-castellate"-style country house of the county, having been completed in the "Restoration" period by Robert Trollope of Newcastle—the date of completion is firmly there on the splendid south front. Late Jacobean, its rusticated pilasters used to finish under an overhanging gable, but with the significant rebuild by William Newton, including the more solemn Georgian north front, the pilasters simply conclude before the roof level—they are still a most unusual and attractive feature, as are the swags and sundials decorating this elevation. The north front is solidly northern but attractively welcoming with the modest wings partially enclosing the courtyard, within which the original circular lawn has been reinstated. The grounds too, including the interesting curved drives, prescind from the sometimes overstated grandeur of the Palladian period. A fine landscape in the saloon captures the original hall as designed by Trollope. It is not surprising that this larger house was built in 1688 since the then Sir John Swinburne had some twenty-four children!

The grounds are open, expansive and well landscaped, although an earlier attribution to Capability Brown was mistaken. The present gate piers were originally placed symmetrically south of the south front. Large and imaginatively

ordered walled kitchen garden. Poet, Algernon Swinburne, was a scion of this family and in his youth would spend summers here.

Village rebuilt in model proportions in the eighteenth century; fine Gothick/Georgian villa now acting as Dower House, to the north of the entrance drive and in front of the former stables. Eighteenth-century Clock Mill, 1,200 m northeast, is almost complete with an overshot wheel—closed in the early twentieth century. East Shaftoe Hall (c.1800), 2,000 m northeast, is probably fourteenth century in its origins followed by sixteenth- and seventeenth-century work, before the eighteenth-century reordering. Iron Age hill fort on Shaftoe Crags, 1 mile northwest.

CARHAM

On the banks of the Tweed, just yards from the border with Scotland, Carham is a notable village. Here, in 1018, Malcom II of Scotland defeated the combined Northumbrian forces under Uhtred to establish the border between Scotland and England, although full recognition would not follow until some centuries later. Almost certainly the battle took place on the south bank of the Tweed, immediately behind the Church of St Cuthbert.

The village's eponymous name (the first part is a corruption of Cuthbert) is on account of King Ecgfrith of Northumbria reputedly granting the land to St Cuthbert for a daughter house of the monastery at Lindisfarne—Carham is almost exactly halfway between Lindisfarne and Melrose where Cuthbert had been a novice under St Boisil (Boswell). In 1126, Walter Espec, who had built Wark Castle, some 2 miles east, granted the church to the Augustinian monastery at Kirkham in Yorkshire. The church was built in 1138 but largely destroyed in 1290. A new church was built in the sixteenth century, and by the 1780s was described as a mean church, with thatch in poor condition. The present church was built in 1790 and the chancel and vestry in 1864. The wooden altar table is by Robert Thompson, the "Mouseman" from Kilburn in North Yorkshire—the mouse is easily traced. At the east end of the village is Carham Hall, built on the site of an earlier house in the mid-nineteenth century for the Compton family.

Sunilaws Station is still there, albeit without tracks, trains or travellers. The platforms serve as gardens/access for converted railway cottages. Nearby Carham Station on another by-road is the only station to be named after a place in a different country—it is in Scotland and was built by an English railway company; the former Shidlaw tileworks is close by.

CARRAWBURGH

Two and a half miles north of Newburgh and on the Roman Wall. Brocolitia Fort is prominently visible as a rectangular platform south of the road, although little masonry is exposed; it is probably one of the last forts to be constructed as part of Hadrian's plans c.130. The Roman service road to the fort is clear to the west. In the marshy valley to the west is a Temple of Mithras or Mithraeum which went through a series of developments in the third and fourth centuries. There are three replica altars at the north end and a statuette of an unknown mother goddess against the east wall. On the north wall, there was a relief of Mithras killing the bull at the dawn of Time. Coventina's Well, another shrine, was built next to a powerful spring 200 m northwest of the Mithraeum—16,000 coins were found when the shrine was excavated in 1876.

↑ **CAWFIELDS** disused quarry

CARTINGTON

Hardly anything but a castle, and amazing to think it's a parish. But the castle is interesting. The mediaeval part is fourteenth and fifteenth century, but it was altered and rebuilt in the sixteenth and seventeenth centuries. There had been at least three towers. Lord Dacre stationed his troops here on a march to the north to join the Earl of Surrey before the Battle of Flodden. Margaret Tudor (Henry VIII's sister and widow of James IV of Scotland) stayed here with her baby daughter, Margaret, in November 1515, on her way south from Harbottle Castle. Ruinous by the early nineteenth century; Lord Armstrong, from nearby Cragside, partially restored the castle to avoid its complete disintegration.

CAWFIELDS

Cawfields Fortlet is some 2 or 3 miles west of Housesteads. It includes Milecastle 42, similar to that at Housesteads, but it is built on a particularly steep sloping site just below the crags of the exposed Whin Sill. It was built c.105 as a base on the Stanegate. There is good exposure of Roman camps, of the wall and the Vallum nearby.

CHATTON

Small, well-kept village with an excellent modern development by the Duke's Estate and surviving blacksmith's forge. Chattonpark is a large Victorian farmhouse built for the duke and bearing his crest. Holy Cross Church is of 1770 with an 1846 north aisle by Salvin, mediaeval cross slabs built into baptistry

floor. Cup and ring marked rocks on Weetwood Moor. Cairns, 3 miles east-southeast, with Beaker pottery c.2000 BC; Roman flagon found nearby.

One mile to the northwest is Fowberry Tower, originally a tower house but converted into a country house in 1666; it gained its Gothick style in the changes made for Sir Francis Blake in 1776 by Nesbit of Kelso. The final version of the front was made in 1809 for Matthew Culley—very fine interiors. There is also a mid-eighteenth-century gazebo—the lodge and gateway are also part of Blake's alterations. Fine bridge over the River Till, 1825, and also for Matthew Culley.

CHERRYBURN

Near to Eltringham, 1 mile west of Prudhoe, is Cherryburn, where the engraver Thomas Bewick was born in 1753. His birthplace, farmhouse and cottage gardens are now a museum administered by the National Trust; his tools remained in the outbuilding and

local children would use them to carve their names in the frame of the building—ironically, the same tools are now displayed by the National Trust, with a notice saying firmly "Do not touch"! (*qv* Ovingham).

Eltringham House nearby is a three-bay mansion of c.1800.

CHESTERS

The situation of Chesters Roman fort is stunning, alongside the river whose bridge it guarded, and enhanced by Nathaniel Clayton's parkland created from 1796 onwards. Half of its area and three of its gates project north of the Wall. The interpretation on the site gives a clear idea of the placing of the barrack blocks, the headquarters, the bath house and the main gates (remnants of the hinging slots for some of the gates still survive). It is an unusually scattered site partly due to the nineteenth-century excavation for which thanks should be given to John Clayton and his family, owners of the estate on which it sits. To the east of the headquarters is

the commanding officer's house and then closer to the river, and cut into the sloping ground, are the substantial remains of the bath house.

The 1891 museum building is by Norman Shaw. The Roman bridge carried Hadrian's Wall across the North Tyne and evidence of it is visible on both banks. The east abutment of the bridge amazingly still stands 2 m high. The piece of wall here includes Turret 29a. Here is a particularly good stretch of wall, and the Limestone Corner forms the summit with fine views both over Tynedale and also northwards to the Cheviots and the Simonside Hills.

The house (Chesters) which looks down on the fort is substantial and was built by the Yorkshire architect John Carr in 1771. It was much enlarged for John Clayton by

↑ **CHESWICK** Ladythorne House
↙ **CHESWICK** dovecote
→ **CHILLINGHAM** Bull, Thomas Bewick

Norman Shaw in 1891. Shaw added wings to form a forecourt and gave the west front much grandeur, with a curve at the centre of which are detached giant Ionic columns—it is a romantic interpretation of English eighteenth-century tastes. His stables opposite are equally successful, with a bow in the direction of Seaton Delaval and Vanbrugh.

CHESWICK

Just 5 miles south of Berwick, Cheswick is a hamlet grouped around East House Farm and farmhouse of c.1808 with attractive cottages of the same period and a high carriage arch and dovecote. Cheswick House (1862) was built for Robert Crossman, the brewer; Ladythorne House is of 1721. Next door Goswick, a haven for golfers, and the site of train crashes in 1907, 1941, 1947 (tragically twenty-eight were killed and sixty-five injured) and 1953. There are two towers—remnants of the former RAF bombing range.

CHILLINGHAM

The most amazing encounter at Chillingham is with the herd of indigenous wild cattle who live in an equally wild 300-acre park. During the past fifty years, there have been significant threats to their survival with "foot and mouth" outbreaks, but happily very strict security measures have ensured their continuity. Numbers have gone below fifty, but there are now over one hundred animals. A "king bull" reigns until he becomes weak, when another will challenge him as leader of the herd—there are sometimes other "minor royals" leading parts of the herd.

King Edward I stayed in the tower here in 1298. Sir Thomas de Heton built a castle in the mid-fourteenth century. The Grey family would own the estate from this time onwards, and by 1695 they had acquired the title of Earls of Tankerville. Later the family name changed to Bennet when Charles Bennet married the female Grey

heir. The death of the seventh Earl in 1931 saw the estate in poor shape, and the ninth Earl emigrated to the USA, leaving estate management to his stepbrother. Both these generations assured the future of the wild cattle.

By the 1980s, the castle was moving toward dereliction. In 1982, Sir Humphry Wakefield bought the castle and grounds, restoring the fabric and housing his extensive collection of antiquities within it. Wyatville worked on the castle in the early nineteenth century,

giving it a certain serendipity, which has been further enhanced by Humphry Wakefield's esoteric collection. There is much to see, and the grounds are extensive. The West Lodge is a Jacobean fantasy of 1835 by Edward Blore; the East Lodge in the village is by Wyatville. The castle is square in plan, with four corner towers connected by curtain walls. The Great Hall is in the south range with the former chapel in the southeast tower.

The village was effectively rebuilt by the Earl of Tankerville

in the 1830s—again to designs by Blore. The Manor House, once the Vicarage, is also by Wyatville. In farmland to the south is the austere ruin of Hepburn Bastle, and beyond that rises the upland known as Ros Castle—from here, in 1804, a beacon was lit starting a celebrated false alarm of a French invasion. St Peter's Church is stark but for the remarkable fifteenth-century table tomb of Sir Ralph Gray (1443) and the controversial plain-glass east window installed by John Smith in the late 1960s.

CHIPCHASE CASTLE

Four miles northwest of Chollerton. Sited above the North Tyne, the castle is a dazzling mixture of a fourteenth-century defensive tower, a Jacobean mansion and Georgian additions. The Herons, a widespread Northumbrian family, became its owners in 1348, and the tower certainly dates to 1415. There is a wooden portcullis at the entrance, and the tower is interestingly decorated architecturally. Comparisons are made with Edlingham and Haughton with regard to the tower and the possibility of a former complex of buildings as in those places. The Jacobean house (1621) appears to have been based upon an early-sixteenth-century mansion. It is the best of its period in Northumberland. Three storeys, it has a projecting porch with Ionic columns. Bow windows were transformed with mullions and transoms in the nineteenth century probably by the ubiquitous Dobson in 1819.

The interior decoration is mostly mid-eighteenth century for John Reed the Elder, who died in 1754. There is a two-storey music room with a rather coarse rococo ceiling. Also in this room is a sumptuous Jacobean fireplace and Palladian doorways. The chapel, rebuilt for John Reed after 1735, stands opposite the Jacobean range. It has a bell-cote "after Vanbrugh", and the interior has some of the finest church furnishings in Northumberland. Good late-seventeenth-century gate piers north of the castle. Boathouse and ruined Gothick cottage to the south.

CHOLLERFORD

The fine five-round-arched bridge over the North Tyne is by Robert Mylne (1785); at the western end of the bridge stands the substantial George Inn, the oldest parts of which date back to the eighteenth century. Chesters Roman Fort is half a mile west (*qv*).

CHOLLERTON

Much to see hereabouts. Approaching from the north, one passes the impressive and elegant Classical-styled gateway to The Hermitage, leading to the mansion hidden behind woodland. The house is a seven-bay two-storey building with a pediment and faced/chamfered corners to the front. In its present guise, it presents as nineteenth century. The last surviving daughter of the Straker family who owned the property died in 2013, and the contents, some of which had been untouched in a hundred years (including stores of champagne), were auctioned off at that time.

St Giles' Church in Chollerton is fascinating. Externally the building is of the mid-eighteenth century, but internally the story is rather different and dates back to 1150. The early-Perpendicular octagonal north arcade is of the later fourteenth century, but the arcading on the south aisle is formed from four monolithic Roman piers probably taken from the fort at Chesters. This is not the full extent of the Roman material, for one of the two fonts is formed from a Roman altar dedicated to Jupiter. The other font is a plain thirteenth-century bowl set on four shafts with moulded capitals. Reredos formed of Jacobean panelling of domestic provenance, probably from a local manor house. Father Schmidt's organ given to the church in the mid-nineteenth century. Rare post-Reformation cross slab to Henry Widdrington, 1637. Good solid west tower with a two-stage wood-shingled spire of 1873. Early-nineteenth-century

↓ **CHIPCHASE** Castle

church stable and hearse house by the gate.

Chollerton Farm remains part of the Browne-Swinburne estate at Capheaton. It is a fascinating collection of buildings grouped next to the understated but perfect five-bayed pedimented farmhouse. A history of mechanization is played out here, beginning with the seven-storey windmill constructed for threshing rather than grinding. Then immediately adjacent is a mid-nineteenth-century engine house as steam superseded wind power. There are cottages, stables and a carriage house just north of these buildings.

Just under a mile southeast of Chollerton stands the shell of the late fourteenth-century Cocklaw Tower with barrel vaulting in both the basement and first floor and including fragments of sixteenth-century wall paintings. Two identical farmhouses and a limekiln close by. More limekilns at Colwell, 3 miles north of here.

Great Swinburne, 2 miles north of Chollerton, boasts two castles, though one has been entirely lost. The eighteenth-century house which replaced it has also gone, although fragments remain including the seventeenth-century manor house (later the west wing of the former eighteenth-century mansion), stables, orangery, and the barn, which carries a good coat of arms. There is an impressive south-west gateway with elongated Tuscan columns. Modest Roman Catholic Chapel of St Mary close by. The most powerful standing stone of the county (3 m high) 800 m south of the castle.

CORBRIDGE

On crossing the impressive seven-arched stone bridge of 1674, one enters one of the most fascinating small towns of Northumberland. Not only is the nearby Roman site of Corstopitum an indicator of a long history, so is the Church of St Andrew, for, alongside the crypt at Hexham Abbey, it is the oldest Saxon church in the county. Much can be learnt from its turbulent history which includes: the death of King Ethelred of Northumbria in 796; Ragnal, the Danish king's defeat of the English and Scots in 918; the occupation by David I of Scotland in 1138; and also, the successive burnings of the town by William Wallace in 1296, Robert Bruce in 1312 and David II in 1346. One is reminded of how late on the present border between the two kingdoms was finally established.

Despite this violent history, St Andrew's Church still boasts a west tower, the foundations and lower stages of which date back to 786, and the top of this slim tower from c.970. The internal tower arch is wholly Roman and may have simply been rebuilt as it originally was in Corstopitum. The nave walls are based on a seventh-century core, and there are two Saxon window heads on the north side. The internal plan of the church is unusual and attractive. Here, thirteenth-century work has survived, including the Early English lancet and other windows. The chancel has an original chapel of four bays. The transepts in the nave are unequal with the north transept including a west aisle. Also from the thirteenth

century is a slab and cross with an inscription to Alicia de Tynedale.

On the south side of the churchyard is the Vicar's Pele, a mid-fourteenth-century tower house entirely of Roman stones; the tower now houses a collection of carved stones. In the churchyard, there is also the grave of Josephine Butler's father, John Grey of Dilston. The old Market Cross close by the tower has a Roman capital as its base. There is a further cross in the Market Place but this time of 1814. There is good domestic housing in what has become a very fashionable town centre.

The Roman base at Corstopitum lies a mile and a half to the north-west, and this too was a garrison town. It was built to guard the bridge which took Dere Street over

↓ **CORBRIDGE** Church

In
Memory of
JOHN RICHLEY
who died
Jan.y 15th 1855, in the
57th Year of his Age.
Also of William &
Henry & of other two
both named John, Sons
of the above John &
Jane Richley, all who
died in Infancy.
ALSO MARY WIFE OF EDWARD SCOTT
OF LYNEMOUTH AND DAUGHTER OF THE ABOVE
JOHN RICHLEY
WHO DIED DEC.r 1st 1869 AGED 38 YEARS.
ALSO JANE RICHLEY WIFE OF THE ABOVE
JOHN RICHLEY.
WHO DIED AT WOOD SIDE AGINGTON
MARCH THE 20th 1872 AGED 79 YEARS

the Tyne. In the 160s, the Romans retreated from Scotland, and what had been largely a fort mutated into a town—indeed it became the most northerly Roman town in Europe; this is indeed what can be seen today, in the excavated remains; these remains include granaries, an aqueduct, temples, houses and the legionary headquarters with the commanding officer's house; a large square courtyard is surrounded by a series of small rooms. The plan on the site gives a good picture of the original town, forsaken by the Saxons for the site further east, which is the basis of modern Corbridge. There is an excellent museum on site, which takes the visitor through the history and development of both the town and military base, and which has windows overlooking the site allowing one to view the remains even in poor weather. The excavations are extensive, but still include only the centre of the town, whereas the entire town occupied some 40 acres. The adjoining fields still keep their secrets although there are annual digs, as there have been effectively for well over a century now.

A number of interesting buildings survive near Corbridge.

Dilston Castle, 1 mile southwest, was originally an L-shaped tower house which was built into a wing of Dilston Hall c.1620; it was the home of the Radcliffe family, later the Earls of Derwentwater, a romantic Northumbrian figure—the final earl was executed for his part in the 1715 rebellion. Greenwich Hospital trustees were the inheritors who allowed the tower to become a roofless ruin.

Stagshaw House, built in the mid-nineteenth century, and its private chapel lie a mile and a half from Corbridge; the house sports a conical-roofed game larder. The chapel is good Perpendicular by Hicks and has stained glass by

Kempe. Fine views to the south and also impressive Straker and Allgood tombs in the churchyard to the south.

Beaufront Castle by Dobson (1840) for William Cuthbert, a successful entrepreneur. The mediaeval tower house has vanished entirely, and the earlier seventeenth-century house absorbed into the new Perpendicular/Elizabethan creation. It is very much a nineteenth-century castle with buttresses and crenellations. Inside, there is a billiard room with a rib-vaulted cloister on three sides. The house is certainly a statement within this part of the Tyne Valley.

← **CORBRIDGE** Vicar's Pele

↗ **CORBRIDGE**
Corstopitum sculpture

→ **CORBRIDGE** Corstopitum

↑ **CORNHILL** Smeaton Bridge

Finally, Aydon, 2 miles northeast, is a "real" castle but most unusually with no keep and surviving almost completely intact despite the ravages and plundering of the Scots. The beginning may date back as far as the very late thirteenth century (c.1280), when the land was bought by Hugh de Raymes, a major Suffolk merchant. Much of the original shape including fourteenth-century additions has been exposed by removing the accoutrements gathered while it acted as a farmhouse. There are spacious courtyards, and the hall range is particularly interesting. Now administered by English Heritage, a visit is educational simply for seeing the development and use of a mediaeval castle.

CORNHILL

The last village in England and the end of the former Alnwick to Coldstream branch railway (curiously named since it never got as far as Coldstream). Here it linked with the Berwick–St Boswells line. At the Coldstream end of Smeaton's elegant 1763 road bridge over the Tweed is a marriage house used by numerous "elopers". On the far side of the town is The Hirsel, the estate of sometime Prime Minister and Foreign Secretary Sir Alec Douglas-Home. Cornhill House, austere and Scottish in feel, is the last house on the left travelling north, ahead of the sharp bend to the right. Described by Mackenzie in 1825 as the "seat of the Collingwoods", a Newcastle family of which Nelson's fellow admiral was a scion. It sounds as if the earliest core of the house was built in defensive proportions. The Collingwood Arms, "the first house in England on this road", is a handsome seven-bay seventeenth-century coaching inn. Cornhill Castle, three-quarters of a mile northwest on a cliff above the Tweed, now just ditches, no masonry; a tower here in 1385. It retains a curiosity in its eighteenth-century "Post Horses" sign carved above the main door.

St Helen's Church, rather bleak from the outside, is 1840 by Ignatius Bonomi using masonry from an earlier church of 1751 and on a site going back to Saxon times. Some good neo-Romanesque detail inside.

COUPLAND

Coupland Castle is a tower house of 1594. It is T-shaped and tunnel-vaulted in its basement. The former hall on the first floor has a large fireplace inscribed for George and Mary Wallis. In the early nineteenth century, Tudor-style additions were built. The house is built of volcanic rock, probably local whinstone. Atop the hill at Lanton is an obelisk, visible from some miles around. It was almost certainly erected in 1827 by Sir William Davison of Swarland Park in memory of his brother, John Davison of Lanton. There is also an inscription reading "Alexander Davison 1795", which may merely record Alexander (William's father) buying Swarland Park (*qv*). Alexander was Nelson's chandler; he set up another obelisk at Swarland.

CRAMLINGTON

Cramlington today suggests little of the atmosphere of a village, which was its origin, but references to it reach back to 1135, when the land was granted to Nicholas de Granville. The actual name may even be Anglo-Saxon. The village survives, however, as another world, a gem within a wider conurbation. St Nicholas' Church by Austin and Johnson (1868) is a good building and with its large tower a focus around which the village is grouped. The Vicarage, Cramlington Hall and other houses are pleasant and with good recent additions form an attractive classical English village ensemble. St John the Baptist Roman Catholic Church is modelled on Ostend Cathedral and was built by Belgian craftsmen. Cramlington Hall is a mid-eighteenth-century

Palladian villa. There are interesting farmhouses in the vicinity, notably at East Hartford and Plessey Hall. Arcot Hall, now a golf club, is late eighteenth century capped by a lead dome—the house was built for George Shum-Storey, an adventurer to India who was present at the siege of Arcot.

Cramlington's designation, in 1964, as a "new town" wrought vast changes—coal mining had admittedly already meant a move away from the predominantly farming culture of earlier centuries; the new town, designated as such by the county and not central government, aimed to remove the long "rows" of miners' cottages and offer new and spacious living conditions. Both here and Killingworth were developed under the auspices of Arthur Lawson, the county architect. The focus here was not "overspill" but rather industrial and residential growth. From a mining village, it has grown into a town of some 30,000 people. In 2017, remnants of an Iron Age settlement were discovered when clearing ground for a housing development. Reference was made by Captain W. E. Johns (of Biggles fame) to the former Cramlington Airfield.

Cramlington has spawned some interesting contemporary architecture. The British Gas Line Inspection Depot (originally built for Courtaulds) makes very good use of curved surfaces with a 1930s-style gatehouse.

Hartford Hall, 2 miles northwest, sits dramatically overlooking the River Blyth with its central bow and lead-covered dome on

↑ **CRAMLINGTON** Northumberland Specialist Care Hospital

the south front—it is very striking. Built in 1807 for William Burdon, by William Stokoe, it was remodelled in 1875 when flanking single storey blocks were removed. The interior is high Victorian from those later alterations. There is an extraordinary wrought-iron gate screen built by the Coalbrookdale Company of Ironbridge, which was exhibited in the Vienna Exhibition of 1873. Hartford Hall later became a Miners' Rehabilitation Centre but was converted into luxury flats in 1994. Hartford Bridge is mediaeval but substantially rebuilt in 1904.

Seghill, 2 miles southeast, had the remains of Seghill Tower built into the Blake Arms Hotel, but they have sadly been demolished, including a rib-vaulted chamber suggesting a building of some significance. Holy Trinity Church by John and Benjamin Green, Early English in style (1849). Seghill Hall (1830)—giant pilasters. Burradon Tower, 1 mile southwest—ruinous sixteenth-century tower house in grounds of nineteenth-century farmhouse—tunnel-vaulted ground floor.

CRASTER

The best kippers in the world—so say the Robson family, who have had curing sheds here for some generations! This tiny fishing village has more than one claim to fame. The tower at the end of the fishing harbour is but the remains of far larger tackle used to load stone from the local quarry owned by the eponymous Craster family who still inhabit the Tower of the same name; it is a three-storey embattled tower mentioned in the 1415 list of castles. A five-bay house was added to the south side in 1769, including a tripartite central doorway with Tuscan pilasters. Further Gothick alterations were made in the late eighteenth century, which added an embattled gateway which spans the road into the village as well as the entrance to the tower.

Dunstanburgh Castle stands just to the north, along an attractive coastal path. On its dolerite platform, part of the Whin Sill, it is the most evocative ruin in Northumberland. Its jagged remains are particularly impressive in wild weather. Probably on the site of an Iron Age fort. The castle was rebuilt after Bannockburn (1314) as a fortified port—the gigantic guardhouse survives, from which runs the main south curtain wall—the north is protected by sheer dolerite cliffs. Only the footings of the barbican, outside the guardhouse, remain. One mile west-northwest is Dunstan Hall, some of which is early thirteenth century. The main block is fourteenth century, and there have followed many remodellings, including the 1939 work by H. L. Honeyman with a charming small dairy and a bell-shaped pantile roof.

CRESSWELL

Cresswell is a name with which to conjure in Northumberland, and indeed a noted scion of the family found herself with John Betjeman (later Poet Laureate) as a suitor many years ago.

This is the village from which the name sprang and Cresswell Hall was the family seat. A large house by John Shaw, it was sadly demolished in 1937. A ruinous Roman Doric gallery survives, alongside the 1829 stables with their enclosed courtyard. The adjacent pele, Cresswell Tower, fourteenth or fifteenth century, has been left roofless and has been refurbished recently in a most imaginative heritage development. The ground floor is barrel-vaulted—the eighteenth-century house which had been added to the tower was demolished in the nineteenth century. A mile further south is the home farm.

St Bartholomew's Church (1836) was built for the Cresswell family in neo-Norman style—interesting white and yellow medallions in the east windows, in thirteenth-century style. Neo-Tudor estate cottages to the east of the church.

CULLERCOATS

Cullercoats dates back to 1539, beginning as a fishing village and later, in 1677, it gained a pier as it blossomed into a port exporting coal and salt. The salt industry declined, and the final salt pans were moved to Blyth in 1726; the pier closed in 1730. There is some interesting architecture in the village including some preserved fishermen's cottages in Simpson Street. The Watch House, built 1877–9 for the Volunteer Life Brigade by F. W. Rich, has elements of early Arts and Crafts about it, with a hipped roof, a clock turret and shingled belfry. The Rocket Garage, also for the Life Brigade, housed apparatus for rockets fired to take lifelines to survivors of ships wrecked on the nearby rocks.

The pride of the village is John Loughborough Pearson's St George's Church (1882–4) standing on the sea front as a notable landmark for mariners. It is a noble building with Pearson's normal eye both for detail and massing. The sixth Duke of Northumberland commissioned the church in memory of his father. It has an aisled nave, transepts, and a polygonal apse. It is unique as the only stone-vaulted nineteenth-century church in Northumberland. It is a study in thirteenth-century Gothic. Stained glass by Kempe in the apse and Art Nouveau light fittings in the aisles by Pearson.

There was a notable artists' colony here in the late nineteenth century, the most famous member of which was the American landscape painter Winslow Homer.

DENWICK

One mile northwest of Alnwick, and effectively an estate village. Plain rectangular chapel of 1872 together with a school of 1907. Denwick House (1808) is a three-bay estate farmhouse, originating as the house for the Duke's factor.

Just over a mile east is Ratcheugh Observatory, an eyecatcher and observatory atop a whinstone crag and the most far flung of the ornamental buildings associated with the Duke's Alnwick estates. It is an embattled gazebo of 1780 by Robert Adam, and being so far from the palace, it avoided demolition or serious rebuilding in Salvin's time.

DINNINGTON

On an ancient site occupied since well before the Iron Age, so pre-700 BC. Its twentieth-century character was much determined by coal mining which began c.1715; the Augusta Pit, the first deep mine, was sunk in 1867, and others followed. The past two generations, following the demise of coal mining, has meant a shift toward commuter residential development. New Horton Grange Farm, 2,000 m north, is an attractive planned farm built in the mid-nineteenth century for the Ridleys—it is effectively a model farm set around a courtyard—good estate cottages just to the west of the farm. St Matthew's Church (1886) replaced an earlier nineteenth-century church; of interest is the reredos designed and given by women of the diocese for the newly inaugurated Bishop of Newcastle's earliest residence at Benwell Towers—the reredos came here in 1959.

↓ **CULLERCOATS** St George's Church, exterior
↘ **CULLERCOATS** St George's Church, interior

↑ Cup-and-ring-marked rocks

DODDINGTON

The Church of St Mary and St Michael is rather hidden, nestling on the west edge of the village and overlooking Milfield Plain and Glendale. Its construction is something of a mystery, but the present rebuilt chancel is 1838 by Ignatius Bonomi. George Reavell rebuilt the roof, south porch and north wall in 1893. Good arcading to south aisle and good font. Fine twentieth-century window in a north lancet by Nuttgens. In the chancel is a memorial to Count Horace St Paul, Count of the Holy Roman Empire, who built Ewart Park between here and Akeld, with its pretty golden lodge gates, but with the house now in a poor state. There is a window to Lieutenant Lambton, of the Earl of Durham's family, who died in the First World War; the Lambtons have property at nearby Fenton, a Tudor–Gothick-style mansion by Thomas Farrer, c.1870, and effectively a hunting lodge. Stone watchhouse in churchyard, 1826, built to deter body snatchers. There is also, close by, a bastle or fortified farmhouse of the sixteenth century.

In the vicinity, much prehistoric evidence—cup and ring marks on Doddington Moor and a hill fort at the Ringses—another Iron Age fort on Dod Law overlooking the River Till and yet another at Fenton Hill, 1 mile north of Fenton.

DRURIDGE BAY

Close by to Widdrington is the panoramic Druridge Bay. The bay is no stranger to controversy, having narrowly escaped becoming the site of a nuclear power station, then more recently an open-cast coal mine. There remains evidence of the extensive Second World War defences, as this had seemed like an ideal site for invasion landings. It is now a country park, bird sanctuary and an SSSI. Amongst the birds to be seen here are the purple sandpiper and the golden plover—the sighting of a slender-billed curlew remains disputed. The only English colony of roseate terns runs from Druridge southwards along the coast toward Cresswell. Of course, here as anywhere the sighting of birds will be seasonal, depending on roosting, nesting and migration patterns. The ecosystems here relate to the presence of the dunes and the pools within them. There is a good visitor centre and excellent waymarked trails.

↑ Roseate Tern

DUDDO

Tiny hamlet with former All Saints' Church a mile to the northeast— good former vicarage next door. On sharp bend in the village atop the hill on the left is just a crag of the former tower—the earliest tower here was 1496. Former Church of St James in village later became a school and is now a private house, as with All Saints' Church. Half a mile northwest, surprisingly invisible from surrounding roads, stand unusual ear-shaped megaliths, the highest more than 2 m high, forming a stone circle from the late Neolithic–early Bronze Age (2400–1000 BC).

→ **DUDDO** Stones

EARSDON

Earsdon's origins are mediaeval and indeed the church which preceded the present building dated from 1250. St Alban's Church as we now see it was the work of John and Benjamin Green, 1837. There is a big west tower, and the church is battlemented with pinnacles. There is stained glass given by Lord Hastings in 1874—he had bought the glass when Hampton Court Hall was being restored in 1840; the windows are attributed to Galyon Hone, Henry VIII's Flemish Master Glazier. Much to excite here—greyhounds, dragons, lions and many coats of arms.

Edward Eccles Church Hall in Front Street (1911)—good Edwardian work. Eighteenth-century work in the Manor House and seventeenth in The Garth; Bleak Hop House is fine nineteenth-century work. The Hartley Disaster Memorial commemorates the terrible disaster of 1862 in nearby New Hartley, when 210 men and boys died in the Hester Pit.

EDLINGHAM

Nestling beneath Telford's Alnmouth–Hexham highway as it crosses Alnwick Moor lies Edlingham with its church, castle and railway viaduct. Each tells its own story. St John the Baptist Church has a low tower with a pyramidal roof. In both tower and north wall, windows are few— defence was the order of the builders' day. Here is real antiquity—the nave may predate the Norman Conquest. Both sets of arcading are Romanesque. A tomb in a nave recess has a pre-Conquest cross slab. The east window with its text "The Sea gave up the Dead which were in it" commemorates Lewis de Crespigny Buckle, who was lost on the all-too-aptly named HMS *Nemesis*.

Next is the castle. A recent archaeological dig indicated its origins in a small castle or fortified manor house. It was probably built in the late thirteenth century by Sir William de Felton and surrounded by a defensive moat. This

would have been a useful first line of defence against any seeking to attack Alnwick Castle.

Finally, the elegant, curved nineteenth-century railway viaduct is further evidence of the former Alnwick-to-Coldstream branch line; probably one of the prettiest of branch lines and shortest lived. Opened in 1889, it closed to passenger traffic in 1930, although parts of it were used for freight even as late as the early 1960s.

EGLINGHAM

Eglingham Hall has 1728 imprinted on a rainwater head, which probably dates the rest of the building with its seven-bay front and a recessed three-bay centre. It was built for Robert Ogle in whose family it has been vested for much of its history. It may be the work of one of Vanbrugh's assistants at Seaton Delaval. The northeast wing by Temple Wilson is of 1903. The arched gateway at the west end is seventeenth century.

The church dedicated to St Maurice (a very rare dedication in England) is aisleless but with north and south chapels making it feel almost transeptal or cruciform. The church is mediaeval but rebuilt in the seventeenth century. In the south chapel, a number of memorials to the Carr-Ellison family include a modern pastoral-styled stained-glass window commissioned by Sir Ralph Carr-Ellison to commemorate both his mother Hermione and his first wife Mary Clare; the estate is at Hedgeley, 3 miles to the west.

The village has some attractive buildings including the village hall which is a converted watermill. One curiosity is the Second World War pillbox in the lane to the east, at the north end of the village—not clear what it might have been defending or why the enemy was likely to come this way! Harehope Hall (1848), one and a half miles west, is an elegant Tudor-style hunting lodge, looking down to the Breamish.

Shipley, 3 miles south toward Alnwick, is now just a cottage, but there are earthworks marking the lost village which had eleven taxpayers in 1296 and a charter for a market. Was it lost as the Alnwick/Percy estate expanded, taking the main throughway in a different direction?

ELLINGHAM

As with its sound-like, near neighbour, Eglingham, just 8 miles to the southwest, the church has the same rare dedication to St Maurice. Rebuilt in 1862, it breathes a certain austerity, but there are noble features and excellent stained glass in good condition—the south nave window takes one on a remarkable gallop through history from the building of the Ark, purportedly some four and a half millennia back, to the construction of this church! Good monument to Sir Carnaby Haggerston, whose family built Ellingham Hall and indeed the Chapel of Our Lady of the Rosary there in 1897.

Preston Tower is just over a mile east of Ellingham. Described by Nikolaus Pevsner as "amongst the most spectacular pieces of mediaeval masonry in England", it was originally a "hall" pele tower of the fourteenth century. Sir Guiscard Harbottle was the owner at the time of the Battle of Flodden in which he was slain. The local Baker-Cresswell family have lived here for a number of generations; one of the Cresswells, an amateur horologist, made the clock in the tower. There are three fine fireplaces and good vaulting in the basement. Next to the tower is the house bearing the same name and built by another local Northumbrian family, the Crasters. The classical garden front of five bays includes a Doric porch and pediment.

Nearby is Chathill Station—another Tudor-style gem from Benjamin Green and cheek by jowl with the delightful Arts-and-Crafts-style former post office.

↓ **ELLINGHAM** Preston Tower

ELLINGTON

Ellington had the distinction of being the last surviving deep coal mine in northeast England. In its later life, it was part of the Ashington group of pits and latterly became a single colliery unit with next door Lynemouth. It is an ancient village, and the north edge retains that atmosphere with some older buildings grouped near the pub. The pit was a little further south to the west of the main road—it extended for a considerable distance under the sea where the seams were thick. The pit figured in the film *Billy Elliot*. The village was owned serially by different local landowners from the De Vescy family onwards, with the final

single owners being the Cresswell family. Richard Runciman Terry (later Sir Richard Terry), the son of the schoolmaster in the village, was born in 1865 and was responsible for the preservation of *Billy Boy* and numerous other sea shanties; later he became Director of Music at Westminster Cathedral.

Next-door Lynemouth was the site of an Alcan aluminium smelter from 1972 (it had its own power station, and this survives at the time of writing)—the smelter closed in 2012. Close by is Linton which is also a former colliery village.

ELSDON

A real village grouped around a broad triangular green and overlooked by both St Cuthbert's Church and the amazing pele tower, the erstwhile vicarage. Recorded as "vicar's pele" in 1415, it was rebuilt in the sixteenth century. The crest of the Umfravilles, who built it, remains, but there are also the crests of the Percys and Howards of Overacre. The ground floor was decorated with fine stuccoed ribs sometime after 1812 by Mr Singleton, then the incumbent. Gothick decoration on the first floor—probably by Mr Dutens, vicar in the late eighteenth century.

The church was once larger than it is now, and its architectural history is complex. The two west buttresses are, for example, the remains of a west tower. This left the church with an unusual ornate bellcote (1720), with two tiers of ball finials and a stumpy spirelet. The earliest visible work is twelfth century, but there was a substantial rebuilding in the

fourteenth century. The narrow nave and transept aisles with their quadrant vaults are the most memorable features of Elsdon Church. Good, large, restored Perpendicular windows in the chancel and transepts, and attractive varied windows in the south wall of the chancel. In the north aisle, there are two Roman inscriptions—a gabled Roman tombstone from High Rochester fort and a dedication slab from Risingham.

The castle at the north end of the village is a well-preserved motte and bailey, again probably built by the Umfravilles to protect their demesne of Redesdale, of which Elsdon was the ancient capital. There are bastles around, and notable is Winter's Gibbet high up and 2 miles southeast on the old drovers' road. The replica gibbet replaces that on which hung the body of William Winter, convicted of the gruesome murder of an old woman, Margaret Crozier, who lived in a lonely pele. A stump of the mediaeval Steng Cross lies next to the gibbet. Manside Cross, an Iron Age fort, lies 3 miles east-southeast.

EMBLETON

Holy Trinity Church with its fourteenth-century western tower dominates the village. The porch is also late mediaeval and the three-bay nave arcades thirteenth century. John Dobson and F. R. Wilson did much rebuilding in the nineteenth century, including the chancel, all of a high standard of design and workmanship. North of the north aisle is the Craster Chapel. The church has links with interesting personalities;

↑ **EMBLETON** Mandell Creighton bust

there are tablets to the Greys of Fallodon—Lord Grey of Fallodon was Foreign Secretary for much of the First World War with his prescient words "The lamps are going out all over Europe, and we shall not see them lit again in our lifetime". Mandell Creighton, later Bishop of London, was Vicar of Embleton from 1875–84 and writer of the acclaimed *History of the Papacy in the Period of the Reformation*; many believed that but for his premature death he would have become Archbishop of Canterbury. The former vicarage is thought by many to have been a vicar's pele as at Elsdon and Alnham—a combination of dwelling and defensive structure.

Fallodon Hall, built originally in 1730 for Thomas Wood but passing to the Grey family in 1755; it is brick and of seven bays. The main house was completely remodelled internally with a second floor being removed after a serious fire in 1924. Nearby there was a private railway station on the main line, now demolished.

Low Newton (or Newton-by-the-Sea) is two and a half miles north on Embleton Bay. The square of cottages and the Ship Inn, with its microbrewery, is owned by the National Trust. It faces the sea on the craggy coastline down towards Dunstanburgh. Newton Hall and Newton House, both eighteenth century, are close by.

ESHOTT

A small village known for its Second World War RAF aerodrome (qv. Felton), and for Eshott Hall, built in 1660 by Robert Trollope and recast in the nineteenth century. There is sumptuous plasterwork

↓ **EMBLETON** Fallodon Hall

↑ **ETAL** Village

in the drawing room which now forms part of the facilities of a country house hotel. The original front door of the Hall has curiously been used at nearby Eshott Haugh, a nineteenth-century farmhouse! Half a mile north there is evidence of the moat, curtain wall and angle towers of the former castle, first crenellated by licence to Roger de Mauduit in 1310 and owned by Sir John Heron from 1415.

↓ **ETAL** Castle

ETAL

One could be forgiven for thinking one was in southern England, with the picturesque, whitewashed estate cottages and Northumberland's only thatched pub. All this is down to Lord Joicey, who bought the estate in 1907. Etal Manor is a restrained Georgian house of 1748 and 1767, built for William Carr and extended in 1888 for James Laing. There is a fine gateway to the south with

views of the house at the end of an avenue of trees. The small Church of St Mary the Virgin, near the entrance to the grounds of the Manor, is a perfect miniature by William Butterfield in 1858 and was Lady Fitzclarence's memorial to her husband who had died in India four years earlier.

The road through the village takes one first to Etal Castle dating back to the licence to crenellate given to Robert Manners in 1342. It has not always been as peaceful as it now feels. In 1428, there was a battle here between the Manners and Heron families, and in 1513, it was briefly captured by King James IV of Scotland on his ill-fated expedition to Flodden. Near the castle is the terminus of the Heatherslaw Light Railway which runs for a mile or so along the bank of the River Till to the eponymous hamlet and mill. Heatherslaw Mill is a fully operational water-powered corn mill producing a range of useful products. At the far end of Etal village is a fast-flowing deep ford over the Till, at the site of an earlier bridge. Within living memory, a rope-slung, pedestrian suspension bridge survived until destroyed by vandalism. Ford and Etal Estates are a model of rural development with good facilities for visitors.

EWART

Ewart Park was built for Count Horace de St Paul. St Paul was a Count of the Holy Roman Empire and designed this slightly eccentric house for himself in Gothick style. It was completed in 1790. There are two lodge gates and that on the main road takes one to the main front with its circular tower—the idea originated from Twizel Castle (*qv* Tillmouth) which was built at the same time. The 1794 lodges are in good order, but the house sadly appears semi-derelict.

The road past the east lodges allows one some interesting encounters. First is the signal box next to the former Bendor level crossing on the erstwhile Alnwick–Coldstream branch line—the signal box, probably c.1887, is in surprisingly good condition. Next, on the left are the eastern lodge cottages to Ewart Park from which one can catch a glimpse of the derelict Hall. Soon after this, also on the left, are the remains of the former brickworks which provided the bricks for Ewart Bridge/Causeway over the Till. Perhaps most surprising of all is Ewart Newtown: this amazingly long building (seventeen bays) with a raised central section, now farm buildings, was intended as a grand hotel standing alongside the branch railway to Coldstream; the course

of the line was changed, leaving the intended hotel "beached" in this isolated position—it still looks well. Finally, past the 1870 Italianate villa, Thirlings, and on the left are the remains of the entrance to Milfield Second-World-War RAF base. Alongside the decaying huts are two globes surmounted by eagles, built by Italian prisoners of war while held in captivity here.

FALSTONE

Now lying just beneath Kielder Dam, Falstone is the last village before the lake and Kielder village itself. The farmhouse has a door lintel dated 1604 in an otherwise eighteenth-century house. The bridge by Henry Welch (1843) is on the toll road to Scotland surveyed by Telford. Bastles nearby and an Iron Age/Romano-British settlement one and a half miles south-south-east. Two hostelries in this remote village. St Peter's Church—1825 by John and Benjamin Green but badly hit by a fire in 1891—some interesting headstones.

FARNE ISLANDS

On a calm day, these extraordinary dolerite excrescences (the most easterly outcrop of the Great Whin Sill), appear almost like surfacing submarines on the near horizon. There are some twenty-eight islands, the largest of which is Inner Farne, and they are in the care of the National Trust. The tale of the rescue of survivors from the *Forfarshire* by Grace Darling is told elsewhere (*qv* Bamburgh), but the story reminds one only to embark on a trip in a good sea—as well as being kitted out with robust headgear.

Most significant historically are the associations of the islands with St Aidan and St Cuthbert. Aidan occasionally retreated here, and Cuthbert built a cell on Inner Farne within which he died in 687. Remains of the later 1246 monastic cell can still be seen. St Cuthbert's Church dates from 1370 but was much restored in the nineteenth century—indeed some of the furnishings of Durham Cathedral were brought here. There is a monument

↓ **EWART** Italian globes

↓ **FARNE ISLANDS** Grey Seals

to Grace Darling with an inscription by Wordsworth which begins "Pious and pure, modest and yet so brave . . . ". There is the base course of another church dedicated to St Mary, and west of St Cuthbert's Church is Prior Castell's Tower, erected by the prior c.1500 but with some earlier work. Fragments of a Benedictine cell, built c.1360, lie to the left of the path from the landing stage. The celebrated Longstone Lighthouse, of which Grace Darling's father was the keeper, is 1826 by David Alexander, who also built the lighthouse on Inner Farne.

The islands are, of course, immensely important ecologically, as a wildlife sanctuary and especially for bird life, so all visitors are reminded to act responsibly. Arctic terns abound in the summer months, and in the nesting season they can be quite fierce, hence the need to take a hat with you—they are not keen on human intruders and will happily dive and attack with their sharp beaks. Puffins are also a speciality here, as the National Trust publicity suggests; eider ducks and grey seals also abound. Eiders are also known as "cuddy ducks" because of their association with St Cuthbert. The Farnes are just a magical place.

FELTON

A former coaching stop on the Great North Road, Felton boasts two bridges over the Coquet, the old bridge probably dating back to the fifteenth century and still used for wassailing at Christmas! Riverside includes some good houses— No. 6 is particularly interesting,

intersected as it is by a stone-walled cross passage; the room to the east of the passage was once a distillery for the next-door inn. Park Lodge, a former lodge gate to Felton Park, is attractive. The Park itself was of 1732 remodelled in 1799 and much of it demolished in 1951; the east kitchen wing survives. There remains a good greenhouse of 1830 and the Roman Catholic church of St Mary (1857) had been joined to the lost west wing. It includes a brass to Thomas Riddell of Felton Park, "Founder of the Church". The parish church of St Michael reveals a complicated history of construction, best explored in one's visit. The twelfth-century church was probably aisleless with nave and chancel. The fourteenth century brought aisles and a chantry—the porch is c.1400. Some interesting monuments including one to Alexander Davison of nearby Swarland (*qv*), who was surely responsible for the obelisk of 1807 commemorating Nelson "in memory of a private friendship", presumably adding kudos to Davison for his closeness to a national hero.

Just northwest is evidence of the former rural gasworks, including the retort house at Gasworks Farm. Felton Mill is the focus of some attractive buildings which probably date back to the thirteenth century. The mill building itself is of interest and the wing downstream housed a drying kiln and low kiln for making "crowdie" cheese. In the 1970s, there was a speedway training track at what was then called Bockenfield Aerodrome. It has now reverted to its original name, remembering its

role in the Second World War as RAF Eshott, training Spitfire pilots. It is now home to two flying training bases including one for microlights.

E. M. Forster spent youthful summer holidays with his uncle at Acton House, a mile north. Oliver Cromwell stayed at the former Old Angel Inn on his way to the Battle of Dunbar.

FORD

Ford, like Chillingham slightly further south, is a powerful example of the quadrilateral type of castle with towers at each of the four corners. The licence to crenellate was given to William Heron in 1338. Two of the three towers appear to survive, the largest being the King James Tower at the northwest corner. The north range was rebuilt as a mansion in the Elizabethan period. Strawberry Hill Gothick was introduced into the castle in the eighteenth century under the Delavals. Later, from 1861–5 under Louisa, Marchioness of Waterford, some mediaeval flavour was revived particularly by replacing the Strawberry Hill windows. The portcullis gate is an extraordinary feature with complex decoration. Parson's Tower to the northwest of the church and southwest of the castle is a massive Northumbrian pele—there are similar vicar's peles at Embleton, Alnham, Elsdon and Corbridge (*qv*).

The village is "model" which is variously received by the critics. The earlier houses are dull but those added in the Edwardian period by Lord Joicey are attractive. There is a pretty smithy with an unusual horseshoe door surround. There is also a fountain memorial to the Marquis of Waterford. The Waterford Hall, originally built by Lady Waterford as a school, is now used as a museum and village hall. Lady Waterford painted fresco-style scenes in watercolour onto paper— all are in a Pre-Raphaelite style. They form a period piece.

One mile east at Ford Moss are the remains of a colliery dating back to the seventeenth century. The remains of thirty colliers' houses can be distinguished, and there are various semi-ruinous buildings relating to the former pit. There are other planned farms and small industries discernible from the past three centuries; this ingenuity prospers still in the variety of activities pursued on the united Ford and Etal Estates.

The thirteenth-century Church of St Michael and All Angels has a plain exterior but a most unusual bellcote with a pyramidal roof. Dobson over-restored the church in 1853—his work includes the north aisle and the east bay of the chancel. There is some good detailing in the interior and notably the dog-toothing and double chamfered arches. There is a monument to Louisa, Marchioness of Waterford, partially by G. F. Watts, which includes two kneeling angels holding a shield with the Waterford arms. In front of this is a recumbent Celtic cross.

George Culley's grave is that of one of the most influential farmers of eighteenth-century Britain. Both the first and second Baron Joicey are buried in the churchyard in family plots immediately to the east of the east wall of the church.

GILSLAND

The last outpost of Northumberland just below Spadeadam rocket range, the village is divided by the Poltross Burn between Northumberland and Cumbria.

Wardrew House, 1 mile north, was once a hotel which hosted both Robert Burns and Sir Walter Scott, who met his wife here.

GLANTON

Originally sporting two pubs, two shops, a post office, and a World Bird Research Station, Glanton is now much reduced with the loss of even the tin tabernacle which served as the Anglican church. The Queen's Head survives as does the neat United Reformed Church (formerly Presbyterian) at the west end of the village, its earliest part dating to 1783; Presbyterianism became stronger as one approached the border. Some fine houses, including Glanton House and Glanton Pike three-quarters of a mile to the west. Glanton Hill is crowned with a sturdy wooden mast.

GREENHEAD

Glenwhelt, on the north side of the Military Road just before the Tipalt Burn Bridge, is of six bays (1757), perhaps incorporating a bastle, and was for a period a coaching inn. St Cuthbert's Church is a fine study in Victorian nineteenth-century architecture, by John Dobson (1828). The nave is tall and noble, and the lancets echo those at Haltwhistle; the equally attractive chancel

(1900) by Hicks and Charlewood has good geometrical tracery in the east window.

Another good station house on the Newcastle–Carlisle railway, Carvoran, is not visually impressive with just a rectangular platform traceable and next to the Roman Army Museum. "Join the Roman Army here", as the proprietors of Vindolanda and this museum suggest—a very useful introduction to the Roman military who would have patrolled the wall.

GUYZANCE

In a hollow by the Coquet stand the sturdy but scant remains of the small Brainshaugh Premonstratensian nunnery (c.1147). Northern and western walls of nave stand high. Guyzance is but a single street with an "improved" country house in the form of Guyzance Hall, which is an eighteenth-century farmhouse extended by W. H. Knowles in 1894. Attractive watermill half a mile to the southwest.

HAGGERSTON

Haggerston has had an unsettled history. Of the castle, only the stable block (1908), rotunda (the former entrance) and water tower survive. The ancient seat of the recusant Haggerston family was rebuilt in 1777, 1805, then very substantially in 1893–7, and finally, in grand proportions to designs of Norman Shaw— this time for Thomas Leyland, the new owner. Following a fire in 1903, it was restored, only to be demolished in 1933. The remnants give some idea of the grandeur of the final mansion—there are sunken

gardens and pergolas—all now within a well-managed and laid-out caravan park. The monumental water tower is visible from a good distance on the Great North Road.

HALLINGTON

The hall is of 1768, with a perfectly proportioned front. Built for Ralph Soulsby, it is of five bays and three storeys with pedimented door and flanking Venetian windows. Pleasant, neat courtyard.

HALTON

A delightful group of buildings. Halton Tower began with the late-thirteenth-century tower to which a most attractive late-seventeenth-century house was attached to the east. One doorway survives from

c.1400 and is built from Roman stones. The 1696 additions are just two storeys high, and there is a staircase with strongly twisted balusters. There is a walled garden with a Roman tombstone built into its wall.

Again, a most agreeable building, St Oswald's Church stands snugly to the east of the house. There may be some Saxon work in the northwest of the nave, but the chancel arch is plain, understated, and undeniably Norman. The church's present character is almost entirely late sixteenth century. In the churchyard, there is a weathered Roman altar.

At Haltonchesters, the Roman fort is crossed by the main road and by the north drive of Halton Tower. The fort itself had an interesting and extended process of development.

↓ **HALTON** Church

HALTWHISTLE

This feels like a town happy in its own skin. Its unusually isolated location between the Roman Wall with Spadeadam Forest and its former rocket-launching base to the north and Allendale, the South Tyne and Alston Moor to the south has given it its character. Unpretentious buildings throng the main street, and somehow it has weathered the death of at least two industrial eras.

On the north edge of the town along the Haltwhistle Burn are the remains of early-nineteenth-century industry. Here were collieries, limekilns and a woollen mill dating back to 1762. Haltwhistle Ironworks was established in 1856 but lasted little over a decade. The whinstone quarry to the north was served by a "tubway" from 1902–52, which incorporated offshoots to the collieries and even delivered concessionary coal to the colliery men of Oakwell Terrace. To the south of the town lies the Hadrian Industrial Estate which hosted paint factories in the mid-late twentieth century; this site too is now largely disused.

The town centre focuses on the tiny Market Place next to the Black Bull Inn. Across the road and slightly to the east is the Centre of Britain Hotel (this boast of the town's location is echoed by other businesses), which was formerly the Red Lion; unusually incorporated is a "town" three-storey tower house/pele tower. There are a number of bastle houses (including Manor House Hotel) on the street. Further east on the north side of the main street is the seven-bayed former Town Hall of 1861, now hosting "Georgie's Unisex Hair Salon and Beauty Boutique". On the same side of the street further west is the former Mechanics Institute (now appropriately the Library and Information Centre)—a good pilastered building of rock-faced stone (1900), standing next to the Methodist Church.

The railway station just to the southwest of the town retains its cast-iron water tower designed by Peter Tate in 1861; the 1900 signal box survives as does the cast-iron footbridge and other station buildings. Later, the station formed a junction which acted as the northern terminus of the Alston branch. The platform for that line still remains and may well yet be reused—as attempts are made to restore services on the branch line. George Barclay-Bruce's Alston Arches Viaduct, 400 m southeast, is a six-arch structure also carrying the former branch line.

Holy Cross Church is a beautiful thirteenth-century Early English gem. The chancel is a treasure house with three fine cross slabs in the sanctuary and lancets with glass by Morris and Co.—Edward Burne-Jones, Ford Madox Brown, and Philip Webb. The sixteenth-century ledger stone to John Ridley, with its extended rhyming inscription, is on the south wall; chancel and aisle windows by Kempe. The nave lancets are mainly part of the 1870 restoration by R. J. Johnson—the west end, including the bellcote, appears to have been rebuilt at the same time. The font is of 1676.

Bellister Castle, 1 mile southwest, is a fortified hall house similar to Haughton and Langley Castles—a noble statement with a John Dobson house next door and farm buildings with square gingang. Blenkinsopp Castle (1415) ruins are 2 miles west, and again a castellated house by Dobson next door. Blenkinsopp Hall, owned for a long time by part of the Joicey family, is of 1812 with Dobson additions of 1835.

HARBOTTLE

One of the last villages in Coquetdale with its pretty main street, there are many historical associations. High up on a ridge above the Coquet are the remains of the castle, begun by the Umfravilles for Henry II, in 1157, as a motte and bailey fort, and rebuilt in stone in the thirteenth century. In the fifteenth century, it passed to the Talbots, who exchanged it with Henry VIII for another property elsewhere. Margaret Tudor, Henry's sister, who had married James IV of Scotland, was granted asylum and residence at Harbottle Castle after the death of her husband at the Battle of Flodden. Of the castle, there remains a stretch of curtain wall some 40 m long and 5 m high with an angle tower at the north—fragments of the keep can also be discerned.

Castle House (1829) by Dobson, built for Thomas Clennell, replaced an earlier house of the same name at the north end of the village—some materials from the earlier house were included. There is a Presbyterian chapel of 1854 with an octagonal bellcote over the gable.

The Drake Stone, a 10-m-high boulder of Fell Sandstone, was legendarily reputed to have healing powers and is associated with Druid rites.

↑ Old **HAYDON** Church

HARTBURN

Set high above the two streams of the Hart Burn, St Andrew's Church is of considerable interest, built as it is on Saxon foundations, including massive pre-Conquest nave quoins. The south doorcase is attractive including the vertical dog-toothing which is popular in these parts (cf. WHALTON and BOLAM). The west tower is c.1200, as is the chancel which has three lancets on the south but a rather blank forbidding north wall. The interior arcading has octagonal piers. Mediaeval stone coffins and an east window by Kempe (1904). Best collection of eighteenth-century headstones in the county in the churchyard. The adjacent Old Vicarage probably has sixteenth-century origins. A lancet-shaped arch survives from Dr Sharp's (eighteenth-century incumbent) footbridge on the way to his grotto. Old schoolhouse nearby also by Dr Sharp.

Middleton, 2 miles west, is an attractive hamlet with a former Congregational church, built as one with its manse. Next door are adjoining cottages and the Ox Inn. Earthworks of a lost village 1,200 m southwest.

Meldon Park, 1 mile east, 1832 house by Dobson for Isaac Cookson, with its park bordering the north banks of the infant Wansbeck. The villa has a four-column Ionic porch—also an imperial staircase altered by Lutyens (1930). The village lies 1 mile south. The tiny church of St John is early thirteenth century, restored by Dobson (1849)—only a nave and chancel with Minton tiles in the sanctuary. Thirteenth-century cross slab. Meldon is one of a handful of "thankful villages" which lost no one in the First World War.

HAYDON BRIDGE

The "modern" village, largely a creation of the Greenwich Hospital Commissioners, is clustered around the two bridges over the South Tyne.

The older bridge dates from 1776, although it was much rebuilt in 1824, following floods. The eighteenth-century Anchor Hotel is impressive on the banks of the river and the Commissioners' Shaftoe Terrace almshouses, on the hill just above the town, are good.

St Cuthbert's Church (1796), again by the Commissioners, has a north transept added in 1869 to accommodate the Shaftoe Trust School. There is Kempe glass in the chancel and a damaged fourteenth-century effigy brought from Haydon Old Church. The Old Vicarage is a fine three-bay house of 1820.

The old church, also dedicated to St Cuthbert, stands on the hill, half a mile north of the present village, and where the original village was located. Although it is effectively just the east end of the earlier complete building, it is something of a delight, with a Roman altar refashioned as a font and with much Roman fabric used in the church's construction. The chancel is early twelfth century

and the north chantry chapel fourteenth century—the two-bay arcade is nineteenth century—the restoration was by C. C. Hodges in 1882.

The Newcastle–Carlisle railway runs through the village and the former stationmaster's house and ticket office have been refashioned as Station Cottages. John Martin, the painter was born here in 1789. Philip Larkin was a regular visitor.

Some interesting houses nearby including Alton Side, originally a sixteenth-century bastle, 1 mile east; Lipwood House, 2 miles west, is c.1800; Threepwood Hall, 1 mile south, is in origin late seventeenth century but remodelled in the late eighteenth century—the stable block has a pedimented centre. Finally, Elrington Hall, one and a

quarter miles southeast, is again late seventeenth century, refenestrated in the nineteenth century but retaining collar-beam truss roofs.

HEALEY

St John's Church by C. E. Davis. 1862 Neo-Norman, apsidal east end, extraordinary western rose window. Three good windows by L. C. Evetts and 2011 award-winning window by Ann Vibeke and James Hugonin. Healey Hall (1834), on site of a former bastle house.

HEDDON-ON-THE-WALL

On the fork where the military road branches away from the main Carlisle highway, it is a clustered village with the church atop a mound. Good stretch of wall to the east as one approaches the village. The church of St Andrew is interesting inasmuch as there are, as the old Shell Guide put it, some Anglo-Saxon "bits"! Part of the southeast corner of the nave includes some stout Anglo-Saxon quoins—the west end of the chancel is early Norman with a very narrow blocked priest's door crowned by a plain tympanum; there is a further tympanum over the door to the vestry. It appears that an earlier apse was replaced with the present squared end. It is a fascinating building in regard to its architectural history and a must for the enthusiast. East window by Kempe.

Houghton is an attractive hamlet 800 m to west. Heddon Hall, eighteenth century and 1824, down a narrow road to the southeast with the Tidestone on the bank of the Tyne nearby, marking the tidal limit of the river; several other houses and farm buildings of some note. Close House, now at the centre of a prestigious golf course, is 1,200 m southwest—1779, for Calverley and Mary Bewick and perhaps by Newton. Pedimented front; one room includes rich eighteenth-century stucco, possibly by the Duke's team at Alnwick. Fine grounds with an orangery and an eighteenth-century bridge. The cricket scoreboard is 1894 by Septimus Oswald.

Rudchester, 200 m west-north-west—Georgian five-bay house with Gothick windows. Rudchester Roman fort nearby but only a rectangular platform discernible.

HEPPLE

Wonderfully placed in the Coquet Valley, Christchurch was built in 1897. Good interior colour scheme and linenfold panelling in the chancel. Neo-Perpendicular with bell turret between nave and chancel. The fourteenth-century Hepple Tower is pretty complete apart from battlements and crenellations. Hepple Whitfield, 1 mile south, beautifully situated nineteenth-century country house built for Sir J. W. B. Riddell. Nearby is a niche gin distillery. There are several

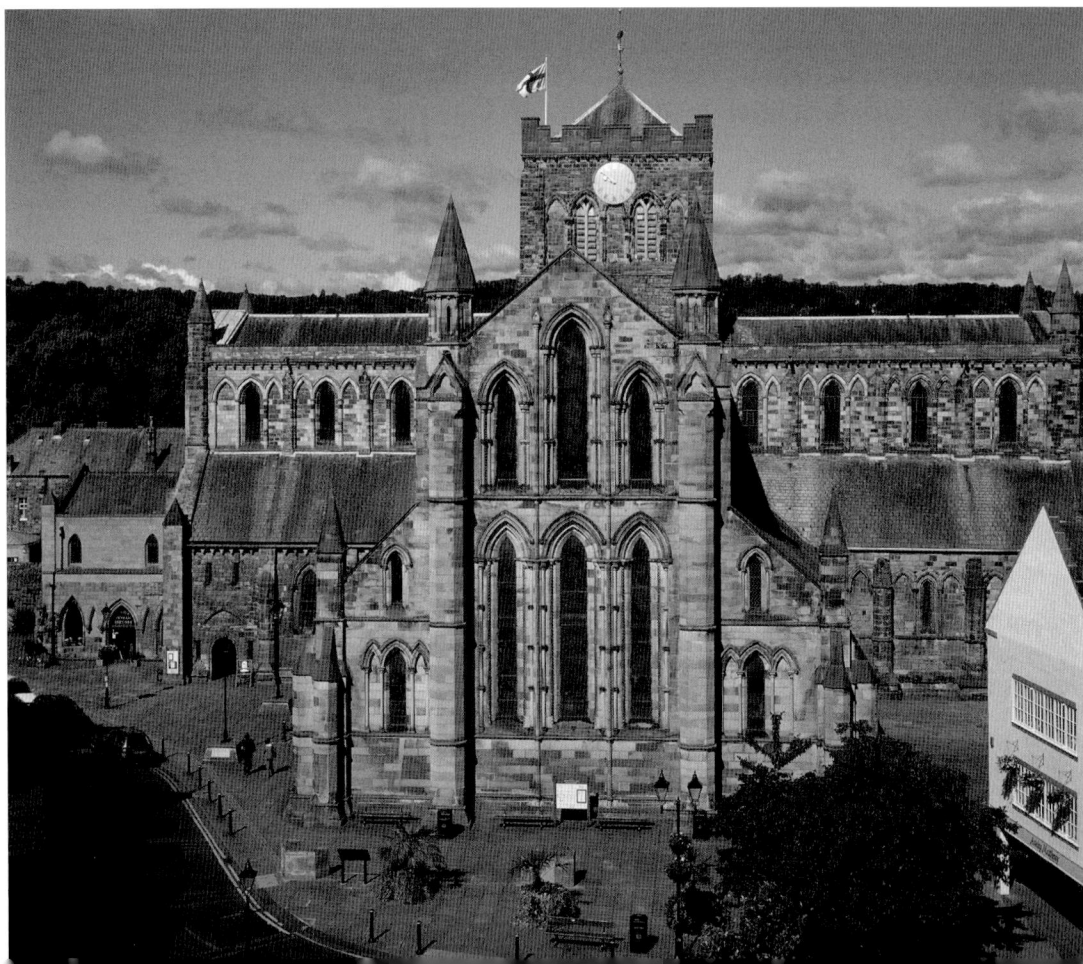

bastles on the moors west of the village. Witchy Neuk, atop Swindon Hill, 1,200 m west-southwest, is a well-preserved Iron Age camp.

HEPSCOTT

Two miles southeast of Morpeth, the key landmark is Hepscott Hall, a three-storey rectangular pele tower which is too thinly built ever to have been defensive. In the village is a late-eighteenth-century smithy.

HEXHAM

Hexham has not been blessed by modern development, since if one approaches this ancient town from east or west along the Tyne Valley, one is greeted by plumes of smoke from a paper factory. Then closer in still there are vast macadam spaces surrounding the supermarkets, all skirting the hill which is surmounted by the abbey which gives Hexham its fame. Like Corbridge, its neighbour, it has lived through a turbulent history. Pillaged and plundered by the Danes in 876, it suffered further indignities when burned by the Scots on several occasions in the fourteenth century. The Battle of Hexham, in 1463, within the Wars of the Roses, was fought on the banks of Devil's Water some two and a half miles south of the town, and Henry Beaufort, the defeated Lancastrian commander, was executed in Hexham Market Place. In 1761, there was a fierce riot here in a protest against the calling of people to the militia—fifty people died and a further thirty were injured. Nonetheless, despite—and to some extent because of—all this, it has much to draw the traveller from near or far.

The abbey is undoubtedly the jewel in the crown. Eddius, St Wilfrid's first biographer, describes Wilfrid's church as "supported by various winding columns and many side aisles" and also "spiral stairs leading up and down". The sole survivor of this church is Wilfrid's crypt, which is almost entirely intact—a catacomb but without burials; a step down into the crypt offers one a moment of awe. Hexham was an episcopal see from 681–821, so from the time of Cuthbert until the sacking by the Danes. Little is known thereafter until the Augustinian foundation which began in 1113. The canons rebuilt the church with a nave and north aisle—the lower western and southern walls survive despite later rebuildings. Otherwise, today's church is the product of the survivals of the mediaeval foundation, built during the period from 1180–1250, and then the "modern" work from 1858 and 1910. The Victorian east front is a slightly underwhelming piece by Dobson, who used Whitby Abbey as his model. The chancel and tower are clearly of the late twelfth and early thirteenth centuries. The east mediaeval parts were built all of a piece with no changes of plan. The nave is an estimable piece by Temple Moore in simple Decorated style and was added 1907–9.

There are some unique survivals at the east end. Not least of these is the splendid "night stair" in the south transept, by which the monks gained access to the choir to say or sing the night "hours". The other remarkable survival is the "frith

← **HEXHAM** Abbey, exterior
→ **HEXHAM** Abbey,
night stair detail

↑ **HEXHAM** Abbey, re-use of Roman stones

stool" in the chancel/choir, a stone chair, or rather the episcopal *cathedra*, or throne, dating from probably 675–700. The crypt, also unique, is built of Roman stones, many carved with inscriptions—here would relics have been enshrined.

There is so much to absorb generally in the architecture alone. On either side of the sanctuary are chantry chapels, to the south that of Prior Ogle and to the north of Prior Leachman. The crossing has tall arches springing from powerful piers. The colourful rood screen includes an inscription commemorating Prior Smithson, who died in 1524. In the south transept is the Roman tombstone (c.80–98) of

Flavinus, standard-bearer of a prestigious Roman regiment. Bishop Acca's cross (he died in 740) is opposite the Roman headstone. The effigy of a knight in this transept is of Sir Gilbert de Umfraville and his lady; he died in 1307. In the nave is a Roman altar alongside other sculptural fragments. Misericords in the chancel with fairly plain carving.

The cloister, as in most monastic houses, lay south of the nave and elements of it can still be seen. The lavatorium (c.1300), where the monks washed their hands on their way into the refectory, is still intact with its seven gabled blank arches. A reconstruction of some of the monastic buildings, completed

in 2014, hosts an interesting historical exhibition about the abbey and there is further space for other occasional exhibitions.

The Market Place which looks out onto the abbey has at its heart the Shambles, a noble open building resting on Tuscan columns, built by Sir Walter Blackett in 1766. There are some good houses bordering the square and the remains of the parish church of St Mary are built into a more modest row of cottages. The Hallstile Bank includes an eighteenth-century brick building at the rear. The Moot Hall, which housed the courthouse of the Archbishop of York, stands on the east side of the square. Its castle-like appearance bears some similarities to Haughton, further up the North Tyne. A vaulted passage runs all the way through the building at the south end. The second floor houses the main hall; significantly this is unique in being built as the Archbishop of York's own prison. The 1684 Grammar School lies along the lane leading from the prison.

There is a good town centre including Market Street which becomes Gilesgate and Fore Street. Hexham House is mid-eighteenth century, and the House of Correction is an interesting building. Time spent walking these streets will reveal a number of good buildings which have each had a variety of uses in their time.

Further off and dropping down to the north brings one to the nine-arched Hexham Bridge (1793) over the Tyne; like that at Corbridge, it is the work of Robert Mylne, but based on the drawings produced earlier (1756) by Smeaton.

The south bank of the river to the west of the bridge is now a highly attractive piece of parkland, affording good walks along the river.

Dotland Park, two and a half miles south, was the former hunting lodge of the Priors of Hexham—the arms of Prior Smithson (*qv* Hexham Abbey above) are there on the west gable. The former village, still extant in 1769, is now only earthworks.

↑ **HOLBURN** St Cuthbert's Cave → **HORNCLIFFE** Union Chain Bridge

HOLBURN

Tiny hamlet, 3 miles northwest of Belford. Just a mile south is St Cuthbert's Cave, known variously as one of the locations where the monks rested Cuthbert's coffin as they sought sanctuary for it from Viking invaders, and also possibly where Cuthbert sought solace as he lived out a partially eremitic life.

HOLYSTONE

The Lady's Well is a quarter of a mile northwest. Restored in 1788 with a statue imported from Alnwick Castle which was meant to represent St Paulinus, who it was thought (incorrectly) baptized multitudes here. It feels to be a holy place and stands close by to the course of the Roman road running from Bremenium (Rochester) eastwards. Only a tiny fragment of an Augustinian canoness' priory is extant in the nave of St Mary's Parish Church (possibly some more in the churchyard wall and in Mill Cottage), which was rebuilt in 1848. An attractive village, with seventeenth-century Priory Farm and early-nineteenth-century Holystone Grange with a beautiful garden and garden house, dismantled from its original location at Haggerston Castle and rebuilt here in 1933; dramatic Woodhouses Bastle just over the wall standing to its full height and one of the best in the county.

Iron Age fort at Campville Farm. At Five Kings, four standing stones (the fifth removed to form a gatepost!), then Five Barrows, half a mile south, and Harehaugh Iron Age fort to the east—so plenty of evidence from prehistory, despite or perhaps because of its remoteness.

HORNCLIFFE

Horncliffe House—elegant seven-bay pedimented sandstone house— good arcades leading to symmetrical pavilions—beautifully positioned in grounds. Just to the left and down the hill is Robson's amazing honey farm—one can see the bees about their work in a glazed hive—tractor museum attached and very good facilities for children, along with refreshments in a retired bus.

Further down the hill is a wonder of the world, the Union Chain Bridge of 1818–20, designed by Captain Samuel Brown RN. This cast-iron suspension bridge is the oldest suspension bridge anywhere in the world still carrying vehicular traffic. The chains are suspended from a support tower on the Scottish side, but they are anchored into the rock, 13 m above the road level, on the English side. Full-scale restoration completed in 2020–2, celebrating the second centenary of its completion.

A mile and three-quarters east is the High Gothic Longridge Towers built in 1876 for Sir Hubert Jerningham, former Governor of Mauritius and then of Trinidad and Tobago, and sometime Member of Parliament for Berwick. Now a school.

HOUSESTEADS

Three miles north of Bardon Mill lie the most remarkable ruins of a Roman fort in Britain. Administered by the National Trust, the ruins lie on the line of the Wall. The Whin

Sill acts as a further defence to the north. The site developed into a more obvious "civil" and less military community in the third and fourth centuries, with terraces and arable farming. There is an excellent museum and explicit interpretation after one has entered the site by the South Gate (which was later converted into a bastle). Any number of buildings survive, including the gatehouses, the Commanding Officer's House, the hospital, two granaries, barrack blocks and the nearby Milecastle 37—not to forget the latrines. There is a good (eight-mile) "wall walk" from Housesteads to Steel Rigg.

There is another Roman camp 1 mile northwest of Housesteads and an Iron Age fort 200 m east-northeast.

HOWICK

Here the dolerite of the Whin Sill outcrops, offering exciting exposed coastal rock formations. The estate village replaced the original settlement near St Michael's Church.

The Long Row, Tudor-style cottages with their terracotta chimney pots, offer an attractive quirkiness and notably with the central gabled tower sporting the Grey crest and motto. St Michael's Church is of 1746 but remodelled in 1849, and it contains the white marble table tomb of the Whig politician, the second Earl Grey, prime minister and architect of the Great Reform Bill of 1832. There is also a memorial to Sybil Grenfell by Eric Gill (1907).

Howick Hall, home of the Grey family, was built in 1782. It is nine bays wide with one-storey wings leading to five-bay pavilions. The drive originally led to the south front, but this was changed by George Wyatt in 1809 and the entrance moved to the north side. The house was remodelled by Sir Herbert Baker in 1928, following a serious fire. The interior of the house is now largely empty, and the west pavilion now acts as the family residence. The gardens are very fine and open to the public. There is a wooded lake and a stone bridge over the public road connecting the different parts of the garden; the walled garden is just under 200 m northwest of the Hall.

HUMSHAUGH

Just off the military road built by General Wade, after the 1715 Jacobite rebellion, Humshaugh is contiguous with Chollerford on its south boundary. The former paper mill by the river was built in 1788 and was used by William Pitt in 1793 to print fake French banknotes which were to flood France

↓ **HOUSESTEADS** Fort

→ **HOWICK** Hall

and force devaluation of the currency. The expedition to Flanders related to this eccentric plan was unsuccessful.

The first official Boy Scout Camp in 1908 took place near here at a site known as Look Wide near to Fourstones, where a memorial marks the spot.

Much of the land in these parts became the property of Greenwich Hospital in London and the churches both here and in Wark, 6 miles north, were built in 1818 and paid for by the hospital. Both churches are by H. H. Seward in plain Gothic with a flat white ceiling. St Peter's, Humshaugh has a Kempe window in the south wall. The village is picturesque and there is significant new development. The entrance to Haughton Castle is here (*qv* Barrasford) with the pleasant five-bayed Wester Hall 400 m east of the castle. Humshaugh House is an eighteenth-century five-bayed brick house with an earlier core.

ILDERTON

First attested in Charter Rolls, 1125, and beautifully positioned on a road only adopted as far as the village. The pink sandstone Church of St Michael has a crenellated west tower, the only mediaeval survival from a raid by the Scots c.1300—the rest is late eighteenth century. The church is set attractively within its churchyard. The churchyard contains a fourteenth-century cross slab and the 1795 Roddam Mausoleum, which includes the tomb of Admiral Robert Roddam of that same family, who were previously squires of nearby Roddam Hall. The Hall is

1733, also in pink ashlar. Middleton Hall, 3 miles north-northwest, built in 1807 for the Greenwich Hospital Commissioners who had acquired the land from the Earl of Derwentwater's estates after the 1715 rebellion—rear courtyard. North Middleton Hall (1830–40), 2 miles north-northwest—unusually faced. Railway station, 1 mile north—briefly a restaurant in the 1990s—guests dined in refrigerated conditions on the former platform!

Middleton Old Town—half a mile west of North Middleton—earthwork remains—eleven tenants still living here in 1580. Threestoneburn, 1,200 m west of Roddam—stone circle on edge of forest, and Tathey Crags, Bronze Age settlement 800 m further west. Brands Hill, 1 mile west of North Middleton, late-prehistoric and Romano-British landscape—Bronze Age cist exposed in burial mound near river.

↙ **INGRAM** Valley, Linhope Spout ↑ **KIELDER** Water from Kielder Viaduct

INGRAM

The Ingram Valley is one of several valleys running east–west into the Cheviots. Higher up these valleys the countryside can be wild and remote—indeed Peggy Bell's Bridge, the furthest bridge along the valley, marks a Victorian tragedy. Peggy Bell rode through the Breamish here on horseback during flooding and was drowned with her mount in the storm-swollen river. The valley is marked out as having one of the darkest skies, if not the darkest sky, in England—good for the astronomer.

The valley also has the remains of a number of prehistoric forts and other sites, in better preservation than in most places, and on account of the lack of ploughing high up in these wild parts. Brough Law, Grieve's Ash, Wether Hill and Old Fawdon Hill are four of these, and there are former settlements at Hartside and on Ingram Hill. Haystack Hill marks a Romano-British settlement. Also, Hartside and Alnhamsheles are sites of deserted mediaeval villages. Life

will have been tough and weather fierce for much of the year, perhaps accounting for the abandonment of these townships.

St Michael's Church has a western tower, nave and aisles rebuilt in 1879, but still with very much the atmosphere of a mediaeval church. Memorials to the Roddam family from nearby Roddam Hall (which features in its unaltered state in one of the windows). The font is dated 1662, the year of publication of the Book of Common Prayer.

KIELDER

Those of us who can remember driving up the North Tyne Valley in the 1960s will have a powerful picture of the changed landscape. Heralded as the largest man-made lake in north Europe and set within the landscape of the largest man-made forest within north Europe, this is "Panavision country". The lake has a 27.5-mile shoreline holding 44 billion gallons of water—at its deepest it is 52 m deep. Alongside the reservoir, a water grid was constructed allowing

water to be moved as far south as the industrial areas of Teesside. The lake and forest now host a wide range of sports and important animal habitats; like the Ingram Valley, it has some of the darkest skies in England. It is also host to the largest hydroelectric plant in England. The Bakethin Nature Reserve allows opportunity to enjoy and study a very wide range of species and natural phenomena. Birds of prey abound, including goshawks, peregrines, merlins, kestrels, sparrowhawks and ospreys in the summer.

Of the earlier history of these remote, wild and moorland parts, there are many legends and tales. Sir Walter Scott, quoting the Duke of Northumberland, recounted some of these: " . . . the women had no other dress than a bed-gown and petticoat. The men were savage . . . and sang a wild tune . . . " Kielder village lies next to Kielder Castle, effectively an eighteenth-century shooting box built for the Dukes of Northumberland in 1775 in a loosely Gothick style. There is a good exhibition here and also a café. The village itself is similar to Byrness and built in the 1950s for the Forestry Commission. The Presbyterian church of 1874 is by F. R. Wilson. The viaduct (John Furness Tone and Robert Nicholson) was completed in 1862 for the Border Counties Railway and survives with its fine skew arches and castellated parapet. Devil's Lapful, 1,200 m southeast of the castle, is a Neolithic long cairn, and near the Tower Knowe Visitor Centre is a submerged homestead reoccupied in the Roman period. Bloodybush Pillar stands on the border, 4 miles west-southwest, as a toll road marker. The road was built by the Swinburnes of Capheaton for the transport of coal, Telford being the surveyor. Plashetts, 2 miles southeast, former colliery.

KILHAM

Travelling northwest alongside the Bowmont Water, Kilham is a tiny hamlet to the southwest of the road going into the Cheviots. Walking up towards Kilham Hill are good footpaths offering a chance to catch sight of wild Cheviot goats. Bronze Age sites abound. On the corner of the junction with the Howtel Road is the site of the former Kilham sidings, one of the few places where supplies could be brought by rail to this remote corner.

↓ **KIELDER** Dam

↑ **KILHAM** Cheviot mountain goat

↑ **KILLINGWORTH** former Gas Research Centre

Howtel, 2 miles to the east, has the ruin of a fifteenth-century tower; Bowmont House, halfway to Howtel, is a former Presbyterian chapel and manse.

At Pawston, further west from Kilham, is the estate of another former house of the influential recusant Selby family. Pawston Hall, the mansion, is now gone completely. Here is the site of the deserted village of Thornington, first mentioned in 1296; a country house and farm nearby recall that name. Further west still is Mindrum, a tiny hamlet with a substantial farm and estate, almost on the border with Scotland. Here too was the final station on the Alnwick–Coldstream line, before it reached Cornhill.

KILLINGWORTH

Killingworth village, the original settlement, lies just north and west of the "new town" development. The earliest reference is 1242, when Roger de Merlay is named as landowner; in 1373, thirteen tenants were registered as living here. St John the Evangelist Church (1869), the church of the old village, is in West Lane; on the buttresses is the crescent motif of the Dukes of Northumberland.

North Farmhouse is dated as 1725 on a lintel, and there are several eighteenth-century houses despite the infill. Sadly, no trace survives of Killingworth Hall built by Lancelot Coxon; it was demolished in the 1960s. Half a mile east of the village is Killingworth Cottage, eighteenth century with an ornamental "overlight".

Dial House, south of the new town centre, is eighteenth century.

Of no architectural merit, its significance lies in its having been the home of George and Robert Stephenson from 1803–15; it was they who made the sundial over the door while Robert was still a schoolboy. George had been a brakesman at West Moor Pit, and his engineering genius was first seen in his improving of the pumping engine at Killingworth High Pit, with his development initially of static steam power; on 25 July 1814, *Blucher*, his locomotive, first ran on the nearby wagonway, which was effectively the oldest railway in the world, albeit on wooden rails! Ten years later, he designed *Locomotion No. 1* for the world's first public railway, running from Stockton to Darlington.

Despite Stephenson's fame, Killingworth is probably now best known as one of the two regionally developed new towns in Northumberland, alongside **CRAMLINGTON** (*qv*). Killingworth is undoubtedly superior when it comes to contemporary architectural merit. Sadly, that inheritance has not been well stewarded. Norgas House (1963–5), by Ryder, Yates and Partners, was allowed to crumble into desuetude and was demolished in 2013; Stephenson House nearby suffered a similar fate. Another building for the gas industry, however, the Engineering Research Station, by the same architectural partnership, has happily survived albeit now being used for another purpose, along with the pioneering, concrete School of Engineering next door. Derelict pit sites were reclaimed, and a fifteen-acre lake formed south of the town centre.

KIRKHARLE

Most famous now as the estate first employing Lancelot "Capability" Brown. His baptism in 1716, in nearby St Wilfrid's Church, is noted by a facsimile register in the porch as well as by a memorial plaque to him in the chancel. The present farmhouse is the partially rebuilt mansion of the Loraine family. Kirkharle Manor, just to the south of the church, is the former vicarage—an estimable early-nineteenth-century three-bayed house. The Church of St Wilfrid dates from 1336, although it was rebuilt in the 1770s and restored in 1884. Nonetheless the chancel windows are original, and the church retains a proper sense of holiness. Fine fifteenth-century Perpendicular font decorated with hatchments and originally from the mediaeval All Saints' Church in Newcastle. One curious memorial in the church refers to "Richard Loraine Esq, who was a proper handsome man of good sense and behaviour: he dy'd a Batchelor of Appoplexy walking in a green field near London, October 26th 1738, in the 38 Year of his Age". On a mound close to the church stands the 1728 memorial stone to an earlier Loraine, Sir Robert, "who was barbarously Murdered in this place by the Scots in 1483".

Kirkharle is an ancient religious site, and "harle" comes from *herle*, meaning "a temple grove". The courtyard has been decorously restored by the Anderson family, revealing ancient flagstones, and developing the farm buildings as a craft centre and café/restaurant/gourmet farm shop. The lake,
cascade, and tree planting, originating from plans by Capability Brown, have been partially recovered, offering attractive walks.

KIRKHAUGH

Bastle houses abound including Whitlow, White Lea (foliage lintel dated 1682) and Underbank; Low Row half a mile north is late seventeenth/early eighteenth century—although there was hardly a need for fortified houses at this time. Church unusually dedicated to the Holy Paraclete (1868) and designed by the incumbent, Octavius James. There is a real thirteenth-century two-light window, included from the old church. Saxon hammerhead cross in the churchyard.

KIRKHEATON

Captivating cul-de-sac village with church, farm and tiny green all grouped together. The manor is a sixteenth-century bastle with a mid-sixteenth-century front; the ashlar tower to the right is c.1740 with Georgian sash windows—this part of the house includes a panelled room on the first floor. The house which had become ruinous was restored in 1930—nice wall and rusticated gate piers at the front.

The Church of St Bartholomew is 200 m to the southwest and was rebuilt in 1755 and later Gothicized by the then curate in 1867. It has an amazing western bellcote with volutes, trefoils, and obelisk finials.

Devil's Causeway runs a mile to the east. There are nineteenth-century limekilns 500 m to the south of the village.

↑ **KIRKNEWTON** Church, Magi relief

KIRKNEWTON

Set in the north of Glendale close to the border, the village has an intriguing history. The Church of St Gregory yields much of interest. The nave by Dobson (1867) is plain but with very accomplished arcading. The south transept (the Burrell Chapel) and the chancel are gems, both tunnel-vaulted. Andrew Burrell's headstone (1458) is fine although with metal from the faces and hands now lost. On the wall to the north, as one approaches the chancel arch, is a very fine primitive twelfth-century relief of the three Magi. To the west of the tower in the churchyard is the tomb of the social reformer Josephine Butler (1906). Butler campaigned for women's suffrage, worked to abolish child prostitution and then human trafficking of young women for prostitution; she is now noted as an early feminist. She was a member of the well-known Grey family of Reform Bill fame and was married to an Anglican divine. There is a striking centenary window and sculpture by Helen Whittaker with lettering by Charles Smith, using the quotation Butler took from St Catherine of Siena: "She loved, she prayed, she endured." The copper sculpture is of lilies with bindweed.

In the churchyard, two rows of Commonwealth War Graves remind one of the proximity of the former airbase at Milfield. Also in the churchyard is a strong but slightly forbidding vault for the Davison family of Swarland (*qv*) and nearby Lanton—the Davisons lived at Coupland Castle. Alexander Davison erected the obelisk on the hill to the northeast in 1827 in memory of his brother, John. Ann "Nancy" Lambton, of the landed family, and sometime Professor of Persian at University College, London is buried nearby with a modest headstone, belying her stature as a scholar but reflecting her personality.

Another good disused station by Bell on the former Alnwick–Coldstream line.

Close by is Hethpool with the ruins of a tiny tower and the present Hethpool House rebuilt in 1919 by George Reavell for Sir Arthur Munro Sutherland, a Tyneside industrialist. It is inspired by Charles Rennie Mackintosh's Hill House at Helensburgh, but there is evidence of old masonry and a dated door surround of 1686. It was Robert Mauchlen in 1928 who added the Mackintosh touches and built Hethpool Cottages, also with an Arts and Crafts feel. Wild Cheviot goats are frequently seen in these parts. College Valley runs westward into the Cheviots and has splendid walks amongst Bronze Age forts; a day pass is required, and visiting is restricted in the lambing season—permits online or at the Cheviot Centre in **WOOLER**. See also **YEAVERING** (*qv*).

KIRKWHELPINGTON

Quite a large village just off the main road, which once expected to be larger, inasmuch as Henry III gave it a charter for a market. The growth never occurred, however, and the charter was revoked on account of markets not happening. Perched high above the Wansbeck, you enter from the south over an attractive bridge, built in 1819, through the efforts of John Hodgson, the local

↑ **KIRKWHELPINGTON** Church

historian who lived in the village. Nice double-gabled house, the Old Temperance, to the south of the churchyard. Next door, another good early-nineteenth-century house, Cliff Edge, the former police station, now a private residence, is across the main street to the north of the church.

St Bartholomew's Church is long and large with a strong west tower—both nave and chancel are aisleless, although clearly there were both aisles and transepts. There is Norman and then thirteenth-century infilling at the tower arch; very good wooden nave ceiling. The church seems to have had a complex architectural history. Fine, airy and light chancel, recently very well restored, with an unusual "Festival of Britain" reredos—plain but with a series of tiny crosses and some sculpted figures; good east lancets and plain glass windows. Some good monuments, especially relating to the Aynsley family; a number of mediaeval (and one post-Reformation) cross slabs. Plain seventeenth-century font, recently repositioned in an excellent remodelling of the west part of the church.

Sir Charles Parsons, the inventor of the steam turbine, who later lived at Ray, 2 miles to the east, attended church here, and both he and his wife are buried to the north of the church. Katharine, his wife, was also an engineer and a suffragette; along with their daughter, she founded the Women's Engineering Society.

Evidence of the mediaeval lost village of West Whelpington, 800 m west. It was deserted by 1720 and earlier on had been victim to Scottish raids. Iron Age hill fort at Great Wanney and Romano-British settlement to the northwest of Catcherside—bastles abound.

KNARSDALE

Sometimes spelt Knaresdale in the Pennine South Tyne Valley. The Hall is a seventeenth-century house set on a steep defensive site—mullioned windows. Burnstones Viaduct on the former South Tyne branch close to the roadside is eccentrically built in two reverse skews over the burn. St Jude's Church (1833 with 1892 chancel) is a Gothicized preaching box. Mediaeval cross slabs including one with shears in the chancel; 1904 east window by Kempe.

LAMBLEY

Fine thirteen-arched viaduct over the South Tyne, which carried the former branch line over the river—maybe in use for the same purpose in the not-too-distant future. St Mary and St Patrick Church (1885) by W. S. Hicks. Aisleless, but very attractive in a thirteenth-century manner. Vaulted chancel and fine timber nave roof and two bellcotes. Site of former priory—Benedictine or Augustinian nunnery founded before 1190—masonry reused in house and farm buildings of Lambley Farm.

Two miles east on the right-hand side of the road to Whitfield, just before Garbutt Hill Farm and next to Burn House Farm, is a delightful 1760 Friends' Meeting House. Rusticated quoins and good doorway. Movingly attractive interior with a cast-iron grate at the north end beneath the gallery—a building not to be missed.

LANGLEY CASTLE

One of the most impressive of the larger tower houses in the county, all the more impressive on account of the work of Cadwallader Bates who restored it in the 1890s; clearly it had been built robustly early on, for so much of the structure to have survived—it had been ruinous from 1405 onwards, due to damage sustained when Henry IV was putting down Archbishop Scrope's rebellion. It is built to an H-plan with a large undivided central apartment. Owned later by the Earls of Derwentwater, it was confiscated following the Earl's part in the 1715 rebellion; a memorial of 1883, on the main road, commemorates the involvement of the family in both the 1715 and 1745 uprisings—they were beheaded at the Tower of London. Since its restoration, the castle has also hosted a school and now a hotel. There is an unusual turnpike cottage just by the castle.

Significant ruins of Stublick Colliery remain 1 mile south with

↑ **LAMBLEY** Coanwood Friends' Meeting House and headstones

a Cornish-style flue and buildings—coal has been mined here since at least 1700. Other lead industry buildings abound.

Staward Pele, 2 miles southwest, stands on a precipitous spine of rock above the River Allen—much Roman stone is incorporated—the pele is first noted in 1327. Staward Manor nearby is the result of a "merger" between two bastle houses remodelled in the late eighteenth and mid-nineteenth centuries. A blocked upper door is dated 1688. A Roman altar—on the lawn—was earlier at Staward Pele.

LEMMINGTON

Set under the lee of the hill with the remarkably effective eyecatcher, Lemmington Branch, keeping watch. The hall is a mid-eighteenth-century house altered by William Newton at the end of that century and then restored in 1913. A quarter of a mile southeast is a column by Sir John Soane, a memorial to one James Evelyn, a relative of the diarist. Originally in Felbridge Park in Surrey, it was moved here in 1928.

LESBURY

A village of bridges, and now stunningly approached by the 2004, slightly out of context, steel bowstring bridge with the bows leaning away from the road. Fine fifteenth-century stone bridge close by and remains of good steadings sadly mutilated in the road improvements. There is a good Robert Stephenson eighteen-arch viaduct 800 m northwest. Lesbury House, good five-bay villa of c.1800 overlooking the River Aln. St Mary's Church much restored in 1849; east end three-light window of c.1300—interior history very puzzling. Some attractive contemporary mock-Georgian boxes in Aln View.

LILBURN

Lilburn Tower itself was built in 1828–9 by Dobson for Henry Collingwood, a really splendid house in the Tudor style. It includes a ballroom with a coffered ceiling and a Gothick staircase with cast iron balusters. John Collingwood again used Dobson to make changes in 1843, inserting a ceiling into the hall and partitioning off the staircase. The porte-cochère was moved a little to the left at the same time. There is a large garden and an observatory with a coppered dome and embattled parapet.

A quarter of a mile west are remains of a chapel set next door to the ruined fifteenth-century West Lilburn Tower. The chapel is early Norman and comprises a nave and chancel—in the south chapel two mediaeval grave slabs survive, one with the inscription "Alexander".

A little north of Lilburn is the Hurl Stone, which is a mediaeval standing cross. Close to the Hurl Stone is Hurlstone Tower, a fanciful but attractive millennium folly, commissioned by Duncan Davidson and designed by Harry Potts as an observation point and a "meetings venue". It is a noble building and received an Oscar from the Master Builders' Federation. There is also a standing stone with cup markings northwest of the tower and about 270 m from Newtown Mill—it stands alongside the course of Devil's Causeway.

LINDISFARNE

The wooden stakes marking out the walkers' pathway across the sands at low tide carry the traveller back fourteen hundred years to Aidan's arrival in 635, from the monastery on Iona, at the behest of King Oswald of Northumbria. Thus began a golden age in the development of Christian culture in England culminating in the Lindisfarne Gospels (there is an exhibition in the Visitor Centre). Lindisfarne, also known as Holy Island, had been inhabited during both the Old and New Stone Ages. Aidan, of whom there is a fine twentieth-century effigy in the churchyard, set up a monastery here and became the first Bishop of Lindisfarne. We cannot be sure of the site of the wooden buildings set up by Aidan. St Cuthbert followed later in 665, and in 684 he also became Bishop of Lindisfarne. St Cuthbert's Island, just at the southeast corner and near the small fishing harbour, is said to be where

he spent time in retreat—there was a monastic cell here in earlier times.

The priory is an evocative ruin with one of the ribs of the crossing vault surviving and apparently suspended in mid-air, and frequently described as the "rainbow arch". The Benedictine ruins date from about 1140. The former church has a short nave and chancel with an apse, later replaced with a squared-off east end. The main monastic footings are clearly exposed, and there is a large outer courtyard to the south. Next door to the priory

stands the parish church of St Mary which itself, although appearing as a thirteenth-century building, has tell-tale signs of Saxon origins. The church is broad with substantial north and south aisles, and the chancel is lit by three Early-English-style lancets. Both aisles are lit by lancets of different designs, and the arcading—Romanesque on the northern side and Transitional on the southern—is delightfully composed of alternating strands of red sandstone and white limestone. There is a very powerful elm

↓ **LINDISFARNE** Priory, west front

→ **LINDISFARNE** pilgrim stakes

sculpture by Fenwick Lawson of monks carrying Cuthbert's coffin, along part of its long journey, after the saint's death. In the outer courtyard, there is a further sculpture of the saint himself, also by Lawson.

Holy Island Castle is a small fort, one of a number built by the Crown c.1549. It stands as if mounted on a plinth on a whinstone outcrop. In the early twentieth century, it was rebuilt by its new owner, Edward Hudson, the editor of *Country Life*—his architect was Sir Edwin Lutyens. Lutyens worked with great sensitivity producing a modestly sized country house of great character—as elsewhere, his fellow designer was Gertrude Jekyll, who laid out the walled garden.

There are limekilns in the lee of the castle, and the path of a former tramway to transport the lime is easily identifiable. One mile south of the island on Ross Sands are two stone navigation beacons with an almost ancient Egyptian feel to them, also used for timing the passage of vessels. Built between 1820 and 1840 for Trinity House, they stand about 150 m (500 ft) apart.

→ **LINDISFARNE** Church,
Fenwick Lawson,
"The Journey"

LONGFRAMLINGTON

As the name suggests, a long village on the Coldstream Road and to the east where the fast-growing village centre is focused. There was a pit here, and Longframlington also narrowly escaped being on a mid-Northumberland branch railway. The pit was on the site of the present-day Fram holiday park. Attractive houses on corner of Front and Church Streets; Embleton Hall c.1730 now a hotel. The nave and sanctuary of St Mary's Church are c.1190, and some fabric may be earlier still; the west end has a buttress dated 1740 and probably was built along with the bellcote; chancel is late nineteenth century.

The fine eighteenth-century Weldon Bridge was bypassed in 1969; the bridge replaced an earlier crossing of the Coquet lost in floods in 1744 and 1752. Next door, the Anglers Arms is a five-bay eighteenth-century brick house. Weldon Mill, built in honey-coloured sandstone, was the last complete watermill to be built in the county. Milling continued until 1964, when the building was adapted as residential accommodation.

A mile and a half west is Brinkburn Priory, founded in c.1130 as a community of Augustinian canons. Its position is idyllic in a deep cleft of the Coquet and almost encircled by a meander. The church was rebuilt from ruins in 1858 at the expense of the Cadogan family. The six-bay nave is Transitional, although many of the windows remain round in a Romanesque fashion. Of the nave's three doorways, the north door is the richest and most elaborate. The church has a splendid acoustic and has been host to a music festival. Little survives of the monastic buildings, and the most substantial remains have been built into the adjacent manor house previously owned by the Fenwick family. The house was remodelled in Gothick style in 1810. The priory drain is still discoverable and later became the millrace. The nearby watermill is first noted in 1535, although the present buildings are nineteenth century. Above the priory is the site of an Iron Age fort. Brinkheugh, a little upstream, has some elements dating back to the sixteenth century.

LONGHIRST

An attractive nineteenth-century estate village. The Hall is a very good Dobson villa of 1824 for William Lawson. The jewel in the crown would have been the inner hall (now sadly sub-divided into apartments) with an apse at either end, visible from the exterior of the house. Conservatory has Tuscan pillars! On the western side, there is a large porch with enormous Corinthian columns. St John's Church (1876) is by Sir Arthur Blomfield—nice, tiled floors and carved benches.

↓ **LONGFRAMLINGTON** Brinkburn Priory

↑ **LONGHORSLEY** Linden Hall Hotel

LONGHORSLEY

Small watering place on the Morpeth–Wooler road, with a rather sad abandoned, now partially ruinous church, set attractively in the middle of a field to the southeast and near to the sewage farm. The nave was 1783 and the chancel 1798.

St Helen's Church in the village is nineteenth century and was the former village school. The porch, however, was brought from the old church in 1982. Next door is a schoolmaster's house of 1751. The cruciform Roman Catholic Church of St Thomas of Canterbury is of 1841. Horsley Tower is early sixteenth century but with a mid-seventeenth century north wing. The third floor was used as a Roman Catholic chapel before the church was built. Good early-nineteenth-century former vicarage.

Linden Hall, just over 1 mile north, is a noble but plain ashlar house of 1812, built for Charles William Bigge; heavy Greek Doric porch, well converted (including stable block and outbuildings) by Ainsworth Spark in 1980, and the entire campus is now a hotel and golfing centre.

LONGHOUGHTON

The ancient Church of St Peter and St Paul has a chancel of the mid-eleventh century, an early-twelfth-century tower, and a south aisle of c.1200. Some of the moulding is intriguingly plain although the tower arch has more elaborate work. In the churchyard is a small cross which could be pre-Conquest. Sturdy early work at Longhoughton Hall farmhouse. The village was colonized by the RAF for housing for nearby Boulmer—there was even a NAAFI in the village, which later became the village store.

LOWICK

Fairly large and expanding village on the old north–south Roman road known as Devil's Causeway. The earliest known church here dated from the early twelfth century, but the present parish church of St John is 1794, by Henry Penny Selby Morton (on an inscription over the doorway)—Classical but Gothicised in the early nineteenth century, with a chancel and vestry by F. R. Wilson (1887). Good vicarage, on west corner of Eelwell Road, in Georgian style but of 1879. South of the church, earlier three-bay vicarage of the late eighteenth century, later a Roman Catholic convent and now privately owned. Former

Roman Catholic church of 1861 by Stevenson of Berwick. Presbyterian church of 1821 at Cheviot View with three-bay manse attached.

Curious tale of war memorial—the present column at centre of village is of traditional design, with the inscribed names of the dead. The original memorial consists of huge pieces of whinstone simply etched with 1914–1918. It was commissioned by the Sitwells of Barmoor, then moved by the villagers and placed to the east of Barmoor Castle. Opposite the Sitwell memorial are Arts and Crafts-style cottages at Barmoor Lane End. Barmoor Castle stands on an ancient site. There was a tower house on this site from the fourteenth century, and the Muschamp family enlarged and crenellated it. William Carr of Etal bought it in 1649, before it passed to the Sitwell family in 1791. John Paterson built the present house for Francis Sitwell in 1801 in "castle style", of which it is an excellent

example, and a mixture of Gothick and Classical. The Sitwells were of the same family as the twentieth-century literary family of Edith, Osbert and Sacheverell Sitwell.

One and a half miles east is evidence of a castle, near Lowick Low Steads: earthworks—banks and outer ditches. Two miles east is St Nicholas' Church, Kyloe, now residential. Saxon cross in churchyard, and the tower of 1792 is rebuilt Norman. The Kyloe Hills are part of the crescent of sandstone hills running south then west and north via the Simonsides. East Kyloe Tower is of the fourteenth century and now attached to a farm building. Bronze Age burial relics found in quarry in 1927. Beal, still farther east, is on the main railway line and used to host the station for Holy Island; 1674 farmhouse. Low Lynn, to the northwest, is a ruined eighteenth-century house with lodge on the Great North Road.

↓ **LOWICK** Sitwell war memorial

↓ **LOWICK** Barmoor Castle

LUCKER

Lucker's transformation has been almost entire. From a rather sleepy and even dull village, it now has a prosperous feel. Its bucolic origins—Lucker comes from the Norse/Old English word meaning "marsh with a pool"—had set the scene. But now pub and restaurant—Apple Tree and Apple Core, set by the old bridge over the Waren Burn—suggest comfort and cheer.

St Hilda's Church boasts of being the sixth on this site. The first (wooden) church was replaced by a Saxon stone building rebuilt in Norman times; later a mediaeval building was succeeded by an eighteenth-century church. The present neo-Romanesque building is by George Reavell (1874); the apse is an attractive feature. Nearby Lucker Hall had fallen into desuetude and was finally demolished in 2009; now the village shop, at the heart of a "holiday village", stands on the site.

MATFEN

A village made particularly attractive by the stream, a tributary of the River Pont, running alongside its main street. Holy Trinity Church (1841–54) was designed by Sir Edward Blackett, who lived at nearby Matfen Hall, which he had also designed for himself. Topped by a large spire, the church is quite a statement. Some interesting features inside including four alabaster reliefs and a lectern designed by an Italian artist also working in Alnwick Castle. The Hall, begun in 1830, has an Elizabethan feel, although the vast great hall by Rickman is unquestionably Gothic! Eighteenth-century gate piers west of the house. Corneyside a mile north of Matfen is the most perfect classical Georgian house in the county (c.1735).

At Ingoe, two and a half miles north-northeast, is the "Warrior Stone", a prehistoric standing stone almost 2 m high; there are hut marks nearby, and Bronze Age relics were discovered in the nineteenth century. South Hall is a fine early-eighteenth-century manor house with a complete interior.

MILFIELD

Stands on the edge of the eponymous plain as a tiny watering place on the Wooler–Coldstream road. This area is scattered with former henges and other evidence of early habitation. Just to the left of the main road, travelling south, Maelmin, a replica of a Neolithic henge, has been erected (2000) close to the site of a seventh-century palace similar to that at **YEAVERING**. The existence of many of these early structures has been uncovered through cropmarks. There is good interpretative material and background to the former RAF aerodrome and training base. Primitive Methodist Chapel of 1855 in the village.

↓ **MILFIELD** Maelmin Henge

MITFORD

Formerly a market town which competed with nearby **MORPETH**, as in the ancient rhyme:

Mitforde was Mitforde when
Morpeth was none,
and Mitforde shall be Mitforde
when Morpeth is gone.

Sadly, for Mitford, something of the opposite happened. One branch of the Mitford family (the Mitford family had held the manor from Norman times) became famous—or even infamous—in the twentieth century!

The castle watches over Mitford on the top of a sandstone prominence, just south of the village, and the River Wansbeck. Originally motte and bailey, a later shell keep was built, perhaps as early as 1138—part of this survives on the west. There is a vaulted basement, a significant amount of the bailey's curtain wall survives and there is a fragment of a late-twelfth-century chapel. There has been some exciting history with William the Lion of Scotland taking it in 1175 and the English King John in 1216, just a year after the signing of Magna Carta. Then it was the headquarters of the rebellious Sir Gilbert Middleton in 1317 and of Scottish outlaws a year later—this was the time of it moving towards a ruinous state.

The Church of St Mary Magdalene is attractively set amidst woodland. Like the castle, the church has suffered from periods of violence. There was a substantial twelfth-century Romanesque building, and of this, three and a half bays of the south arcade have survived.

The violence of 1216 had its impact on the church, as did King Alexander of Scotland's plundering in the following year; the present chancel was built later in the thirteenth century. In 1327, the church was described as "wholly burned" soon after the castle was laid in ruins. The nave was gutted again by fire in 1705—it remained a ruined shell until about 1840, and R. J. Johnson, in a wholesale restoration, extended the nave half a bay in 1870. There is a Kempe window to the Mitford family in the south aisle, and a monument to Bertram Reveley of 1622—nice lychgate of 1889.

The old manor house southwest of the church is largely ruinous, although the tower survives as does the rear wall of the main block. The north-western range was remodelled in 1961–2. Two good bridges over the Font and Wansbeck, of the eighteenth and nineteenth centuries. At Spital Hall, north of the Font Bridge, is the site of a mediaeval hospital, probably a lazar house and now sporting an eighteenth-century villa. Mitford Hall is by John Dobson for the Mitford family (1828). Part of it was demolished in 1970, but the three-bay front remains with its Greek Doric porch. Two unusually connected five-bay houses form Nunriding Hall, almost 2 miles northwest.

MORPETH

Morpeth succeeded **ALNWICK** as county town of Northumberland. Set on the River Wansbeck, but eccentrically the town grew on the northern bank whereas the major buildings including the castle and parish church were built on the southern bank. The name seems to be associated with a murder on the Great North Road! Entering from the south and coming down the broad curve of the bank into the town, one is greeted by the fortress-like Court House by John Dobson (1822–8). Inside there is an imposing stone Gothic imperial stair. The octagonal gaol was demolished in 1891. One is transported over the river by Telford's "New Bridge" of 1829–31—of the Old Bridge only the central pier and abutments survive. There is also an iron footbridge of 1869.

The first castle was built on Ha' Hill, in Carlisle Park, and destroyed in 1216 by King John. The second castle, 200 m south of Ha' Hill, was built later in that century by the de Merlays; the 1604 map shows a keep in the middle of a bailey with a gatehouse and outer ward—only the gatehouse and a fragment of the curtain wall survive. The top two floors of the gatehouse were restored in 1858 for the Earl of Carlisle—some Tudoresque-Gothic stables were also built in the nineteenth century.

The Town Hall was originally by Vanbrugh, but it was severely damaged by fire, requiring the front and back to be replaced by R. J. Johnson in 1870. It has a noble five-bay front with a pedimented three-bay centre. Johnson added a wrought-iron grille to the originally open arcade—his interior staircase is imposing and includes a bust of the seventh Earl of Carlisle by Foley. The Clock Tower in the middle of Oldgate is a rarity and one more town landmark; it houses the earliest example of a ring of "civic" bells.

There are three churches in the town. The Chantry was originally All Saints' Church and then acted as a bridge chantry (as in Rotherham and Wakefield in Yorkshire), founded by Richard of Morpeth in 1296; western end of this building is relatively complete, but the south and east sides were remodelled in 1738 with attractive round-arched windows. Since ceasing to be a place of worship, it has had several incarnations. At present, it is both a craft centre and a bagpipe museum. (Northumbrian smallpipes differ from Scottish pipes in being entirely bellows-blown, that is without a mouthpiece.)

Then, St Mary's, the ancient parish church, has some Early English features but is effectively a fourteenth-century building, with a low west tower. The chancel priest's door is original and retains its iron hinges and door knocker c.1350. The south porch is probably sixteenth century. The church has survived without any major rebuilding. The pitch of the chancel roof is far loftier than that of the nave offering an unusual exterior profile. Good mediaeval glass, with a stunning Jesse-tree east window—the best piece of mediaeval glass in the county and sensitively restored by William Wailes; thirteenth-century octagonal font. Suffragette Emily Davison's tomb in the family vault to west of the church. Davison was a militant campaigner for her cause, being arrested on nine occasions, on hunger strike seven times and force-fed on forty-nine occasions. She died after attempting to halt the progress of the 1913 Derby and falling beneath the King's horse Anmer. Her funeral was an extraordinary event when 5,000 women formed a procession, which stopped briefly at St George's, Bloomsbury in London before the coffin was transported to Morpeth via Newcastle. The funeral in St Mary's Church was private, as was the interment.

It seems likely that originally there were two settlements in Morpeth, north and south of the Wansbeck, hence the presence of the church and

↑ **MORPETH** St Mary's Church

castle on the south bank. There is a nineteenth-century watchhouse on the south side of the churchyard—built as a lookout for body-snatchers!

The third church, Benjamin Ferrey's St James' in Newgate Street, in the town centre, is approached by an attractive avenue of trees. The nave is strong and powerful nineteenth-century Norman, and the church was inspired by one of the Grey family spending time in Sicily—excellent neo-Romanesque detail. There is an attractive screen of Romanesque design, heralding the church from the main street. Newgate Street has a succession of good buildings including a bank and The Beeswing. The former girls' grammar school is here. Old Bakehouse Yard is one of the best preserved of the yards behind these buildings and at the foot of the yard are the Bakehouse Steps, the only surviving stepping stones over the Wansbeck.

Collingwood House in Oldgate was the residence of Cuthbert Collingwood, Nelson's Flag Officer at Trafalgar. Houses of his scions pop up all over the north of the county, even as close to the border as Cornhill-on-Tweed. Also in Oldgate are some good 1970s developments including Bondgate and Collingwood Court.

County Hall (1982) is a good piece of contemporary architecture with an imaginative use of brick—interesting roofs and good window registration. The lobby includes rubbed brick historical reliefs by John Rothwell. Bridge Street is the bustling heart to the town with good mixed elevations above the shops, despite the all-too-frequent proliferation of insensitive shop facias. The Sanderson Arcade (2009) is well conceived and leads through to the bus station behind. The Black Bull is interesting with its bow window and Regency façade.

Between Bridge Street and the river is Oliver's Mill—the stone-built part is of 1830 and the brick building is of 1899. Here is an interesting example of the use of water power.

Newminster Abbey ruins lie 1 mile to the west. Newminster was a

↓ **MORPETH** Emily Davison statue

Cistercian foundation of 1137 and a daughter house of Fountains Abbey. Reconstructions of the former monastery have been made, including the cloister arcade, but the ruins are scanty.

NENTHEAD

Like Alston, Nenthead sits within a tiny corner of Cumbria but still within the Diocese of Newcastle. On a sunny day, the views are marvellous, but in other weathers it can be bleak and unprotected. The manor was forfeited by the Earl of Derwentwater after the 1715 rebellion and given to Greenwich Hospital, which came to own large tracts of land in Northumberland. It was dominated by lead mining which continued until as recently as 1965.

St John's Church is by Ignatius Bonomi (1845) and was restored 1907 by Hicks and Charlewood in Decorated style. The bus garage of 1909 is notable, having been built as a dressing mill.

Perhaps most important of all here is the Rampgill Mine, now in the hands of the North Pennines Heritage Trust and comprising the mining offices, a smelt mill site and an assay house. There is a barracks opposite. Big Wheel Pit on the hillside above. The capped head of the Brewery Shaft can be seen; it is thought it was sunk to connect with the Nenthead Level (*qv* Alston).

NETHERTON

Six and a half miles from **ROTHBURY**, Netherton has a celebrated pub, The Star Inn, listed by the Campaign for Real Ale (CAMRA) for its unusual interior; it remained in the Good Beer Guide for forty consecutive years. There has been a pub on this site since 1788. There is one public room—large, plain and square with a nineteenth-century feel but with a 1950s fireplace—best to check first before travelling, opening hours are variable!

NETHERWITTON

In the valley of the River Font and beneath the Simonsides. The Hall dates from 1685, probably designed by Robert Trollope (as at Eshott Hall) for Sir Nicholas Thornton. There are three bays and pedimented windows throughout. There are sundials with mediaeval-style frames; the rear part of the house is older, perhaps sixteenth century. There is Queen Anne panelling within. In the grounds are a wide stable yard, a game larder and notable banded gate piers, probably

of the late sixteenth century. There is a large mill of some eleven bays by the burn—originally a cotton mill, it was transformed successively for wool and then timber—now well restored as residential accommodation. In the Civil War, Cromwell quartered a significant force in the grounds of the Hall, later paying £96 5s 6d for damage done by troops—ironically, a century later Lord Lovat, the Jacobite leader, took refuge in a priest's hole in the upper part of the Hall.

St Giles' Church has a mediaeval chancel with a fifteenth-century east window and a priest's door dated 1691; the nave is eighteenth century but then remodelled a hundred years or so on. The font may be as early as thirteenth century, and there is a cross slab top dating from the same period.

At Witton Shields, a mile and a half north, is a tower house reduced from three to two floors in the early twentieth century—the top floor had once housed a Roman Catholic chapel.

Two miles east-southeast on the Font near Stanton Mill is the site of a Roman camp and fortlet.

Fontburn Reservoir is 2 miles to the west-northwest.

NUNNYKIRK, 2 miles to the northwest, is universally admired as one of John Dobson's finest houses, which he remodelled in 1825 for William Orde Jr. Some suggest that Dobson borrowed the French Neo-Classical style from his close friend, Ignatius Bonomi. Dobson refronted a five-bay Queen Anne façade on the

garden side. On the entrance front, again of five bays, he included a loggia of three pairs of Ionic columns. In the middle of the house, which is now a school, is an oblong hall with a coffered dome and coffered segmental vaults at either end. There are fine plaster ceilings in the house and an eccentric marble fireplace in the drawing room. There was a ninth-century Saxon cross shaft in the garden, now in the Newcastle Museum of Antiquities.

NEWBIGGIN-BY-THE-SEA

Standing together on a white fabricated platform to greet you—should you arrive by sea—is Sean Henry's unusual sculpture *Couple*. All part of the renewal of this ancient place, a maritime centre in the time of Edward III and later a grain port comparable to London and Hull. The beach too, once scarred with deposits of sea coal, has been restored to seaside status by importing 500,000 tonnes of sand from Skegness. Keeping watch, on its bare headland, as sentinel over all this are the tower and spire (intended originally as a beacon) of St Bartholomew's Church. Likely to have had pre-Conquest origins, the capital of the chancel arch is twelfth century and the delicate nave arcading from the thirteenth. The architectural development of the church is interesting and complex with significant restoration in the nineteenth century—an important collection of cross slabs. Powerfully coloured modern east window.

Newbiggin was placed at the end of the first sea cable to Scandinavia, with its east end in Jutland in Denmark. The lifeboat station is the oldest operational lifeboat house in the British Isles. There is still some fishing; the colliery and pit closed in 1967. The small seaside centre breathes modest but faded glory. Sadly, the annual street fair ceased in 2004.

NEWBROUGH

Wandering village in the beautiful South Tyne Valley. St Peter's Church (1866) in plain thirteenth-century style—aisle window by Kempe; remounted Jacobean panelling on interior of west wall. On an ancient site occupied from fourth century by a Roman fortlet.

Cute 1876 Italianate Town Hall and early-eighteenth-century Red Lion Inn; segmental bridge of 1830. Newbrough Park (1790) is built facing the river and with its rear to the main street; Newbrough Hall half a mile north, an early Dobson mansion. Thornton Tower is a rectangular mediaeval tower house.

↓ **NEWBIGGIN** The Couple

On the edge of lead mining here, High Stonecroft is the remains of a Cornish pumping-engine house.

Fourstones, 1 mile east, has a paper mill, established in 1763—the country's earliest Fourdrinier paper-making machine (1860) is preserved within the complex. Nearby, the stationmaster's house of the erstwhile station survives and just west of the station, five substantial limekilns. St Aidan's Church is a tiny attractive, green-painted wooden building.

NEWBURN

Only 5 miles from **NEWCASTLE** city centre, Newburn, with its neighbour **LEMINGTON**, with which it is now contiguous, has a long history. Some Roman material here, and then mediaeval history with Copsi, the Earl of Northumberland being murdered here in 1069. Later Newburn was caught up into the Civil War, which was preceded by the Battle of Newburn, when the Scottish Covenanters subsequently occupied Newcastle-upon-Tyne. Having been one of the richest vegetable-growing areas of the county, Newburn was later taken over by heavy industry, particularly engineering. In 1822, Spencer's steelworks was established—the site of the steelworks is now a country park. William Hedley built his *Puffing Billy* steam engine here two years before Stephenson's *Blucher* began its work in Killingworth.

Lemington Glassworks has now gone but one of the pyramidal kilns still stands proud.

St Michael's Church is one survivor from mediaeval times, with an early-Norman west tower; large quoins around the blocked west door may well be Saxon as indeed with the quoining at the southeast angle of the nave. There is much to explore of the architectural history of the interior. Some good stained glass and memorials to the Hedley family including one of the pioneering railway engineers. Some interesting waterworks nearby. Good steel lattice girder bridge of 1893. The wagonway which connected with Wylam, and thus also Stephenson's cottage, ended here.

↓ **NEWCASTLE** Tyne Bridge with the Sage Gateshead below

NEWCASTLE-UPON-TYNE

Newcastle is, without a doubt, the regional capital of Northumbria and one of the great cities of England. First known as Pons Aelius (Aelius was Hadrian's family name), referring to the Roman bridge over the Tyne. The bridge was probably built at the turn of the second/third centuries at the north end of Cade's Road. This road is thought to have passed through Concangis (Chester-le-Street) and Brough to Eboracum (York). Fragments of Hadrian's Wall survive in Denton, in Westgate Road at Benwell and in Byker. On the seaward edge of the city (*qv* Wallsend) is the east end of the wall at Segedunum.

Evidence from mediaeval times also survives. Pre-eminently, of course, the castle is a symbolic reminder of this; rather like Berwick Castle, it was dealt with in a Philistine manner by the railway engineers, although what remains is impressive—and particularly from the train! Stretches of the thirteenth-/fourteenth-century town wall, and notably to the west some mediaeval houses, are still extant. The remains of Blackfriars Dominican friary are very substantial, in extent perhaps second only to Norwich among Dominican friaries in England. Some timber-framed buildings are visible, and there is some good Georgian work. Newcastle is remarkable for the planned environment of Grainger Town. Developer Richard Grainger and architect John Dobson left an astonishing legacy in Grainger Street, Grey Street and, before the rapacious 1970s developers ruined it, Eldon Square. Central Station is a triumph.

The twentieth century has, however, not been entirely destructive and even elements of the urban motorway have added some elan. The Civic Centre is a fine piece of municipal architecture, and the series of bridges over the Tyne (some nineteenth century), along with the new and refurbished buildings on both north and south banks, add enormously to the excitement of the riverscape. It is the riverside with which we shall begin.

↓ **NEWCASTLE** Central Station

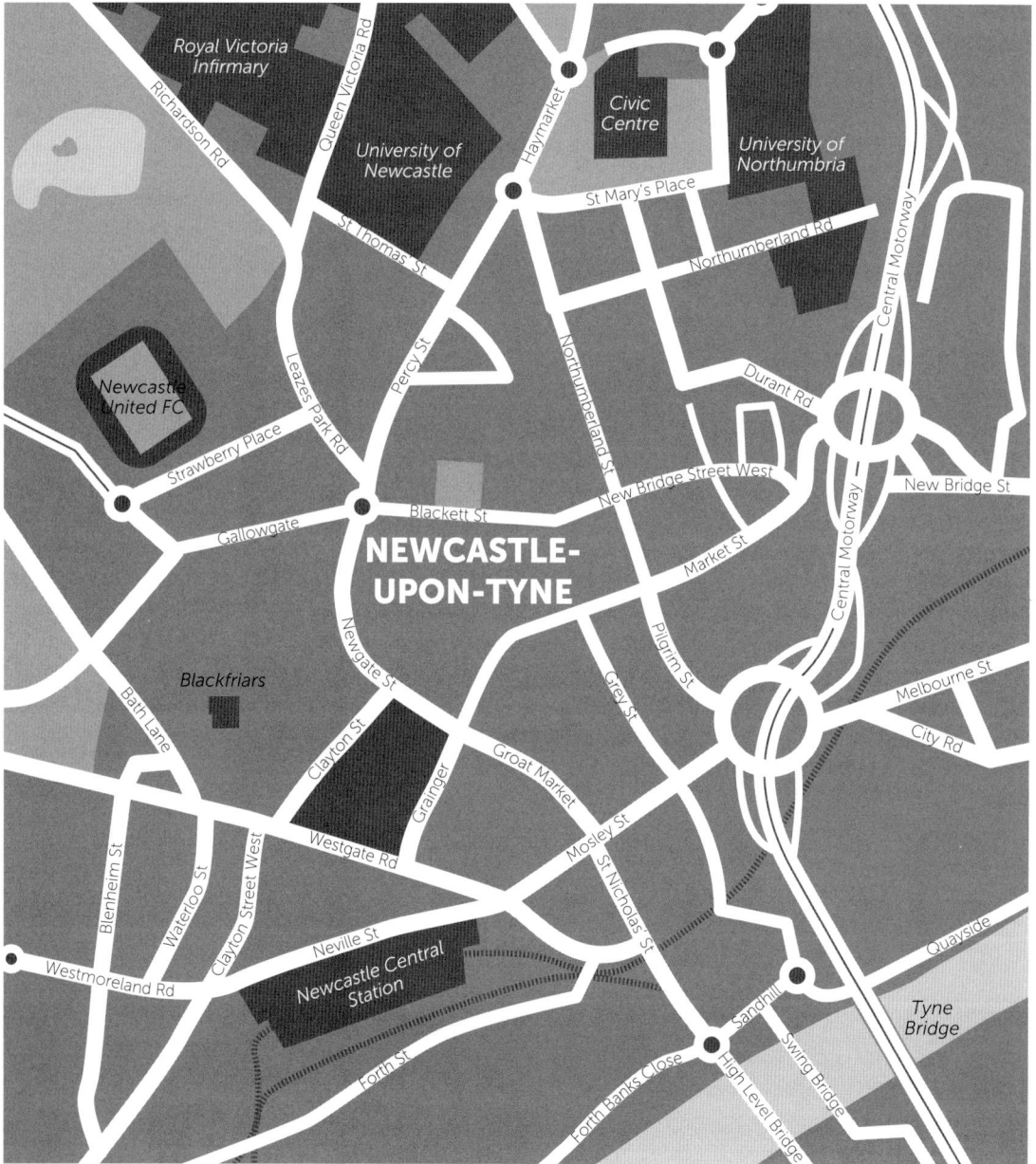

The Riverside. Crossing the Tyne travelling north, either by road using the Tyne Bridge or by rail on Stephenson's High Level Bridge, is now breathtaking. Both banks of the river have been transformed, and although the Baltic Centre for Contemporary Art and the Sage Centre are on the south side in Gateshead, any description of Newcastle's quayside cannot omit them—they help fashion the overall riverscape. Foster + Partners brought together a star-studded cast to produce the undulating silver roofs of the Sage; the Centre is also a key contributor to the cultural fabric of Tyneside and the region. The radical redevelopment (1998–2002) of Mouchel's flour mill, built originally for Joseph Rank in 1950,

offers a further dramatic contribution to the skyline.

Having started life as a bridge, Pons Aelius, Newcastle never disappoints with its multifarious river crossings. The longest surviving of these is Robert Stephenson's High Level Bridge from as early as 1845–9. The combination of a road and rail bridge was a radical advance in design, prefiguring the huge rise in road transport in the twentieth century. It is almost the twin of Stephenson's Britannia tubular bridge over the Menai Strait built in 1850. Then, following this, came William Armstrong's Swing Bridge of 1868–76. It replaced Mylne's eighteenth-century bridge offering flexibility for river traffic. Armstrong's Elswick

↑ **NEWCASTLE** Civic Centre, David Wynne, "Swans"

↑ **NEWCASTLE** Castle, Black Gate

Redheugh road bridge, 1983, carries the Spine Road.

Less spectacularly, but still attractively, the quayside on the north bank has been transformed with new housing, restaurants, and office accommodation. Along the riverside, there are important older buildings. Trinity House has been home to the Newcastle Company of Mariners since 1505. The present buildings include a mediaeval house, a chapel, almshouses and a nineteenth-century gatehouse. The yard beyond the gatehouse is an attractive feature. The buildings include the 1721 Banqueting Hall and an entrance hall with an impressive flight of steps. The former Custom House is of 1766 and is now barristers' chambers. Broad Chare, nearby, was the only "chare" wide enough for a cart.

All Saints' Church is magnificent and replaced the mediaeval church; the present church was built between 1786 and 1796 by David Stephenson. The coming together of spire and west front is perfect; the unusual and splendid semi-oval interior has survived, with its superb mahogany furnishings. Sadly, the location is such that it can no longer be used as a parish church, but it is now used by an Old Catholic congregation. Further east, in City Road, the Keelmens' Hospital (1701–4) is interesting with its quadrangle and slightly eccentric square-domed tower sporting both a clock face and a sundial. The former early concrete CWS building by Mouchel (1900) is now the Malmaison Hotel. The Ouseburn Valley offers several interesting modern buildings alongside

Works was already established, and the hydraulics employed in the Swing Bridge were an early example of Armstrong's extraordinary creativity. The emblematic Tyne Bridge, designed by Mott, Hay and Anderson and built by Dorman Long of Middlesbrough (who, almost concurrently, had built the longer Sydney Harbour Bridge), did not arrive until 1928; it was the largest single-span bridge in Britain when it was opened.

The Queen Elizabeth II Metro Bridge was completed in 1980 and is one of the larger pieces of civil engineering associated with this rapid urban transport project— unique in its scope in the UK. The Millennium Bridge (sometimes called the Winking Eye) is novel as the "world's only tilting bridge" and, similar to the London Millennium Footbridge, is only for pedestrians and cyclists. The King Edward VII rail bridge is of 1906, and the innovatively converted warehouses and factories.

Further west at Sandhill and The Side, there are timber-framed houses overlooking the river. Bessie Surtees' House was so named after her eloping, in 1772, with John Scott, later Lord Eldon; the house is now administered by English Heritage with some rooms open to the public; Derwentwater Chambers is part of this grouping. Watergate Buildings are shops and offices by John Dobson (1850) and The Quayside pub is the only surviving former warehouse here. More timber framing at The Cooperage in The Close; some remains of the thirteenth-/fourteenth-century town walls a little further along. The Side, steep and sharply curved, takes you up towards the castle quarter and the historic centre. At the foot of Sandhill is the Guildhall, whose present appearance owes most to the rebuilding by Dobson (1825) with its attractive D-shaped end. Robert Trollope was responsible for the original building (1655), and much of this survives internally; this includes the fine plaster ceiling of the Mayor's Parlour, and the hammerbeam roof of the Town Court.

The Centre. On our way to the castle, we can pass through the Stephenson Quarter— Eduardo Paolozzi's bronze Vulcan heralds this as we encounter the former Stephenson Locomotive Works, with the interesting 1862 Stephenson Monument by J. G. Lough. Close by, on the corner of Orchard Street, is the Neville Hall (The Common Room). Within the building, the Wood Memorial Hall is itself a testimony to the engineering genius of the city—the lantern-style roof, and the main window which fills almost all its west wall, are just part of this. The "Lit and Phil", that is the Literary and Philosophical Society's building, pedimented and Greek Revival, dates from 1825, and the Moot Hall, also strongly Greek Revival, is just slightly earlier from 1812—it now serves as the Crown Court.

We are now ready to visit the castle and a succession of important buildings in this same quarter. The castle was constructed by William the Conqueror's eldest son, Robert, in 1080 and was built on the site of the Roman fort on a plateau overlooking the lowest bridging point. Henry II strengthened it and work was completed in John's reign. All that survives however, after the rampages of the nineteenth-century railway-building race, are the twelfth-century keep and the thirteenth-century Black Gate—the outer gateway. The keep was built 1168–78. It is approximately square and on its east side is a restored

↓ **NEWCASTLE** City Walls, round tower

↑ **NEWCASTLE** The Side

forebuilding—here is a fine ground floor chapel with a room above reached by an external staircase off which is a landing and stairs to the Great Hall. There is one principal room on each floor. Included are both a King's and a Queen's Chamber. Parallels with the design of the keep include the White Tower in London and Castle Hedingham in north Essex. The Black Gate was begun in 1247 and is roughly oval— the portcullis survives; two storeys were added to the Black Gate in the seventeenth century, and it became crowded in with housing which disappeared with the construction of St Nicholas Street.

Just along St Nicholas Street is the Anglican cathedral after which the street is named. Its "crown spire" with its lantern, designed to guide vessels along the Tyne, is one of the emblems of the city. Almost certainly, the design came from London's pre-Great Fire Church of St Mary-le-Bow. Later St Giles' High Kirk in Edinburgh would use a similar design. The Diocese of Newcastle dates from 1882 when the parish church became the cathedral. The origins of the church can be traced to 1194, and a cruciform building with tower was completed c.1370; James Gibbs added a vestry in 1736, and John Dobson, John

Green and Gilbert Scott added the north and south tower porches in the nineteenth century. The northeast hall and vestries were completed by W. H. Wood in 1926. The fifteenth-century tower dominates and is just short of 60 m high; the crown spire is probably c.1435, although the internal ribbed vaulting of the tower bears the arms of Robert Rhodes MP who died in 1474. There are fourteenth-century windows in the transepts, south aisle, and clerestory. There was some insensitive restoration by David Stephenson and William Newton in the late eighteenth century; the chancel screen, stall and reredos are

by R. J. Johnson in the 1880s. The octagonal piers from which spring chamfered arches bring a lightness giving a greater sense of length to the interior. In the north transept east aisle is an unrestored mediaeval window.

The font with its blue heraldic shields, sitting beneath the tower, has a very fine fifteenth-century wooden cover with gables, pinnacles, crockets, and foliage. In the 2020 refurbishment, the cover was raised and the base lowered; "the water of life" now flows continually through the font. The 2020 refurbishment also included the altar and ambo by Dan Rose of the RASKL partnership; both

pick up the dark blue from the font decoration and are fashioned using modern materials and finished with patinated pewter. Very good seventeenth-century organ case built for a Renatus Harris organ and modified in 1891 and 1932. Some very fine nineteenth- and twentieth-century glass by Clayton and Bell, William Wailes, C. E. Kempe, Basil Barber and P. C. Bacon—indeed the cathedral offers a feast of stained glass. Behind the reredos is an interesting sculpture in alabaster and porphyry focusing on Eucharistic images and created by Stephen Cox. Above it is the Thornton Brass, the largest surviving brass in Britain. The

precincts have been relandscaped and fashioned as a pilgrim prayer trail, including modern Beatitudes based on the well-known passage in St Matthew's Gospel.

Moving westward, on the corner of Grainger Street is St John's Church, originally from the twelfth century but now mainly of the fourteenth and fifteenth centuries. It is cruciform with a dominant west tower. The church is the result of a donation from the lawyer, Robert Rhodes. The high altar and organ case are the work of Sir Charles Nicholson (1909) and the fine wrought-iron chancel screen and communion rails are by Stephen

153

↑ **NEWCASTLE** Roman Catholic cathedral

Dykes Bower (1973). Memorial to Richard Grainger, business-man and architect, who with John Dobson conceived Grainger Town and Newcastle's very fine city centre.

Moving further west still with the station almost opposite is the Roman Catholic Cathedral of St Mary. One is greeted by a good, if slightly stumpy, statue by Nigel Boonham of Cardinal Basil Hume, a native of the city. The cathedral (1844) is by A. W. N. Pugin, although the dominant tower and spire are later work (1872) by A. M. Dunn and E. J. Hansom. The interior is noble with a good sense of mystery,

increased in the 1980s reordering which created a large central space. The Caen stone altars, pulpit and font were designed by Pugin and made by Hardman. Again, good stained glass as in the Anglican cathedral, including Joseph A. Nuttgens' modern windows (2006) in the Blessed Sacrament chapel; good, glazed screen to courtyard (2003) by Doonan.

Across Neville Street, Dobson's magnificent Central Station takes pride of place. The remarkable sweep of the platforms and train shed internally is complemented by the broad street elevation with the

reduced porte-cochère by Dobson and executed by the railway's archi-tect Thomas Prosser. The angle pavilions and the Roman Doric pilasters add to the majesty of the composition.

The train shed is in three parallel bays with wrought-iron roof ribs. It covers an area of three acres. The restrained appearance is in contrast to the exuberance of the Burmantoft tiling in the Old Refreshment Room (now The Centurion). The 1985 Travel Centre by Nick Darbyshire has its own style without interfering with the historic structure. The adja-cent Station Hotel is also by Dobson. Viaducts carry the line southwest to the High Level Bridge and northeast towards Berwick and Edinburgh.

We now move north towards the historic centre and Grainger Town. Unfolding in a gentle curve from the cathedral quarter is Grey Street (1837). This is the finest of Grainger's streets, with well-nigh perfect proportions and composi-tion, and reaches its climax with the monument to the reforming Earl at its head. John and Benjamin Green's Theatre Royal is a great feature, a masterpiece of classical design with its Corinthian colonnade and restrained pediment; after a fire in 1899, the interior was remodelled by the esteemed theatre designer, Frank Matcham. Grey's Monument (1838), now coined as a feature of collo-quial speech (Why are you stand-ing there like Grey's Monument?!), is by Benjamin Green. Rising to a height of 41 metres, Edward Hodges Baily's statue stands proud atop the column. (Baily also fashioned the statue of Horatio Nelson crowning

↑ **NEWCASTLE** Earl Grey on his monument

↑ **NEWCASTLE** William George Armstrong statue

↑ **NEWCASTLE** Cardinal Hume statue

the column in London's Trafalgar Square.)

We are now at Grainger Town, that part of central Newcastle transformed by Richard Grainger from the 1820s onwards starting with Blackett Street and Eldon Square; Grainger's grid plan acted as a net to link with mediaeval Newcastle's historic web of streets. Tragically, the construction of the 1970s Eldon Square shopping centre led to the demolition of the north and west sides of the square, and the south side of Blackett Street suffered equally. Blank brick walls with some later lame decoration were the replacement. Happily, elsewhere Grainger Town has fared well. Dobson, Grainger's most eminent architect, designed the splendid Grainger Market (1835), unique amongst English cities for its size and design, with its broad internal avenues and wooden pilastered shops. The Marks & Spencer "Penny Bazaar" dates back to 1896. The long sides on the exterior of the market extend to forty-six bays.

The market faces the Central Exchange Buildings (1838) at its north end. At the corners are ribbed domes surmounting facias with large Corinthian columns. In 1906, the central space was transformed into the Central Arcade with its stunning Renaissance tiling by Burmantofts of Leeds and a floor of Rust's vitreous mosaics—the shops in their variety mirror this glory. Clayton Street completed Grainger's plan in the early 1840s. Throughout there are different and attractive facades often including pavilions, with the Cordwainers' Hall, the Café Royal, Victoria Buildings and then a series of good commercial buildings for banks, insurance companies and other institutions.

Moving further west takes us to some of the most interesting mediaeval parts of the city. Just a little way past the junction of Clayton Street and Westgate Road, the southern extent of a long surviving piece of the town walls is revealed—these stretch all the way to Gallowgate and St Andrew's Church. Three towers remain partially extant. The Heber Tower is almost complete, then follows the Morden Tower with its quirky brick upper storey and finally the Ever Tower—complete as far as the beginning of the arrow slits. The walls date from 1265, when Henry III granted the city permission to charge a murage tax. A lane ran inside the walls and a ditch outside, which has been recently excavated.

↓ **NEWCASTLE** Grainger Town

↓ **NEWCASTLE** The old town

↑ **NEWCASTLE** Central Arcade, corner

↑ **NEWCASTLE** Central Arcade, interior

In 1540, Leland could still say that the walls surpass those of any other city in "strength and magnificence". There is further evidence of the walls near to the Copthorne Hotel not far from the riverside.

At the north tip of the walls stands St Andrew's Church, the oldest of the city churches and possibly the site of a Saxon church, although the oldest surviving parts are of the twelfth century, including the lower courses of the tower and the chancel arch. The chancel, north transept and fine simple Romanesque-style nave arcades are c.1300. It is a noble but not extravagant interior. During the Civil War, the church tower became a gun platform. The churchyard is the final resting place of some notable citizens. St Andrew's Building in Gallowgate was the home of the offices of W. H. Scott and W. M. Turner, who manufactured "Andrews Liver Salts", the best-selling antacid in the world in the early twentieth century.

In Newgate Street to the south is the splendid Art Deco Newcastle Cooperative store (1932) by L. G. Ekins. Ekins was influenced by Dutch and German architecture which he had travelled to study just before designing this building. Then in St Andrew's Street, heralding Chinatown, is the exciting and colourful *Chinese Arch* (2005) by Yonglai Zhang.

Just to the west, on the corner of Friars Street and Stowell Street are the remarkable remains of the Dominican friary (c.1250). The survival of the buildings was assured through them being sold to the mayor and burgesses, who converted much of them into almshouses for the cordwainers, tanners and butchers, with the smiths making their Hall here. The mediaeval kitchen became the cordwainers' almshouse. An arch opens onto the cloister, around which are grouped the refectory and the almshouses. The site of the *lavatorium* is clear and the plan of the aisled church has been revealed. The chapter house and warming room are labelled on the site. The restoration of the friary began in the 1970s.

There are fascinating buildings all around, including old warehouses close by. The former Gaumont Cinema (1912) survives, and opposite, also in Fenkle Street, are the Assembly Rooms (1774) by Newton. Charlotte Square is notable for its similarity to London squares. Further south and just west of Central Station is the eccentrically named Times Square; here is Terry Farrell's International Centre for Life with its lofty-arched and glazed front.

Finally, we move to the north limits of the centre with buildings clustering at the nexus of the central motorway, Northumberland Street and Percy Street. Towards the east side of this quadrant is the impressive frontage of the Laing Art Gallery (1904) by Cackett & Burns Dick—this was a gift to the city from Alexander Laing, a wealthy wine merchant. It now includes Thomas Heatherwick's glass and resin *Blue Carpet* (2001); Heatherwick also designed the timber spiral stair. There are other notable buildings in the area including John Dobson's former Lying-in Hospital and the mediaeval Plummer Tower with its mid-eighteenth-century front. The 1963 Newcastle Development Plan envisaged a brave new world here, but little was built. The MEA building by Ryder and Yates (who were much involved in Killingworth New Town) is an exception: the floors are hung from above, allowing traffic to travel beneath. It was the first British building specifically designed to house a multitude of voluntary services. Another interesting building of Cackett, Burns Dick and Mackellar is the Unitarian Church of the Divine Unity (1940). Dame Allan's Schools were formerly here. Today, the University of Northumbria's City Campus East (2007) is quite a statement with its glass, steel cladding and mesh solar panels.

The outstanding building here is the Civic Centre (1968) by the City Architect George Kenyon, opened by King Olav V of Norway in 1968. It is one of the most confident and enduring of 1960s civic buildings. You approach the building along a Processional Way. Its plan is semi-monastic grouped around a cloister-like square of grass or garth, with lakes, and with offices on three sides. The council chamber is a prominent mushroom-shaped drum. A strong lofty tower and belfry crown the entrance. The council chamber doubles up as a porte-cochère. There are some excellent art works, including David Wynne's *River God Tyne* fountain and his *Swans in Flight*, Geoffrey Clarke's cast aluminium portals, and John Hutton's glass screens engraved with local history. The Banqueting Hall is impressive with its inscriptions by David Dewey.

Note also the South African war memorial of *Victory*, on an octagonal column in the centre of the Haymarket, and the Northumberland Fusiliers memorial, by Sir W. Goscombe John (1923), by St Thomas' Church. Nearby is the Great North Museum, including key antiquities from Hadrian's Wall and elsewhere. It was earlier known as the Hancock Museum.

Finally, in this quadrant, is John Dobson's Tudor-style St Thomas' Church (1830). Set well within tree-lined parkland, it is not a parish church and has often felt like a church in search of a role. It has been used as the base for university chaplaincy and for industrial chaplaincy. Most recently it has become a "resource church" for the diocese and has been the focus of some radical reordering. Gothic in style, the west tower is Early English in feel. Very good organ case of 1837. The original concept felt almost like a preaching box with a small chancel. In the reordering, the galleries have been glazed to allow them to be used for other purposes without losing the internal massing of the building. A cruciform sunken font greets you as you enter from the west door; panelling has been pushed back to reveal a large worshipping space.

Nearby Haymarket Station was arguably far more satisfactory in its first incarnation as a small, neat drum; it has now rather overgrown itself with its monster dome. Just to the west of Haymarket lies the university area. Newcastle University's origins lie in the institutions which merged in 1937 to form King's College, Durham; in 1963, this became the University of Newcastle-upon-Tyne. It has grown enormously and there is space to note just some of the campus buildings. King's Walk includes the neo-Jacobean Students' Union (1925) in red brick and Portland stone—the 1964 extension is by William Whitfield. The Arches, with the fine Tudor-style gate tower, leads to the Quadrangle—more red brick and stone. Beyond lie a number of buildings of various dates in the first part of the twentieth century. The southwest side of the Quadrangle is the buttressed Armstrong Building of 1888 with the Jubilee Tower of 1894. The King's Hall has a hammerbeam roof and minstrels' gallery. William Whitfield also designed the former University Theatre and Gulbenkian Studio, now reworked as Northern Stage. Facing the Great North Road is the Robinson Library (1982) by Faulkner-Brown Hendy Watkinson and Stonor. Dobson's Carlton Terrace (1838) is nearby. In this same area is the Royal Victoria Infirmary (1906) by Newcombe and Percy Adams, with a chapel formed of a Greek cross surmounted by a large dome. Also here is the attractive, gently curved Leazes Crescent (1829) by Thomas Oliver and then the grand Leazes Terrace by the same architect. In powerful contrast in this same part of the city rises St James' Park football stadium, the earliest section of which dates from 1973, the stadium being completed in 2000; it is a mighty statement at the heart of town with its mast-hung tiers. Newcastle College is not far away and perhaps one of the most dramatic buildings is its Lifestyle Academy; its bold blocks are clad with dark and light metal panels.

Outer North. Perhaps most remarkable of all is the Town Moor, comprising a vast area of common land extending over 1,000 acres and larger even than New York's Central Park. As pasture, it dates back to the twelfth century, and freemen of the city still have the right to graze cattle here. It had its own racecourse and later, an aerodrome. In its southeast corner are the remains of the 1887 Royal Jubilee Exhibition of which the only notable survivors are the fine bandstand and next-door lake. Then the 1929 North East Coast Exhibition spawned the former Palace of Arts which later became the Military Vehicle Museum.

To the north of the moor is Gosforth. St Nicholas' Church (1799) is by John Dodds, built on the site of a mediaeval building reaching back to 1153. The church has much fine glass by Kempe, Wailes and others. Elizabeth Barrett Browning's parents were married here. All Saints' is an imposing neo-Gothic church of 1887 with a tower of 1896; the architect was R. J. Johnson. Gosforth Park now houses the racecourse, but it was set out as the park of Gosforth House (1764) by James Paine; Brandling House is its present name, remembering Charles Brandling for whom it was built. The Regent Centre at the crossroads offers less than the name suggests—an office complex with a swimming pool and Metro station. Wideopen is a former colliery village in North Gosforth. The nineteenth-century Sacred Heart Roman Catholic Church, with its good Perpendicular tower, has a fine collection of Pre-Raphaelite windows by Edward Burne-Jones, Ford Madox Brown and William Morris. It was originally built as an Anglican church by the then owner of Gosforth Park for residents of the area and became a Roman Catholic church at the turn of the twentieth century. The Anglican Church of St Columba was built in 1982 and is a flexible building with some good contemporary stained glass.

Jesmond, just to the east, became a fashionable suburb in the mid-nineteenth century. William (later, Lord) Armstrong built his own mansion here. The house has gone, but his greater legacy is the transformed valley (as in his house **CRAGSIDE**) which is now the romantic park of Jesmond Dene; as ever there is a symbol of his engineering prowess in the Armstrong Road Bridge, forged in his Elswick Works, now just used by pedestrians; its bearings made it safe even in the event of mining subsidence. Jesmond is notable for three churches and a former synagogue. The ruined St Mary's Chapel is twelfth century, comprising chancel, sacristy, and a fragment of the nave—all in coarse sandstone. Jesmond Parish Church (1857) is by John Dobson and often styled the Clayton Memorial Church after Richard Clayton, a leading Evangelical of the time. Early English with a handsome pinnacle tower, it is effectively a preaching box of six bays, with galleries which were remodelled in 1907.

Good stained glass by Atkinson, Capronnier and Lawrence Lee.

St George's Church in North Jesmond is more than a statement; its tall campanile is a landmark in the area. The church by T. R. Spence (1890) is Arts and Crafts, the gift of Charles Mitchell, Armstrong's business partner, with no expense spared. The interior too is dramatic with plenty of height and light. Almost certainly, Ravenna was the inspiration for the mosaic procession of saints and the wider scheme of dazzling painting throughout. There is superb stained glass by Alfred Shirley and John W. Brown. The richly carved altar and reredos are of Pavonazza marble; this is a building not to be missed—within and without.

The former Jesmond Synagogue (1915) in Eskdale Terrace is powerfully decorated in red brick with stone bands—the triple-arched porch is particularly attractive. The Royal Grammar School is also nearby. Its original buildings are by Edwin Cooper in low brick and stone, and neo-Early Georgian in flavour.

Outer East. Further east takes us to Byker with the celebrated Byker Wall by Ralph Erskine, who had been involved in designing some of the housing in Killingworth. It is the protective perimeter block which is styled as the Byker Wall (1970–81) and which encloses otherwise low-level housing. The bowl in which the estate is set was used to full effect by Erskine. Motor vehicle access is deliberately restricted. Erskine developed the plan working in the Swedish Arctic. The colour and the

jaunty use of balconies adds to the scheme's individuality and success.

Heaton Park, just to the north, was another gift of parkland to the city by William Armstrong, this time using the valley of the Ouseburn. The Wills Factory, now apartments, continued the Art Deco factory style although built as late as 1946.

Further east is Walker, taking its name from Hadrian's Wall. This includes a small development of modern cottages in Walkerville. From here eastwards, we are well into the former shipbuilding and port areas of Wallsend with the fort at Segedunum marking the eastern extremity of Hadrian's Wall. To the southeast is the Willington Viaduct over the Wallsend Burn with its seven wrought-iron arches set on stone piers.

Outer West. " . . . Gannin' along the Scotswood Road to see the Blaydon Races . . . " sets the scene for the journey westwards out of the city. Here was another industrial powerhouse with Armstrong's Elswick Works which, gradually rebuilt and expanded, became the vast Scotswood tank factory. Almost all of this has gone and much has been replaced by housing. Other things had vanished earlier—three islands in the Tyne disappeared with industrialization. St Stephen's Church (1868) with its spire looks out over this—St Stephen's had been paid for by the Cruddas family; W. D. Cruddas had been one of Armstrong's founding partners. Alongside this too there had been a leather works, gasworks, and lead works. Adamsez also had a drift mine here for clay which they used in the manufacture of their sanitary ware. There had been a chain bridge in Scotswood, built in 1831 and demolished in 1967 making way for the present road bridge. The present wrought-iron rail bridge is from 1871.

Just to the north, in Benwell, are infinitely older historic remains in the form of the Roman wall fort of Condercum. Much of the fort and civil settlement (*vicus*) has been built over, but the Temple of Antenocitus (probably a local Celtic deity) survives—in Broomridge Avenue! Apsidal in structure, with an east side-door. There are replicas of two second-century altars flanking the apse; the originals and fragments of the cult statue are now in the Great North Museum. The Vallum Crossing at the foot of Denhill Park is a unique example of a masonry-revetted original causeway over the Vallum—the west pier of the gate survives. One can thus track the wall between the first three forts of Segedunum, Pons Aelius and Condercum. General Wade's eighteenth-century Military Road is the foundation of West Road. At nearby Denton on the West Road is Hadrian's Wall Turret 7b; this is unique as the only visible example of the original plan incorporating turret and curtain wall. Denton Hall is seventeenth century—marked as 1622 on the porch; for a time, the home of the Roman Catholic Bishop of Hexham and Newcastle.

Benwell Towers, originally a tower house and then a country house, was the site of the Shafto family's country seat. Built by John Dobson (1831), it then stood well outside the city; the Pease family gave it to the newly established Diocese of Newcastle as the bishop's residence. Ironically it is now an Islamic school.

↑ Gateshead & **NEWCASTLE** Tyne bridges

NEWTON ON THE MOOR

On the edge of Alnwick Moor, surprisingly this was one of the first dual carriageway bypasses on the Great North Road in Northumberland, completed as long ago as 1950. On the old main road is the Cook & Barker pub, named not after two professions, but after the coming together of the two eponymous local families in marriage. The centre of the village is to the west of the main road. The Hall (1772), half a mile to the southwest, was remodelled in 1864—Pevsner describes the house as rambling but picturesque. The garden summer house has eighteenth-century panelling originally from **SHILBOTTLE** Church—there is a walled garden 800 m to the southwest.

The Waterloo Stones, 400 m northeast, are three headstone slabs commemorating the battle of that name—two French soldiers are also remembered—they were drowned off the Northumberland coast. Other interesting buildings include the early-eighteenth-century Old Manor House, Newton Low Hall from later in that century, and John Dobson's Villa Farm c.1820. The attractive Jubilee Hall and Reading Room are in the main street.

NORHAM

Later in his life, Joseph Mallord William Turner, the great English landscape artist, revisited Norham before painting a now celebrated oil of the castle—he doffed his hat and bowed low to the gaunt ruin. When asked by his travelling companion why, Turner replied: "I made a drawing of Norham Castle several years since. And from that day to this I have had as much to do as my hands could execute." That early watercolour and the later oil painting frame the artist's career.

The gaunt profile of the castle is very powerful even as a ruinous

↓ **NORHAM** Castle

shell. Its situation is classic, with the sheer bank of the Tweed to the north and west and a sharp ravine to the east. Built originally as a motte and bailey in 1121 by Bishop Ranulph Flambard, it established Norham as part of the County Palatinate of Durham under the rule of the Prince Bishops. Until the late nineteenth century, this fragment of territory was still marked as "Part of the County Palatinate of Durham— Detached". In 1157, Henry II recaptured Northumberland, and it appears that the then bishop built the massive keep and consolidated the outer ward. The various parts of the castle are well signed, including the Great Hall, the Great Chamber, and the kitchen. The gatehouse is partly Norman. Much of the outer wall survives with three turrets, one of which is covered by a Gothick cottage. The castle was besieged and badly battered by the Scots before the Battle of Flodden.

St Cuthbert's Church is suitably large and surrounded by a vast churchyard, with a majestic feel. Much of the present building is the work of Ignatius Bonomi and Gray in the mid-nineteenth century. The Romanesque feel has been retained as have five original windows in the chancel. The south arcade and chancel are original and date from 1170. The nave is of five bays. The seventeenth-century pulpit and stall are from Durham Cathedral, brought here in 1840 by Archdeacon Thorp. There are other good windows by Clayton & Bell and Wailes. Some very good monuments. St Cuthbert's body is said to have rested here on its way to Durham for burial. There was a twelfth-century religious house to the west, probably a lazar house, which survived for less than a century.

The village is large, and the layout suggests something of a small town with a square at the centre focused on a nineteenth-century cross on a mediaeval base.

The strong stone bridge from Norham to Ladykirk was built by Thomas Codrington and Cuthbert Brereton for the Tweed Bridges Trust in 1885, replacing a two-arched timber lattice bridge of 1838 by John Blackmore.

Norham Station is perhaps the best preserved of all the former stations on the Berwick–St Boswells line, partly on account of it having been a railway museum for several years. Another tall slimline viaduct with rock-faced piers over Newbiggin Dene, a mile south, and identical to the Royal Border Bridge but on a smaller scale, so probably, then, by Robert Stephenson.

NORTH CHARLTON

Six miles north of Alnwick, the site of a deserted village can be seen to the east of the Great North Road. Narrow byway to the northwest crosses the remote Quarry House Moor past the substantial Wandylaw Wind Farm and the remains of Blawearie farmhouse to the west— this has mediaeval origins.

NORTH SHIELDS

North Shields (Shield from the term for fishermen's huts known as "shiels") is undoubtedly one of Northumberland's hidden gems, both in its old and new towns. It has a long history having been first mentioned in 1225, when Germanus, the prior of Tynemouth Priory, created a fishing port for the priory where the Pow Burn enters the Tyne. The burghers of Newcastle tried to starve out this upstart port close to the mouth of the river but, despite their efforts, it survived. Originally it was crowded along the river, but in the eighteenth-century a new town developed on land owned by the Earl of Carlisle. John Wright produced plans including a grand processional way (now forming Howard Street) and laying out the splendid Georgian Northumberland Square. The southwest corner of the square was left undeveloped until the 1960s when insensitively the Brutalist concrete library was inserted, defacing the otherwise perfect composition of the square. The north side is the jewel in the crown.

Howard Street is impressive with John Dobson's 1845 Town Hall—originally it also housed the Town Improvement Commission Office, Mechanics Institute, Savings Bank, Museum and Police Station. Along the street are the former Subscription Library (1806), the Salvation Army Chapel by John Dobson and an Italianate-style bank of 1882. At the Exchange Theatre and Café Bar is a stained-glass window honouring Tommy Brown who went to sea at the age of fifteen and played a key role in snatching German code documents (subsequently sent to Bletchley Park) from a sinking U-boat in 1942.

The former Albion Assembly Rooms (1853) lie in Norfolk Street

to the east. Further to the east is Dockwray Square, twice rebuilt and now less impressive. There is a statue of Stan Laurel (as in Laurel and Hardy) who spent much of his childhood here. Nearby too is the New High Light, one of four lights built to aid navigators in avoiding the "black middens", notorious rocks which could be negotiated by lining up the "Lights"—the two early lights were originally from 1539. The New Lights are 1808 by John Stokoe; the Old High Light of 1727 is further along Tyne Street. In Brewery Street is the late-eighteenth-century Low Lights Tavern with its Tuscan doorcase and in Union Road are the sandstone Old Maltings.

Close by is the Union or Fish Quay, famous for its morning fish market. Clifford's Fort, also in Union Road, is a harbour defence of 1672 by the Swedish engineer Martin Beckman. It has been much developed and altered over succeeding centuries, unhelpfully obscuring the Lights, to the irritation of Newcastle's Trinity House. It later became the headquarters of the Tyne Division Royal Engineers (Volunteers) Submarine Squadron. The former Albert Edward Dock was redeveloped to become the Royal Quays—good lock gates and walls and a hydraulic accumulator tower.

Christ Church in its original foundation dates from 1654–68, replacing the decayed church at Tynemouth Priory. The tower was added in 1788 and the organ chamber in 1869. Splendid sundial above the south door. Inside, the aisles have Tuscan columns with Soane-like shallow arches. Interesting monuments and a rather dashing parish hall by Rock Townsend added in 1984. Several other churches including the impressive Memorial Church in Albion Road (1889–91) again with a big tower and a still taller octagonal stair tower.

NORTH TOGSTON

Both a Hall and a House. The Hall began as a bastle, perhaps from 1546 as per a reset datestone. Remodelled in 1685; in the late eighteenth century a five-bay pedimented ashlar front was added; good farm buildings. The seventeenth-century House has a dovecote on the hill to the northeast. Broomhill alias Red Row is pit village-style housing to the south.

NORTHUMBERLANDIA

Just over a mile west of **CRAMLINGTON**, and opened in 2012, this remarkable new country park is centred on what is claimed to be the largest land sculpture in female form in the world. With its woodland, lakes, and amazing vistas, it overlooks the huge adjacent open-cast workings (operational at the time of writing but eventually also to be landscaped). Its origins are in the next-door Shotton Surface Mine—the excavation here was what offered the opportunity for establishing a new and unusual visitor attraction. It is designed by the celebrated American landscape architect, Charles Jencks, on part of the Blagdon Estate, through the generosity and initiative of Viscount Ridley, also an environmental scientist and economist.

OGLE

Ogle Castle is in fact a sixteenth-century house, although previously there was a quadrangular fourteenth-century castle here, licensed in 1341; a round tower at the east end disappeared as late as the eighteenth century. The present house had an L-shaped plan. The house has an attractive south front.

To the north of the present main street are the clearly identifiable turf-covered remains of the former village, running along the south of the former village green. There were sixteen houses around this green in 1632 and the castle guarded the east end.

OLD BEWICK

Tiny hamlet—once a post office served as general store for all. A trackway goes onward and upward to the east into an incline surmounted by hill forts and with cup and ring-marked rocks. Further on at Blawearie and close to the

abandoned farmhouse is a significant Bronze Age burial cairn and another hill fort nearby.

Holy Trinity Church, half a mile north of the village, is something of a treasure. Ruinous, and rescued (1867) by the then rector, R. Williams, it is simply a nave with an apse and semi-dome. It is Norman but almost certainly with some Saxon material surviving. The church once belonged (c.1110–) to Tynemouth Priory. It is set very prettily amongst the trees.

ONCE BREWED

There's much brewing around this scattered hamlet, for not only is the settlement called Once Brewed, the hotel, pub and brewery is called *Twice Brewed*!

There is plenty of interest nearby with **VINDOLANDA** (*qv*), the Roman site just 2 miles to the southeast, but also The Sill, the National Landscape Discovery Centre next door to the pub; its aim is to encourage exploration of the history, culture, and heritage of Northumberland. There is an exhibition, a visitor centre, shop and café. There is also a Youth Hostel.

The hamlet lies on General Wade's Military Road, which was built between 1751 and 1758 for the swift movement of troops, following the 1745 rebellion. The Vallum of Hadrian's Wall also comes past Once Brewed. Different legends surround the name of the inn. The most romantic is that related to the 1464 Battle of Hexham, when a Yorkist

soldier demanded that the ale be brewed again as it was too weak to energize the troops. A second, less exciting explanation says that farmers in the eighteenth century brewed poor ale and that this inn boasted a stronger draft. A more academic attempt points to the existence of two brows of hills over which Hadrian's Wall climbs toward the meeting of two ancient drovers' roads. Writing in 1801, antiquarian William Hutton extolled the inn's food: The pudding was cooked "as big as a *peck* of measure" and "a piece of beef . . . perhaps equal to half a calf!" There is still a brewery and taphouse here and the boast is that beer has been brewed here since at least the mid-fifteenth century but possibly even back as far as Roman times.

OTTERBURN

A rather dispersed settlement and much of it twentieth-century development. Nonetheless, several points of interest in this isolated part. First comes the Battle of Otterburn (1388) where the English were firmly defeated, despite the fact that Lord James Douglas was slain. The battle is the subject of the *Ballad of Chevy Chase*, which begins:

It fell about the Lammas tide
When muir men win their hay
The doughty Earl of Douglas rode
Into England to catch a prey.

One of the Widdrington family fought on, even after having both legs severed. The battle is commemorated by the Percy Cross, 800 m to the northwest—the present cross dates from 1777.

Eighteenth-century Otterburn Mill lies 400 m south. Although weaving no longer happens here, there is much evidence of the former working mill with preserved equipment. Many babies have been kept warm with the unique Otterburn shawl, which is still available at the mill. Also, behind the end of the building are the "tenterhooks" on which the newly washed woollen fabric was stretched.

Otterburn Hall (1870) is an Elizabethan-style mansion built for Lord James Douglas in recompense for the loss of his ancestor in the famous battle. It is now a hotel. St John the Evangelist Church (1858) is by John Dobson in Decorated style with a tiny spirelet—interesting altar frontal in the form of a wood relief of the Last Supper.

Otterburn Tower (1830) is a pleasant castellated mansion but with no evidence of the earlier tower house which once stood nearby.

OTTERBURN RANGES

These are the largest firing ranges in Britain. They include both Otterburn (and the former Redesdale) Camps along with an airstrip and other facilities for military training; the ranges run all the way to the site of the Roman camp at Chew Green (cf. **ALWINTON**). They were established in 1911 and cover 93 square miles of land, most of which is still farmed. Both tanks and rocket systems are used in exercises here. The ranges are frequently open, but care must be taken to check first online, to follow the designated tracks and to watch for the warning flags—there is much debris scattered, some of which may be high explosive.

OVINGHAM

The Saxon name refers to Offa, the first chief of the enclosure, but not Offa of the Dyke. Connected since 1883 with Prudhoe, south of the river, with a metal bridge by Dorman Long of Middlesbrough, Ovingham is the burial place of Thomas Bewick the renowned engraver and of other members of his family—his headstone is now mounted in the church porch (*qv* **CHERRYBURN**). There was a dyehouse here and weaving was a local craft. St Mary's Church has a late-Saxon tower with Saxon windows surviving. The interior is unusual but lofty and noble. The nave is very short as it opens both south and north into broad transepts. The arcading is extensive and fine; the chancel is unaisled. There is a range of Victorian glass with work by Kempe, and Clayton and Bell. There are fragments of two Saxon crosses discovered in 1945 and 1946.

The east end of the Old Vicarage is late fourteenth century, and it was built to house three Augustinian canons from Hexham. Much of the rest is seventeenth- then nineteenth-century work—good seventeenth-century fireplaces. The unusual bulgy rusticated gate piers are c.1700 with garden terraces of the same period.

PONTELAND

Ponteland began as a settlement on the marshy land near to the present St Mary's Church—the name means "Island in the Pont", referring to the River Pont, a tributary of the River Blyth. St Mary's Church, with its strong Norman west tower and tympanum, is twelfth century in its origins, although much of what survives is from the thirteenth, when the noble chancel and north transept were built. The large south transept is largely Norman. There are rare fragments of fourteenth-century glass in the south chancel windows. Various monuments to the Ogle family of Kirkley Hall including an urn in front of an obelisk to Nathaniel (1789). Also in the chancel is a slab telling the tragic history of Anne Byrne's family; Anne died in 1769.

Ponteland narrowly escaped pillaging in 1244 and was saved by the Treaty of Newcastle between

English and Scottish forces—the treaty was signed in the village. Later, in the fourteenth century, part of the castle was destroyed in a prelude to the Battle of Otterburn of 1388. The "castle" was later rebuilt as a hostelry, having been altered and extended by Mark Errington in 1597, and as The Blackbird Inn it still survives; part of the ground floor is tunnel-vaulted. There are the ruins of a fourteenth-century pele tower in the garden of the Vicarage. The tower was rebuilt in the seventeenth century, and much of it demolished in the nineteenth century; it was restored to its present condition in 1971.

Darras Hall, acquired by the Northern Allotment Society in 1907, was the site of a Second World War prisoner-of-war camp and now hosts an expensive modern housing development protected by its own amenity committee. Ponteland is now somewhat overshadowed both by this estate and by the close proximity of Newcastle Airport.

Three miles west-southwest is Dissington Hall—1794 by William Newton for Edward Collingwood; seven bays and much classical detail within, plus an imperial staircase. Other notable sites in the vicinity including the walled garden of Dissington Old Hall, the only remains of the old manor house.

POWBURN

On the Wooler–Morpeth road and effectively on the Devil's Causeway, the Roman road to Tweedmouth, with two bridges over the Breamish and a tributary burn. Crawley Tower, now a maintained ruin, is an early-fourteenth-century pele tower surrounded by a small farmstead. Another good station on the former Alnwick–Coldstream branch—strictly speaking this is at Hedgeley—the two villages are contiguous.

One mile east lies Hedgeley Hall, which began as a small building in the late seventeenth or early eighteenth century including the large Gothick bow window after the style of Adam. Enlarged to the north in the nineteenth century, it was further remodelled 1910–14 in Tudor style by George Reavell for Colonel Henry Carr-Ellison. Some internal detail came from other houses, including Dunston Hill in Gateshead and Hebburn Hall in County Durham. The gatehouse is early twentieth century along with other outbuildings. A mile northwest is the farm to the Hall, at Low Hedgeley, with an interesting set of buildings, some from the late eighteenth century. Beanley Hall, a mile further east, is also within the Hedgeley estate.

PRUDHOE

Set on a hill beneath the town and on the south bank of the Tyne is Prudhoe Castle. It is first mentioned on account of the siege by William the Lion in 1173, although it was originally built sometime in the eleventh century. After the Norman Conquest, it was rebuilt for the Umfravilles, but it passed by marriage to the Percys in the fourteenth century. It is set on a strong natural site, with the keep free-standing within an inner bailey. A late-Georgian house, built in Gothick, a style much favoured by the Percys, stands between the inner and outer baileys. The curtain wall of the outer bailey still stands proud. The gatehouse is splendid, retaining its Norman character and with an interesting chapel on the first floor. An equally impressive barbican was built in the thirteenth century and lengthened in 1326; the entry to the castle is dramatic. The Percys handed the castle over to the Crown in 1966, and it is now owned and administered by English Heritage. There is a mediaeval bridge over the dene to the east of the castle.

Prudhoe Hall was built for the wealthy industrialist Matthew Liddell in 1870. It was sold by the family in 1913, just before the First World War, and has been used as a hospital since then. Liddell, who was a devout Roman Catholic, had a chapel built. Between 1904 and 1905, the chapel was dismantled stone by stone and rebuilt in Prudhoe village. It is a noble building designed by Dunn, Hansom and Dunn of Newcastle. The nave and porch have unusual window tracery. There is a fine panelled and painted ceiling in the apsidal chancel. A sensitive restoration was completed in 2005, including a ministerial chair (loosely using the Frith Stool at Hexham Abbey as its model) and ambo fashioned of Chinese marble. Outside some interesting gargoyles.

RENNINGTON

All Saints' Church (1831) is Early English style with later Gothick additions. The plain octagonal fourteenth-century font came from Embleton church. Little Mill limekilns three-quarters of a mile east form arguably the largest kiln bank in the county.

RIDING MILL

Pleasantly set above the Tyne, Riding Mill has become something of a dormitory for Newcastle, although it has not lost its character; another good station on the Newcastle–Carlisle line. The much rebuilt "Riding Mill" is still very recognizable as one crosses the burn; its origins date back at least to the fourteenth century. Corn-milling continued until c.1900 after which saw-milling took over until the mill was converted into a house in 1972. Almost opposite stands the Wellington Inn with its doorcase dated 1660. The tiny "Roman Bridge" carries the line of Dere Street over the burn—segmental seventeenth-century arch perhaps concealing mediaeval masonry. St James' Church (1858), a neat but imposing building by Matthew Thompson.

Some 6 miles south of Riding Mill is Minsteracres. Formerly residence of the Silverton family, it has been a Passionist monastery and is now a retreat centre. The original house is of 1758 and Dobson made additions in 1816. The chapel of St Elizabeth of Hungary was built for the family in 1854 by Joseph Hansom in free Decorated style.

ROCHESTER

Often pronounced "Row-chester", as in Rotten Row, to distinguish it from the Kentish cathedral city. High Rochester is the site of the important Roman fort of Bremenium,

guarding the ancient Roman "Great North Road", Dere Street. It was one of a series of forts and camps between here and Chew Green. The site was occupied on and off from c.90 to c.312. Although the ditches survive, much of the outer wall has gone, but the west gate remains impressive; there is a large cemetery to the south-southeast with perhaps ninety barrows identifiable.

There are bastles hereabouts, a Neolithic long cairn 2 miles north-northeast at Bellshiel Law and an Iron Age settlement at Woolaw 1,200 m west. Wayside cross bases are found near Golden Pots. In the village, there is a Scottish Presbyterian church of 1826.

Horsley, 1 mile southeast, hosts a further Roman fort at Blakehope with clear ramparts. Holy Trinity Church is by J. and B. Green (1844); in 1997, a west gallery was added with a new organ; there is a Roman altar in the porch. Bastles abound (the Redesdale Arms includes fragments of one) and notably at Old Evistones, a deserted hamlet 1 mile west.

ROCK

St Philip and St James' Church is mid-twelfth century restored in 1855 by Salvin. The Romanesque work is fine with many good details including a "corbel table", fine stonework throughout nave and chancel, and an excellent Norman chancel arch. There is a marble plaque (1850) to Charles Bosanquet, the local landowner.

The Hall, for some years a Youth Hostel, is interesting and of several periods, the earliest work probably

being of the thirteenth century. In 1549, the house was the headquarters of a band of Spanish mercenaries under Sir Julian Romero, hired to fight the Scots. The Salkeld family remodelled the house again in the seventeenth century. John Dobson was engaged in 1820 to add two curious octagon bays to the south front. A further octagon was planned for the northeast corner, but only the ground floor was completed. To the north of the Hall is a chapel, first recorded there in 1359.

ROTHBURY

Rothbury's character owes most to its geographical location. Set between the sandstone scarp of the Simonside Hills on the south, wooded hillsides on the north, the foothills of the Cheviots to the west and Alnwick Moor on the east, its position on the Coquet makes it the perfect nodal centre. Popularity as a resort in the nineteenth century added to all this. Although there are but a few outstanding buildings, the treelined main street is picturesque from all directions. The bridge is mediaeval except for the twentieth century strengthening. Addycombe Cottages built by Norman Shaw for Lord Armstrong for retired staff are interesting—almost like a mini-garden suburb—after the manner of Shaw's Bedford Park in London. Back to the main street from Brewery Lane and turning left, one encounters what was Rothbury Motors—happily the basic frontage is unchanged since 1913, even though it is now host to an intriguing emporium. Beyond are the pleasant but pastiche Tudor-style Armstrong

↑ **ROTHBURY** Cragside

Cottages. At the centre of the village is Rothbury Cross (1902) by C. C. Hodges—all Arts and Crafts, with rabbits, stags, and squirrels. There are some grand houses on the south side of the High Street.

All Saints' Church was regrettably entirely rebuilt in 1850—the most severe loss was a pre-Conquest tower. There is some surviving mediaeval material but nothing before the thirteenth century. The massing of the building from the outside is good, and the church still has something of the feeling of the centrepiece of the town. The bowl of the font is of 1664, but the base is a marvellous Anglo-Saxon cross base—it may date back to the ninth century. There are two mediaeval cross slabs and a twelfth-century fragment in the north wall.

Of course, the other remarkable magnet at Rothbury is Norman Shaw's extraordinary mansion at Cragside, 1 mile to the east, and built for Lord Armstrong, the pioneering engineering entrepreneur from Tyneside. To understand both Armstrong and Shaw's achievement it is instructive to look at the images of the Debdon Burn Valley before Armstrong arrived. The desolation and bare rock faces are an amazing contrast to the richness that one now encounters. It is very different from the elegant London houses and indeed the neo-Baronial, found in New Scotland Yard and in his White Star Building near Pier Head in Liverpool, and for which Shaw is also famous. Pevsner describes the setting as Wagnerian! There is something of a contrast between the comfortable homeliness of the entrance hall and the rooms off the main corridor, and the dining room, library, and gallery with Lethaby's remarkable and extraordinary marble fireplace. There is so much to take in—from the lift and

↑ **ROTHBURY** Cragside, drawing room

its hydraulics to the electric lighting (the first country house to be lit by home-generated hydroelectricity), and then to the expansive kitchens down below. Lakes were created high up in the grounds to allow for an early hydroelectric generator to supply power. A new Archimedean Screw has been installed fairly recently by the National Trust. Armstrong's engineering genius is found everywhere. The iron bridge over the Debdon Ravine was manufactured in Armstrong's Elswick Works on the Tyne. The five-mile pootle along the estate drive is a final bonus. Here, throughout, is the epitome of Victorian ingenuity, inventiveness, and romance.

At Great Tosson, 2 miles southwest and beneath Simonside (470 m, 1542 ft), after which the range of hills is named, stand the remains of Tosson Tower, a fourteenth-century ruin standing to almost 7 m. Although there are no outstanding features, it remains a significant landmark. At Tosson Burgh is an oval hill fort—also a cairn half a mile south.

Whitton, half a mile south of Rothbury, sports two towers! There is a fourteenth-century tower house, rising to four storeys and originally the vicar's pele, that is the residence of the Vicars of Rothbury. The eighteenth-century vicar, Archdeacon Thomas Sharp (a noted local personality), was not content with this and built a 17 m round tower known as Sharp's Folly—it is in a prominent location and a clear landmark; it was said to have been built to alleviate local unemployment and to satisfy his interest in astronomy—and astrology! Whitton Grange is a fine early-twentieth-century house (1921 by Robert Mauchlen).

171

RYAL

South Farm is an impressive mid-Georgian farmhouse including a stair wing added to the rear in 1771 and with a pedimented doorway displaying a pulvinated frieze.

All Saints, the little chapel of ease, is a delight with much old fabric sensitively rebuilt in 1870. Its origins are twelfth century, and the nave retains much mediaeval masonry. There is a good thirteenth-century chamfered chancel arch and built into the western wall is a magnificent collection of nineteen cross slabs. The rebuilding is largely in Romanesque style, although the chancel is Early English in feel.

SCREMERSTON

The broad main street of the village with its green sward reminds us that it formed part of the Great North Road until this most northerly pit village in England was bypassed in 1983. The original village is a mile or so south of the present centre at Scremerston Town Farm, where some cottages survive. The northward move was occasioned by the sinking of the Greenwich Colliery, the remains of which can be seen at the most southerly extent of the present village, a settlement originally named Richardson's Stead.

The remains of the old colliery railway can be traced northwards,

running to the east of St Peter's Church, and passing the cottages which mark the position of the second "restoration" pit. Here the railway went both east and west. The eastward track is the older route which was originally a tramway carrying coal and lime down the cliff to Spittal, where there was then a coal staithe—evidence survives in Spittal with the naming of South Greenwich Road (London's Greenwich Hospital owned substantial tracts of country both around here and near Simonburn and Wark in the South Tyne Valley). The track to the west passed Deputy Row (that name being another sign

↓ **SCREMERSTON** Deputy Row

→ **SCREMERSTON** limekilns

flair, alongside an energetic sculpture of a fisherman. Limekilns speak of another past industry. The former independent branch railway line can be traced past North Sunderland where are situated both Salvin's 1834 Parish Church and the plain but handsome United Reformed Church (formerly Presbyterian chapel) of 1810. The station and its sidings are now the central car park—a symbol of changing patterns of transport! Shoreston Hall, 1 mile north, was built for the Grey family but became the home of the distinguished historian Sir Stephen Runciman in the twentieth century.

SEATON DELAVAL

Seaton Delaval Hall is the last great house by the soldier, herald, playwright and architect, Sir John Vanbrugh. Vanbrugh died before its completion, as indeed did his patron, Admiral George Delaval. It is generally considered to be Vanbrugh's masterpiece in its power, compactness, and maturity. There is an atmospheric painting by the twentieth-century artist John Piper, which captures something of its mystique. The death of architect and patron presaged an unfortunate history. Completed in 1728, it passed through several heirs and the left wing suffered a fire in 1752, but then more disastrously, the central pavilion fell victim to a serious fire in 1822. It has remained an empty shell ever since, and it is only due to the commitment and energy of the late Lord Hastings (1912–2007) that the house has survived at all; the Hastings barony is the oldest in the English aristocracy. The Delaval

of the mining community) to the third site of the colliery a little to the northwest, where Scremerston High Street now meets the road into Berwick.

Scremerston's name as an industrial hub was further emphasized by the lime workings and kilns along Cocklawburn beach at Philadelphia and elsewhere; traces of their cultivated cottage gardens are discernible in the otherwise pleasant wild flora. Hereabouts is ample interest for the amateur industrial archaeologist.

SEAHOUSES

This coastal suburb of North Sunderland has now entirely outgrown its more demure parent with much undistinguished sprawl. It does offer, however, a unique taste of the seaside in these north parts with buckets, spades, candyfloss, and ice cream in abundance. Its fine harbour hosts a modest fishing fleet and plenty of vessels for the frequently bumpy crossing to the Farnes. Lively ponies on the dunes to both north and south. Some more recent building has added some

↑ **SEATON DELAVAL** Hall, stables
← **SEATON DELAVAL** Hall, staircase

family gifted the house and grounds to the National Trust in 2009.

The house comprises a central pavilion and two service wings which extend down to the road, enclosing a forecourt or *cour d'honneur* almost 50 m square. It follows a classic Venetian pattern, bar the attached towers. The west front of the main pavilion has a broad open staircase with an arched doorway, flanked by Tuscan columns. The upper storeys of the stair towers have Venetian windows. The wings are decorated with much rustication. The south side of the house is less dramatic but still sporting elegantly fluted Ionic columns. The Great Hall is large, and stone-faced with very high proportions, and with a second storey which was originally a separate room. The south front houses the saloon which is in three sections and originally included a painted ceiling by Vercelli. The unsupported stone and wrought-iron balustraded staircases were rebuilt by Aynsley and Sons of Newcastle in the 1962 restoration. Beneath the ground floor is a labyrinthine series of vaulted cellars and passages. The centre of the west wing is the kitchen and the centre of the east wing the stables.

There is much of interest in the gardens, including lead statues, an orangery, and an icehouse. The cottages to the west may include fragments of the Delaval family's former tower house. To the southeast is the shell of the 1766 Mausoleum, which follows the pattern of the Temple at Castle Howard in Yorkshire. 800 m south is an obelisk some 18 m high. The walls of the gate screen at the far end of the Avenue—over a mile away—survive.

Barring the nineteenth-century porch, the little church (originally the manorial chapel and a two-cell building) feels Anglo-Saxon in style. Certainly, there is fabric which precedes the twelfth century. The original west door, now covered by the porch, has a zigzag-bordered tympanum. The chancel is Norman except for the fourteenth-century east end which replaces an earlier apse. The fourteenth-century piscina is interesting, as are effigies of Sir Hugh Delaval and of a lady, from the same period.

SEATON SLUICE

There is much history and interest here. Originally known as Hartley Pans, on account of the salt pans which were worked from as early as 1236, the property passed to the de Laval family in 1100 (de Laval was a nephew of William the Conqueror). The family had settled 800 m to the west, the residence eventually being named Seaton Delaval. The tiny natural harbour became known as Hartley Haven. On account of it regularly silting up, Sir Ralph Delaval (c.1670) decided to build a sluice/weir to capture the water at high tide—at low tide the gates

↓ **SEATON SLUICE**

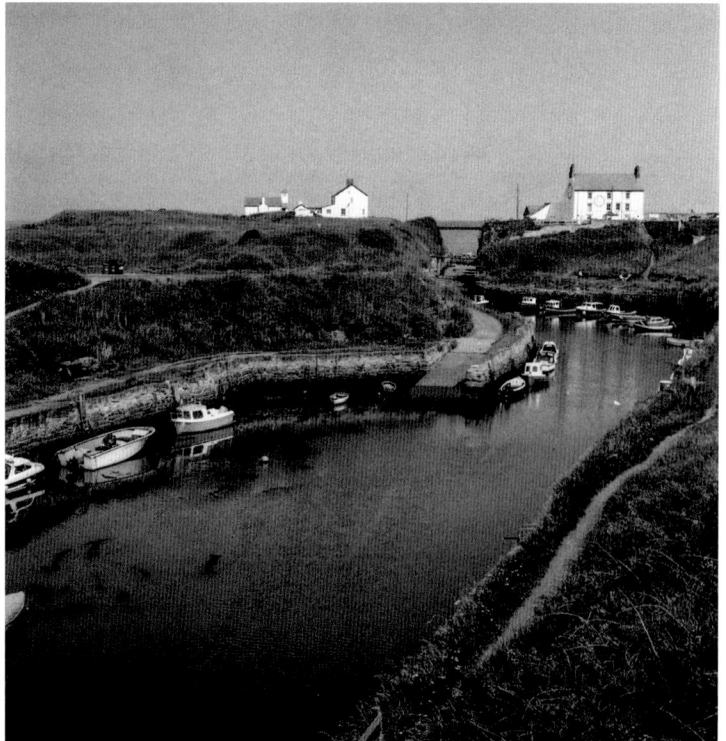

were opened, flushing out the silt. In the 1760s, Sir John Hussey Delaval had a new channel blasted through the rock. So successful was this, that numerous ships used the harbour, largely for the export of coal and salt. Later in the eighteenth century, the Delavals set up a bottle works which finally disappeared in 1896. Both the decline of the coal trade and the Hartley pit disaster led to the demise of this tiny port. There is still space for small craft in the surviving creek.

The Octagon was formerly the harbourmaster's office, which Pevsner describes as an "after-dinner idea by Vanbrugh"—Vanbrugh designed the nearby mansion. Starlight Castle further up the dene is a Gothick gazebo built for one of Sir Francis Delaval's mistresses! Fort House includes an octagonal tower, originally part of Roberts Battery (1917), which housed the Tyne Turrets, guns from the former HMS *Illustrious*.

SHILBOTTLE

Scattered former colliery village and complicated for motor navigation! Two former collieries—Shilbottle and Whittle (a drift mine to the west on the Great North Road and later part of Shilbottle colliery). With its high-grade anthracite Whittle was said to be the legendary supplier of coal to Buckingham Palace. St James' Church is a very fine piece of Decorated architecture by W. S. Hicks, 1885. Splendid wood panelling in the noble and lofty crossing-tower and semi-coffered wood ceilings in chancel and nave; fine nineteenth-century "Norman"-style font. Pele house later converted to the vicarage with an extended mediaeval tower at its west end. The first wedding in the new church was that of Sir Edward Grey, later Lord Grey of Fallodon, to Dorothy Widdrington.

SHOTLEY

Shotley lies 6 miles south-south-east of Riding Mill and is just across the River Derwent from its larger County Durham neighbour, Shotley Bridge. They are connected by a late-eighteenth-century single elliptical-arched bridge.

Shotley Hall was designed and built by its owner, Thomas Wilson, in 1863. It is romantically Gothic with a pyramidal-roofed round tower at one corner. There are marble fireplaces and much painted glass decorating the ground floor windows. The stable block and the north gate lodge are in similar style, the gate lodge including a saddleback tower. Even "The Barn" nearby (two cruciform houses) bears marks of the same creator!

At Snod's Edge, one and a half miles west, stands St John's Church, built in plain lancet style in 1836; there is a monument to the Walton-Wilson family of Shotley Hall at the east end beneath some canopied niches.

↓ **SHOTLEY** Hopper Mausoleum

At Greymare Hill/Kiln Pit Hill, very near to the border with County Durham, is St Andrew's Church, Shotley, now in the care of the Churches Conservation Trust. Cruciform and built in 1769, on the site of a much older church, in the churchyard is the remarkable Hopper Mausoleum. Completed in 1752 for Humfrey Hopper, in memory of his wife Jane Hodgson, it is the burial place also for Humfrey himself and later generations. It is neo-Classical with a dome and cupola, and with pyramidal finials. Both church and mausoleum are fine landmarks on this high point (293 m/1,000 ft) near to the Roman artery of Dere Street.

SIMONBURN

Attractively set around a square village green, Simonburn's church is unusually (for England) dedicated to St Mungo, the early Celtic patron of Glasgow. It is a fine, indeed almost grand, church with a four-bay aisled nave, which retains its noble thirteenth-century arcades. There has been much rebuilding; the aisle walls and south transeptal chapel were removed in 1763, and the chancel was rebuilt a hundred years later. Again, unusually the floor drops to the east such that one looks down toward the altar and east end. Several good windows by Kempe. In the north porch, there is part of a Saxon cross shaft with a vine scroll—there are also other Saxon fragments. Memorials to the Allgood family who lived at Nunwick in the village and to a branch of the Ridley clan who lived at Parkend, north of the village.

Fine former rectory with Vanbrugh influence in the architecture which in its present form dates from 1725, so Vanbrugh's period. Good late-eighteenth- and early-nineteenth-century cottages around the green. The Steward's House is mid-eighteenth century and of five bays.

Simonburn Castle, 1,200 m west, stands on a narrow neck of land and is first mentioned in 1415.

SLALEY

Slaley lies in the middle of Hexhamshire. King Henry I had elevated this area to county status to weaken the power of the Bishops of Durham and their palatinate; it remained a separate county until 1572 and has retained some individuality in the local folk tradition. Effectively Slaley is just one street with some pleasant houses and the Church of St Mary on its north side, built by Milton Carr in 1832 with some alterations in 1907. It is plain and unaisled with an unusual ark-like broad chancel arch; it is a quietly attractive and unassuming building.

Slaley Hall, to the southwest, is an Edwardian-style castellated building of modest merit, but sadly engulfed in an enormous hotel built of ersatz stonework; large, impressive golfing facilities.

North of the village is a disused nuclear bunker closed in 1991.

STAMFORDHAM

One of the most attractive villages in the county, its elegantly broad east–west main street has some fine eighteenth-century houses,

well restored and overlooking wide green swards. Within the central green stands a pretty buttercross of 1735 erected by Sir John Swinburne of Capheaton; square, with rusticated pillars, it has a pyramidal roof topped by a small turret again with a pyramidal roof. Further to the east is the village lock-up, built in the early nineteenth century with a studded floor. St Mary's Church on a mound at the west end of the village is impressive. The quoins at the southeast corner of the nave are probably Saxon, as is the round arch in the west wall of the tower. The rest of the church is attractive thirteenth-century work, but much restored by Benjamin Ferrey in 1848. The east window of 1886 is by Kempe and the south window of the chancel by Clayton and Bell. In the porch, there is a table tomb and cross slabs and in the north aisle a large tomb chest to John Swinburne. The rear of the old vicarage is seventeenth century, and Dobson added more in 1847, including the Tuscan door surround. The front of the house is pedimented with a Latin inscription dated 1764.

Hawkwell is a tiny but attractive hamlet south of the river with the three-bay Hawkwell House including some seventeenth-century work—tall, rusticated gate piers.

One mile south is the former Ouston airfield, an important RAF fighter base during the Second World War, whose life was extended as a dispersal airfield for key squadrons during the Cold War; it now houses Albemarle Barracks. A further mile southwest, near Harlow Hill, are the Whittle Dene reservoirs, an impressive, interconnected group of water treatment and water supply facilities. At Harlow Hill itself, the 1891 Bell Methodist Memorial Chapel (now residential) is both neat and modest, with an added flourish in the turret at its southeast corner.

Horsley-on-the-Hill is slightly further south, sixteenth-/seventeenth-century cottage on north side of village street and an attractive inn of 1718. Welton Hall, 2 miles northwest, is a ruined fifteenth-century tower with an L-shaped house attached, apparently of 1614, as noted over the doorway. The south side includes a period piece which is built from a thirteenth- and fourteenth-century house—a most interesting building. Welton deserted village—earthworks lie close by. Nafferton Castle, one and a half miles west of Horsley, dates back to an unlicensed castle of 1218 built by Philip of Ulcotes but demolished by order of the monarch. Much of it was probably built of wood—there is a simple semi-rectangular tower of the fifteenth or sixteenth century.

STANNINGTON

Effectively the estate village for nearby Blagdon, the seat of the Ridleys; there is a good church rebuilt at the expense of Sir Matthew White Ridley Bt. in 1871 by R. J. Johnson. The strong west tower has some echoes of Durham Cathedral but may have been modelled on Bedale in North Yorkshire. The original church was as early as 1190, and some evidence of that building survives in the north arcade including some good waterleaf capitals. Some fourteenth-century window heads were included in the new tower. The recumbent bronze effigy of the first Viscount Ridley (1904) is by Sir West Reynolds Stephens and is set on a marble plinth by Detmar Blow. The five-bay Old Vicarage is of 1745, and its garden includes architectural fragments from the old church.

In the village main street are two bus shelters by the artist Laurence Whistler, given by Viscount Ridley in celebration of the coronation of King George VI. North of the Ridley Arms, an attractive and spacious hostelry, is the village "Hearse House" dated 1871. Catraw Farmhouse, 1 mile west, is by Lutyens. Bellasis Farmhouse, 2 miles southwest, is dated 1694. The attractive old hogback bridge here has two segmental arches.

Blagdon Hall, to the south, was built c.1735, incorporating elements of its seventeenth-century predecessor. In 1778–91, James Wyatt made alterations. The plain north wing (c.1820) is by John Dobson, and then Joseph Bonomi worked on the house in 1826 and 1830. Following extensive fire damage, there was a significant restoration by Robert Lutyens in 1949 which retained the east front with its giant eighteenth-century pilasters. The south front is of similar proportions but includes a three-bay pediment. The architecture is not extravagant, and all is enhanced by the gentle pale-coloured stone. There is an imperial stair rising from a columnar screen and concluding with another screen at the upper landing. The stables are by Wyatt and the gardens remodelled by Sir Edwin Lutyens (1938). The grounds are fine and include a lake, made from the damming of the Snitter Burn and bridged in three places with two iron bridges and one from stone. There is much else to see in the grounds including an icehouse, a sculpture garden, a Gothick ruin, a circular temple and a mediaeval cross. The south lodge is by Wyatt and the north lodge by Lish. Just inside the north gate is the re-erected Cale Cross, originally a conduit head, from The Side close to the Tyne Bridge in Newcastle; it was designed by David Stephenson,

↑ **STAMFORDHAM** buttercross

↑ **STANNINGTON** Laurence Whistler bus shelter

↑ **STANNINGTON** Cale Cross

the architect of All Saints' Church, and given to the city by the Ridleys. Milkhope farm buildings to the south are now an attractive farm shop and country shopping village run by the estate.

STOCKSFIELD

Stocksfield lives in the shadow of Bywell, its attractive and grand neighbour. It is a dispersed community with a few interesting houses including the original stationmaster's house on the Newcastle–Carlisle line. Stocksfield Hall stands on a hillock southeast of Bywell Bridge. Little survives of Ridley Mill. Wheelbirks is an extended farmhouse transformed in the early twentieth century by a Quaker, David Richardson, in the Edwardian period. Cottages were built and a modest estate established. He left, unfinished at his

death, a sanatorium for TB sufferers. Over the fields on the banks of Stocksfield Burn stand the remains of a sixteenth-century blast furnace! At Hedley-on-the-Hill, 3 miles southeast, are marvellous views over the South Tyne—a Methodist church (1837) is now a house. Two miles southeast is Whittonstall—St Philip and St James' Church (1830) by Jonathan Marshall—striking chancel of 1893; thirteenth-century slab with no cross.

SWARLAND

Here is a village with three incarnations; the surviving Old Swarland Hall bears witness to the earliest history with late-sixteenth-century survivals at the rear; there is also a doorhead bearing a 1730 date. Next came Swarland Park, which was grouped around Swarland New Hall, built in 1765 and demolished

in 1947. Alexander Davison, who owned the house in the early nineteenth century, was a great friend of Nelson and planted trees on his estate to represent the position of the fleets in the Battle of the Nile. Just two gate lodges and some buildings from the home farm are evidence of his estate.

Next, in the 1930s, came the Swarland Settlement set up by Commander Clare Vyner, the then owner of Studley Royal and Fountains Abbey in Yorkshire. Set out as a garden village with workshops to retrain the unemployed from Tyneside, the regular pattern of housing with a tiny central square is effectively all that remains; 3 or 4 miles away on the old Telford Road towards Wooler was an outlier to all this in the former Swarland Brick Company—following a disastrous fire, this is now a trout farm.

↑ **SWARLAND** Old Hall

↑ Former **SWARLAND** brickworks at Thrunton

THOCKRINGTON

Just a hamlet perched on high ground with its church and a few dwellings, it is but the remnant of a former village whose remains are visible in the form of earthworks surrounding this isolated settlement. The Church of St Aidan is Norman in origin, and this is clear once inside the building, with its plain chancel arch and a similar arch at the east end pointing to the existence of a now vanished apse. Lord Beveridge, the architect of the modern welfare state, is buried (1963) just to the west of the tower, alongside his wife who predeceased him. Constance Leathart, the pioneering woman aviator, is also buried here.

THORNEYBURN

Four miles west of Bellingham, a tiny, scattered village with the Church of St Aidan (1818) just south of the main road, built as in other places hereabouts by the Commissioners of Greenwich Hospital, and by H. H. Seward, the same architect as in Humshaugh and Wark—a neat building similar to the others; again, as with the others, rectory, stables and church-yard walls all grouped together— perhaps all slightly urban for such remote surroundings. Redheugh farmhouse 1732 for the Charltons as in Hesleyside.

At Gatehouse, 1 mile north, are a collection of bastles, including that at Black Middens. High Green Moors, 2 miles northeast, rather out of context in these austere moors, a late-nineteenth-century country house for Mr Morrison Bell.

↑ **THOCKRINGTON** church

Tarset, 1 mile south of Thorneyburn, boasts a castle, the property of the Scots until 1244, licensed to crenellate for John Comyns in 1267; it was burnt by the Scots amidst local intrigue in 1525. The castle was partially destroyed by the building of the railway and plundered for stone when the nearby Reenes farmhouse was built. Redmire Bridge over Tarset Burn early nineteenth century and then the railway bridge of 1860—bastles abound.

THROPTON

Two miles west of Rothbury, Thropton is a long village sitting beneath the Simonside Hills with a bridge of 1810 over the Wreigh Burn. The late-eighteenth-century All Saints' Roman Catholic Church has a remarkable pendant screen of three arches. The United Reformed Church of 1863 has an unusual porch-cum-turret. The Three Wheat Heads Inn (what an extraordinary name!) has interesting eighteenth-century work from three different periods. West is The Peel, a well preserved bastle with a good late-twentieth-century extension.

TILLMOUTH

Tillmouth is effectively a lost village whose name endures, largely through the country house hotel at Tillmouth Park. The name pinpoints the estuary of the River Till (in its upper reaches it is known as the Breamish) as it joins the Tweed. Just a few hundred metres from the confluence, the rock-faced stone 1849 viaduct which carried the Berwick–St Boswells branch line crosses the Till, and nearby is the shell of St Cuthbert's Chapel, first mentioned in 1311, although the present ruin is an eighteenth-century structure built by Sir Francis Blake. A boathouse, a cottage and the former stationmaster's house are effectively all that comprise contemporary Tillmouth; the site of the former station built for the estate is easily discernible.

Francis Blake left significant footprints. Later Francis Blakes (there were several) were equally industrious, as for example with Tillmouth Park, built in 1882 by Charles Barry for the same family; the present house replaced an earlier building of 1810—its fireplaces were built into the new mansion. The same Francis Blake also began a new bridge over

↓ **TILLMOUTH** Twizel Bridge

the Till which was never finished—only one arch stands.

On the south-eastern edge of the park at Castle Heaton are remains of a mediaeval building but the castle itself built by the Grey family is gone. The dower house opposite the lodge to the park is picturesque Strawberry Hill Gothick, remodelled in 1976 and formerly a farmhouse.

Twizel Castle high up on the ridge of the glen is the most visible of all footprints left by the late-eighteenth-century Sir Francis Blake. Now but a Gothic ruin—in every sense—it was in course of building for fifty years but never completed. Set around the remains of a mediaeval house; a footpath takes one close to the ruins.

Twizel Bridge was completed in 1511 and until the completion in 1727 of the Causey Arch, it was the largest single-span stone bridge in Britain. It allowed Thomas Howard, Earl of Surrey, to get his troops across the river such that he would outmanoeuvre James IV of Scotland before the Battle of Flodden. With its single-chamfered ribs, it leaps over the Till in athletic fashion.

TRITLINGTON

The five-bay Hall is nineteenth century, but the nearby Old Hall, with its magnificent early-eight-eenth-century gate-piers, is a rebuilt mediaeval tower, with a wing added in 1595 and the whole restyled in the eighteenth century when the gateway was adorned with its baskets of fruit and flowers.

One mile southwest is Cockle Tower, now part of the University of Newcastle's research farm. Early sixteenth century, it is interestingly crenellated and L-shaped in plan. Altered in the seventeenth century on the west with mullioned and transomed windows, it is a handsome but robust statement. Barrel-vaulted at one end, on the first-floor level was a solar.

A mile further south is Hebron, just a few cottages, a farm and with the delightfully situated tiny church of St Cuthbert approached over a burn. Twelfth-century masonry in chancel and fourteenth-/fifteenth-century chancel arch—otherwise all rebuilt in 1793.

TYNEMOUTH

Saving Whitby, Tynemouth Priory is undoubtedly the most impressive monastic ruin on Britain's east coast. Set on a limestone promontory, it stands proudly as a sentinel defending the Tyne estuary—this was the site of an Iron Age fort followed by Roman occupation and then a monastery in the time of Bede: St Oswin's resting place is said to be here, following his murder in 651. The sacking by the Danes in 875 is mentioned by Matthew Paris. Ecclesiastically it has belonged to various congregations, beginning with Evesham, the Jarrow and Durham monasteries and finally St Albans. It remained throughout a fortress as much as a religious house, and in its steep rocky location it is in a powerful defensive position. The gatehouse is later, having been completed by Richard II and John of Gaunt in the early fifteenth century; there is a barbican through which the gatehouse is approached, as at Alnwick.

↓ **TRITLINGTON** Cockle Park Tower

← **TYNEMOUTH** Priory
↙ Tyne estuary, north
and south piers

↑ **TYNEMOUTH** Priory and King Edward's Bay

The pattern of the Norman priory church is clearly seen although not surviving to any height—there was a chancel of two bays with an apse and then a nave of seven bays. It is the church (Early English, begun c.1190) which gives the priory its present profile, with its sheer east wall. With less decoration externally, the interior is more richly adorned. The architecture is very impressive and innovative, and there was vaulting throughout. The former cloisters are mapped out on the ground to the south and included here was a vaulted thirteenth-century chapter house. There was a prior's hall and prior's chapel and originally several more buildings to the east. The Percy Chantry lies at the east end of the church; it is a small, vaulted chapel of the fifteenth century restored by Dobson in 1852.

Ironically, the priory and castle were virtually all there was of Tynemouth until the nineteenth century. It was "discovered" and became fashionable residentially. This is very much the air one breathes on entering contemporary Tynemouth, and with the advent of eating alfresco, there is even a faintly continental feel about the town. The breadth of the public spaces helps here. The Queen Victoria Memorial is the centrepiece (1902) and is a fine study of the monarch. There are good war memorials. There are attractive streets which are worthy of a perambulation. The former Newcastle and Berwick Railway Station is another strong building by Benjamin Green—the adjacent modern development is less successful. The Master Mariners' Homes are also by Green with cottages in a pretty Tudor style. The 1861 polychrome brick Clock Tower forms a pleasant focus. The Collingwood Monument is 1847 by Dobson; nearby are the scant remains of the Spanish Battery, and still further east are the remains of twentieth-century gun emplacements. The Tyne North Pier heralding the estuary salutes its almost identical neighbour which worms its way out from South Shields.

ULGHAM

Counter-intuitively pronounced "Uffem". Near the source of the River Lyne, this is an ancient place with the stump of a fourteenth-/fifteenth-century market cross, almost obscured by being inset into the wall at the centre of the village. When the plague hit Morpeth, the market was displaced to Ulgham. On the east wall of the north aisle of St John the Baptist Church is a tiny piece of Norman art in the form of a small Gothick window head with an almost child-like carving of a woman with two birds over her shoulder and an "Uffington"-style horse beside her, a man in the saddle. There is a similar undecorated stone from a window head in the middle of the outer west wall of

185

the church. Much restored manor house to the south of the church, with a dog-leg stair of c.1680.

VINDOLANDA

The story of the discovery and development of the Vindolanda site is fascinating. Antiquarian William Camden made record of the site in 1586. In 1702, Christopher Hunter visited the site to find the *thermae* (bath house) still partially roofed, and in 1715, an excise officer, one John Warburton, found an altar here, which he removed. It was, however, the work of a clergyman, Anthony Hedley, that marked the beginnings of archaeological research; Hedley died in 1835 before writing up his discoveries.

Then finally, it was the purchase of the property by the archaeologist Eric Birley that marked the vision for properly excavating the site. His sons Robin and Anthony continued the work, as has his grandson, Andrew. The Vindolanda Trust, which owns and administers both this site and Carvoran (with the Roman Army Museum), was established in 1970 and is also taking forward the excavation.

There is an excellent museum and very good interpretative material on the sites. Included on this site is a former civil settlement, the fort, its bath house, the headquarters building, and a mausoleum. Some didactic reconstruction was completed between 1971–4 indicating the construction of the Wall, including stone, timber, and turf; there is naturally some conjecture in the final building, including the final height of the wall, the parapet walks and the roofing. There is no firm knowledge of the form of the crenellation.

There is a Roman milestone in its original position, where Stanegate crosses a ford northeast of Codley Gate farmhouse. At Barcombe Hill, 1,200 m northeast, there is a univallate Iron Age fort. Also, 800 m west is the remarkable survival of a heather-thatched house, dated 1770.

WALL

Attractively laid out around a large square, within which the church and one or two dwellings form an island. St George's Church 1895 by Hicks and Charlewood—slightly solemn Perpendicular rectangle, but well-built and furnished. Originally the green was almost certainly larger, with a series of bastles, surviving mainly on the north side. Greenhead House is the best example and includes a lintel dated 1631; St Oswald Cottages have early features, including a doorway of 1642

↓ **VINDOLANDA**

built as the bastle was remodelled. A section of Hadrian's Wall survives on Brunton Bank, 800 m north— Brunton Turret, 2 m high, is one of the best-preserved wall turrets.

One mile northeast is St Oswald's Chapel, in a very fine position on a ridge. It was built in 1737 to commemorate Oswald's victory at Heavenfield over Cadwallon of Gwynedd, in 634, reuniting the two sub-kingdoms of Northumbria— Deira to the south and Bernicia to the north. Oswald would fall seven years later to the pagan Penda of Mercia at the Battle of Maserfield (modern-day Oswestry, so incorporating the monarch-saint's name). The chapel is a rectangle remodelled by Hicks in 1887. It contains a Roman altar decorated with a sacrificial cleaver, a wine ladle, vine branch and grapes. There are fragments of a mediaeval cross-shaft in the porch.

WALLINGTON HALL

Wallington began life as a pele tower, which belonged to the Fenwick family from 1475. Following the Fenwicks' financial problems, Sir William Blackett bought the estate in 1688 as a country retreat. He demolished the pele tower and built a hall house which was then substantially remodelled. It was built in Palladian style, from 1727 onwards, by Daniel Garrett for William's great-nephew, Sir Walter Calverley Blackett, who created the house much as we know it today. The grounds were also reconceived; Walter built the three-storey clock tower and gateway, crowned by a cupola, lantern and open-columned rotunda. Built of a honey-coloured stone, the house is of two storeys with a Tuscan eastern doorway. To the north is a large stable yard. Sir Walter reduced the size of the inner courtyard.

The principal rooms are sumptuously decorated, notably with stucco plasterwork, provided by an Italian group who Blackett housed in Cambo. There is a full life-size portrait of Sir Walter by Reynolds. The dining room is screened at its east end with Corinthian columns; the library sports Ionic columns. Wallington eventually passed to Blackett's sister's son, Sir John Trevelyan. The Trevelyans, with advice from John Ruskin, further remodelled the house, this time with the work of John Dobson. It was at this stage that the courtyard was roofed in, and the walls painted by a follower of the Pre-Raphaelites, one William Bell Scott, the subjects largely being characters associated with local history. In times past, the last surviving Trevelyan daughter would play the Northumbrian pipes for visitors, in the covered courtyard.

↓ **WALL** Heavenfield cross

↓ Dragons, originally from Bishopsgate, London

↑ **WALLINGTON HALL** bridge

↑ **WALLINGTON HALL** atrium

The gardens are fascinating in themselves. The walled garden is a little way to the east and follows the course of a stream offering a picturesque and less formulaic design than many such gardens. There is a summer house with a Roman Doric screen. On the north horizon, The Arches is an eye-catcher, such focuses being much favoured in the county. The Trevelyans were themselves an interesting family. Sir Charles Trevelyan was a radical Liberal politician who became a minister in the first Labour government; it was he who gave the entire estate as an early gift to the National Trust in 1942. Thomas

↓ Rothley eye-catcher

Babington Macaulay, brother-in-law of Sir Charles, wrote his history of England here; historian George Macaulay Trevelyan was also part of the same family.

Four miles northeast of Wallington, at Rothley, lies the northernmost part of the estate. Sir Walter Blackett in c.1755 engaged Daniel Garrett to design the Gothick eye-catcher with tower and castellations; there is a smaller eye-catcher 1 mile north at Codger Fort, this time c.1769 by Thomas Wright—both very dramatically placed. In the valley below, Blackett engaged Capability Brown to create two fishing lakes one on either side of the road.

WALLSEND

As the name indicates, this was the eastern end of the Roman wall, which had originally ended at Pons Aelius, modern-day Newcastle; some five years later it was extended eastwards, probably to defend Pons Aelius. In 1997, substantial excavations took place at Segedunum, the Roman fort. Then, in 2000, the present museum and exhibition opened together with its 35 m high viewing tower. Parts of the foundations of the wall are visible

↓ **WALLSEND** Willington viaducts

and a reconstruction of a Roman bath house, as at Vindolanda. The museum is housed in former buildings of the Swan Hunter shipyard—terraced housing was demolished to reveal the site of the fortress.

The shipyard closed in 2007—this brought to an end more than 100 years of shipbuilding—the RMS *Mauretania* was built here, as was the 1980s aircraft carrier HMS *Ark Royal*. Coal mining drove the growth of heavy industry here. Burn Closes Bridge is another structure built by the ubiquitous engineer L. G. Mouchel, as at the Royal Tweed Bridge in Berwick and Spanish City in Whitley Bay. Near the end of this bridge are a village green and the mediaeval Chapel of Holy Cross.

Two substantial Anglican churches; St Luke's (1885–7) has an east-end tower. The overall style is Early English with a marvellous First World War window by Wilhelmina Geddes. St Peter's Church (originally 1802) stands at the opposite end of the Burn Closes Bridge from Holy Cross. In Perpendicular style, all signs of Georgian have gone, but there is a fine hammerbeam roof by Hicks and good glass including another window by Wilhelmina Geddes.

Willington Viaduct with its seven arches is further to the southeast again bridging the Wallsend Burn—the attractive skew accommodation arch is nearby. A walk around the old town reveals some good building and two fine war memorials.

WARDEN

Two miles northwest of Hexham and very close to the confluence of the North and South Tynes, St Michael's Church nestles among the trees on a site traditionally associated with an oratory of St John of Beverley. Unaisled and cruciform, its origins are pre-Conquest. Long thirteenth-century transepts with lancets; chancel rebuilt in 1889 by the incumbent, the industrious George Cruddas; much Kempe glass of this period including four depicting the evangelists and some early-eleventh-century glass. Very early (seventh century?) village cross in churchyard alongside some fine headstones. The entire setting with the church is a gem.

↑ **WARKWORTH** Castle

WARK-ON-TWEED

Wark Castle is now "naught but a mound", but it was once one of the most important of the border fortresses. It was built as a motte and bailey castle by Walter Espec in the early twelfth century and was frequently besieged by the Scots. Like nearby Etal Castle, Wark was captured by James IV of Scotland just before the Battle of Flodden. This led to a massive rebuilding programme and stationing of a garrison, but by the early seventeenth century the castle was in an advanced state of decay and the Royal Artillery was withdrawn.

WARK-ON-TYNE

On the opposite bank of the river to **CHIPCHASE CASTLE** (*qv*) is another Greenwich Hospital village, and another H. H. Seward Church of St Michael (1818) in similar style to **HUMSHAUGH** (*qv*) and again paid for by the Hospital. 1900 stained-glass window by the pulpit by Kempe. The former rectory next door also by Seward.

As the former capital of Tynedale, Wark had some pretensions of grandeur with its square, including a town hall which had begun as a Mechanics Institute of 1873. There are several bastles nearby, and Shitlington Cross, 1 mile north of Low Stead, has the base and octagonal shaft of a mediaeval cross. There is a stone circle at Ravensheugh Crags, two and a half miles southwest. Four miles west, Stonehaugh is another village, similar to Byrness and Kielder, designed by Thomas Sharp for the Forestry Commission.

WARKWORTH

An unforgettable sight, its ruined castle still keeping watch over the estuary of the River Coquet, captive within a loop of the same river. Warkworth would be a gem in any county. The northern approach is the most romantic—rather like a miniature Conwy in North Wales; the battlemented bridge was replaced in 1965 and an elegant modern structure now welcomes you. Warkworth is a classic example of ever new vistas: the bends in the main street, the incline leading up to the castle, and the opening to Dial Place and church all offer their own surprises. After the bridge the road curves right and left, and before you stands the five-bayed Georgian Bridge End House with its pedimented front; just along from it is the 1822 Warkworth House Hotel; inside is a patterned wrought-iron balustrade transported from Brandenburgh House, Queen Caroline's residence in London. Throughout, the buildings, including many simple vernacular houses, are exemplary—the journeys to both castle and church delight. The Sun Hotel (1822), at the top of the hill and opposite the castle keep, completes this noble pattern.

So, to the castle. The junior title of the Duke of Northumberland borne by the heir is the Baron Warkworth; the castle is still owned by the Percy family, although it is managed by English Heritage. Beginning as a timber fortress, the present buildings originate from the twelfth century, but not until 1332 did the castle become the property of the Percys. The great building period was in the 1390s, under the first Earl. A deep ditch probably of Iron Age origin completes the defences, provided elsewhere by the river's incised meander. The splendid keep was clearly the work of a talented architect—square plan with polygonal turrets—thirteenth-century origin but remodelled two hundred years later. Hall, buttery, pantry, and kitchen are all visible—a door links to the inner chapel.

The gate tower, of an innovative design, derives from examples built in the crusades; its two towers, along with the Carrickfergus and Grey Mare's Tail Towers, are polygonal in design. The Amble or Montagu Tower at the southeast is late fifteenth century. The extensive outer ward contained the chapel and the Great Hall—the foundations of the Collegiate Church separate the outer and inner wards. The first Earl aimed to found a college of secular priests, but the church was never completed, and what we see today may be all that was built.

Returning to the village, St Lawrence's Church, at the end of Dial Place, is also outstanding. Unique in Northumberland as a virtually complete Norman church, the north wall leans perilously but is well buttressed! The chancel, unusually, is vaulted; the south porch also has a rib vault and an upper chamber which once gave service as the local school. In the south aisle is a fine fourteenth-century effigy of a knight placed on the top of a seventeenth-century table tomb. The western tower is c.1200 with a plain broached spire, probably of the fourteenth century. Interesting wrought-iron communion rail with monogram of Matthew White of Blagdon.

Both Bridge View and The Stanners offer great glimpses of the dramatic loop in the Coquet. The turn into Dial Place has the c.1830 market cross on one side and the former inter-war Co-op acting as a "plane finial" to the sharp corner. Dial Place has some fine houses including the old vicarage. There is a former tithe barn in Bridge Street and the 1736 schoolhouse in The Butts.

Warkworth Hermitage, half a mile west on the north bank of the Coquet, is a curious sacristy and vaulted chapel carved out of the sandstone c.1340; the footings of a kitchen remain. Bishop Percy's (apparently no relation to the Alnwick Percys) *Poetical Relics* include a fictional account of the origins of the hermitage in *The Hermit of Warkworth*.

Coquet Island off the estuary of the Coquet, 1 mile east of Amble, fits most happily here. Bede refers to it as a meeting place for monks, and Cuthbert is said to have accepted the Bishopric of Lindisfarne here, in 684. The present thirteenth-/fourteenth-century monastic remains are of a Benedictine cell of Tynemouth Priory. The 27 m high lighthouse is of 1841. The island, still owned by the Percys, is a remarkable bird reserve with fulmars, kittiwakes, puffins, Arctic terns and many more. There are trips around the island, but one cannot land.

WEST WOODBURN

On the line of Dere Street and used as a watering hole for travellers before reaching Otterburn. Risingham Roman fort is 600 m southwest, built to guard Dere Street where it crosses the River Rede. Occupation of the fort was somewhat sporadic from its original construction in the second century until its final evacuation in the early fourth century. Turf-covered footings of later buildings are scattered in the interior. The lower portion of the Roman sculpture known as Robin of Risingham survives on

↑ **WHALTON** church

Parkhead Farm. At Low Leam, there are two bastles, one of which, at Low Cleugh, is ruinous and the other at Low Leam itself is embedded in farm buildings. All Saints Church of 1906 by Hicks and Charlewood is a quality building with fine woodwork of 1923.

The remains of Ridsdale Ironworks, established in 1836, lie 2 miles southeast—the main survival is the blowing-engine house. One mile east of Ridsdale, at Cold Law, a significant piece of public art is being installed, some 55m in height, in the form of a blade, and titled "Ascendant". It celebrates the reign of Queen Elizabeth II, the longest reigning English monarch, and also commemorates two great Northumbrian engineers, William Armstrong and Charles Parsons.

At East Woodburn, half a mile east, are two bastles, one partly built into Town Foot Farm, with a Roman altar from Risingham; there is an inscription to the local god Cocidius.

Two miles north at Corsenside is the isolated but very attractive Norman church of St Cuthbert, much rebuilt in 1810; the rectory, now a farmhouse, is dated 1686. Nearby, The Brigg and Coldtown are farmhouses based on bastles.

WHALTON

A prosperous village with an extraordinary Manor House of nineteen bays with a central archway. The manor has a complex history having arrived at its present form through the work of Sir Edwin Lutyens in 1908–9. Lutyens combined two former houses—Whalton Mansion and Old Whalton Manor (this c.1700 house had itself already been linked to three cottages by Sir Robert Lorimer in the late nineteenth century)—and the present house appears to go "on and on"! Lutyens inserted the tripartite gateway. The former circular dining room, with its domed ceiling, is said to have been the model for the Viceroy's throne room at New Delhi and has since been converted into a bedroom. The old Whalton Mansion is now a separate dwelling. Lutyens also laid out the garden.

St Mary Magdalene Church is a gem. The west tower is eleventh century, and its tall round internal arch has a distinctly Saxon feel. The nave is spacious, and the chancel has to the north the Ogle chapel with sixteenth-century armorial floor slabs of the Ogle family. The two-bay arcade between the chapel and the chancel is a delight, with a central pier carved with the fine vertical dog-toothing favoured around here. The east window is a gentle piece by Kempe (1877). Just east of the churchyard on the high verge is what appears to be a mounting-step, but which was one end of the vicar's private swing bridge. With bridge in position, the vicar was in church, and the service had begun. The fine Old Vicarage on the east side of the same sunken lane has a fourteenth-century west wing which was probably originally a pele tower.

Outside the Beresford Arms on 4 July, the bale is burnt—this was Midsummer's Day in the old Gregorian Calendar and, in this case, Whalton has not yet embraced the new-fangled Julian arrangements—there is much Morris dancing and a barbecue.

WHITFIELD

Two churches in the one rural parish. St John's is on the site of a mediaeval building which was replaced by Newton's church of 1790; it was not served well by later builders, who demolished three bays of the nave in 1859 to provide

↓ **WHITFIELD** Old Church

↑ **WHITLEY BAY** Monkseaton High School

↑ **WHITLEY BAY** St Mary's Island

stone for Holy Trinity. St John's is prettily situated in its churchyard at the top of the hill. At the foot of the hill and near Whitfield Park is Holy Trinity, a grand cruciform building in the Early English style by A. B. Higham; it is an impressive building and stands proud. Stained glass by Powell and Kempe. Whitfield Hall (1785) for the Ord family is also by Newton. Five bays with a porch of 1969—the earlier tower house is said to be at the heart, but nothing is distinguishable. Cupola Bridge is fine—2 miles north. Bastle-type houses at Westside and Monk.

WHITLEY BAY

Once Northumberland's answer to English holidaymaking: buckets, spades, and amusement arcades—this has become a demure and attractive residential resort. A symbol of the shift is the survival of the 1908–10 dome of Spanish City, but the non-survival of the Spanish City itself, which was a former fairground; it is now residential with some offices. The seaside hordes from Scotland and north England no longer descend upon Whitley Bay. The dome is by L. G. Mouchel, who also designed the new road bridge at Berwick-upon-Tweed, and the Baltic flourmill on the Tyne. The tidal St Mary's Island with its 38 m high lighthouse, at the north end of the bay, is a further landmark, with its pretty c.1800 pantiled stone cottages. Beacon House (1962), rising eleven storeys, a mile north of Spanish City behind the golf links, is by Ryder and Yates, who built impressive modernist structures at nearby Killingworth.

St Paul's Church (1864) in Park View is by Salvin—Early English, with a short octagonal spire—some good stained glass. St Edward's unmistakably Roman Catholic Church (1928) in Spanish Romanesque style with apse and squat crossing tower.

Monkseaton, slightly to the west and now merged with Whitley Bay, is the older settlement. Dating to 1106, it was originally Seton and was then granted as Monkseaton to the priory at Tynemouth. The Monkseaton Arms includes fragments of a mediaeval brewery. Two parish churches here of the 1930s: St Mary's (1930) is brick with an interior much improved by a recent reordering. St Peter's (1938), again brick, has more external style with a small apse and windows by Leonard Evetts.

Monkseaton High School, opened in 2009, was designed by Dewjo'C architects and completed by the Devereux partnership following its merger with Dewjo'C. Its daring profile is based on an oval design with triangular classrooms looking outwards. There are colourful windcatchers to avoid overdependence on air conditioning, and external shades to counter the impact of the sun.

↓ **WHITLEY BAY** Skatepark and Spanish City dome

WHITTINGHAM

Both Whittingham and Glanton, its next-door neighbour, were bypassed when Telford-style improvements were made to the Morpeth–Wooler–Coldstream road. Formerly tracking to the west, it passed the hamlet of Thropton and the then "Castle" coaching inn welcomed you to the village—these buildings are unmistakable as one approaches from the south. Whittingham Station, 1 mile to the east, was the only station on the Alnwick–Coldstream line with an island platform, still visible from the bridge over the former railway tracks.

Fourteenth-century Whittingham Tower was restored in 1845 by Lady Ravensworth, who lived in nearby Eslington Park; Eslington is a large mansion of the eighteenth century originally built for the Liddell family, set in an extensive park, through which one travels on the public highway.

The Church of St Bartholomew contains Saxon work on the south side; in 1840, the then vicar demolished the Anglo-Saxon tower. John Green, the architect vandal who demolished the tower and much of the aisles, left a deadened inheritance. Some earlier work has survived in the south arcade and transept.

A mile and a half to the east, not far from the disused station and just south of the road toward Broome Park, at Learchild, is the site of the former Roman fort of Avna which stood at the crossing of two highways, the north–south Devil's Causeway from Corbridge to Tweedmouth and the highway from Bremenium at High Rochester to the coast. The site can only be discerned from the air in crop patterns.

Callally Castle lies about 2 miles to the west. Owned by the Claverings from mediaeval times, it was bought by the Brownes in 1877. It was imaginatively divided into apartments by Kit Martin in 1987, with cottages even being built into the walls of the walled garden. Innovation, however, was not new here. It was an early example of a house having its own power station to generate electricity. The southwest angle of the south wing is a mediaeval tower, the present wing having been completed in 1707; inside there is some Elizabethan panelling. The west front has two projecting wings, and the east wing was extensively remodelled in the 1930s by Major A. H. Browne, adding a new courtyard and servants' wing. The former chapel was converted into a ballroom, which has itself been cleverly transformed into another separate apartment, with a mezzanine level. The two-storey-high drawing room on the Trollope front is the *pièce de résistance* with Chinese Chippendale-style and Gothick panels alongside marble Tuscan columns.

Lorbottle Hall, 2 miles southwest, is c.1797 with some Venetian touches in both a doorway and upper window.

WIDDRINGTON

Only one terrace of modified cottages bears witness to the old village, almost all of which disappeared during vast opencast coal mining, worked by the enormous "Big Geordie" excavator from the 1960s onwards. The twelfth-century Holy Trinity Church, raised up slightly from the main road, contains good arcading. There is a large pointed-trefoiled piscina with a smaller older pillar piscina next door to it. Of the large recesses opposite, one probably once hosted an Easter sepulchre. The inner lintel of the vestry door is a thirteenth-century cross

↓ **WHITTINGHAM** Callaly Castle, south front

↑ **WOODHORN** Colliery

slab. Earthworks to the east of the church mark the site of the former Widdrington Castle, first a tower house and later a mansion. To the east of the main road is a pleasant United Reformed Church of 1893 with a most attractive octagonal belfry and shingled spire.

WOODHORN

Woodhorn is an ancient village which has been transformed by becoming part of the Queen Elizabeth Country Park with its 40-acre lake. The former colliery has become the mining museum for northeast England. Alongside the mining exhibits there is also a collection of pictures from the Ashington Group of painters known as the "Pitmen Painters". Part of the same site hosts the Northumberland archives.

Woodhorn's history may go back as far as St Cuthbert, as it is some-times identified with Wudecestre, given to Cuthbert by King Coelfrith in 739. The attractive setting of St Mary's Church with its largely Victorian exterior offers much interest inside. The nave walls include some early-eleventh-century work, and the tower's base may be of this same time; the western bays of the arcade are from a hundred years later. The church developed over a long period, with a thirteenth-century chancel arch, and foundations from the same period; there was wholesale rebuilding in Victorian times—an earlier eleventh-century apse has been excavated, exposing two cross fragments from the same period in the chancel. Some interesting memorials. The mediaeval bell inscribed *Ave Maria* is thought to be one of the earliest surviving mediaeval bells.

There is a windmill here c.1880, perhaps the last built in Northumberland.

WOOLER

"Gateway to the Cheviots" is the soubriquet frequently applied to this "townlet" nestling snugly under the hills. There are three churches. The Parish Church of St Mary, wide and aisleless, is of 1751, with a chancel added in 1912. The west window (1903) by Percy Bacon livens the scene; the Roman Catholic Church of St Ninian (1856) lies to the north of the town; the handsome United Reformed Church on the southwest corner of the centre is originally of 1784—all worth a visit. The main street is plain but welcoming with good buildings—the Black Bull pub has an Arts and Crafts feel about it from the work of George Reavell in 1910. Loreto, next to the Roman Catholic church, was Count Horace St Paul's town house. Some masonry rubble close to the war memorial is all that remains of a sixteenth-century tower. Green Castle, three-quarters of a mile west—now just banks and ditches. Caravan sites north and south provide commerce.

Wooler Water runs through the town before joining the Till, just to the northeast; Harthope Burn is a tributary just south, leading to both Harthope and Happy Valleys. Humbleton Hill is the site of the Battle of Homildon Hill (1402), where Harry "Hotspur" Percy and the Earl of March routed the Scots.

In 1879, a Gothick-style fountain was placed at the centre of the town in memory of William Wightman, a bank official who had been instrumental in bringing piped water to the community. In 2020, a new fountain (in the form of a flower feature) was made and placed near the site of the earlier structure, which had been removed after the Second World War. The ever rarer cattle market is

↓ **WYLAM** George Stephenson's Cottage   ↘ **YEAVERING** above Saxon palace site

half a mile east of the town. On the south entry into Wooler, opposite Wooler Water, is the Ad Gefrin distillery and heritage centre.

Further along that same road and 2 miles northeast is the narrow but beautiful single-arch Weetwood Bridge, full of grace and elegance. Weetwood Hall nearby is late eighteenth century with a pyramidally roofed dovecote in the garden.

WOOLSINGTON

An ancient village, first appearing in records in 1204, Woolsington is now known chiefly for Newcastle Airport, which grew out of a Second World War RAF base which itself replaced an earlier pre-war civilian airfield. Contemporary Metro station (1991). Woolsington Hall includes a mixture of styles dating from the seventeenth, eighteenth and nineteenth centuries—the gate piers on the Ponteland Road are early nineteenth century; the orangery is dated 1797. The Hall is in a poor state at the time of writing having suffered from a severe fire in 2015. Eighteenth-century Bullocks Steads makes an interesting ensemble of farm buildings. Trees in Middle Drive, 1968 modernist residence by Gordon Yates for his family.

WOOPERTON

Almost overwhelmed by a vast sawmill and woodyard which envelop another fine station on the former Alnwick–Cornhill line. Railings surround a memorial to the Battle of Hedgeley Moor (1464) just south, where the Percy leader of the Lancastrians was slain. Wooperton Hall nearby.

WYLAM

Here, at the end of the former horse-drawn wagonway to Newburn, is the small cottage where George Stephenson spent his childhood. The core of Wylam Hall is mediaeval with a tunnel-vaulted ground floor—otherwise eighteenth-century work and nineteenth-century Gothic. William Hedley of *Puffing Billy* fame is said to have used the drive to test his steam engines going uphill without rack and pinion! St Oswin's Church is a fine building by R. J. Johnson with a large south tower which also forms a transept—the perpendicular detail makes an excellent statement in Victorian Gothic.

Wylam Station, across the river, is very picturesque with its red-painted footbridge and signal gantry carrying the signal box on high—one of the earliest railway stations still in operation. The West Wylam railway bridge (1876), now disused, is a steel-arched structure, clearly an early model for Newcastle's iconic Tyne Bridge. The road bridge of 1836 started life as a road and rail bridge—originally wooden, it was replaced in 1897 by a steel superstructure which was again replaced by Dorman Long in 1946.

The pumping station 1 mile west is quite a statement. It is a Cornish pumping-engine house of 1874 right on the bank of the Tyne. More was added in 1885, 1894 and finally, new buildings for electric pumps in 1918 and 1950. Hopefully new use will be found for the buildings which looked a little sad at the time of writing.

YEAVERING

Yeavering Bell with its double summit is well worth the ascent, firstly to gain some notion of the extent of the former "Iron Age town". It is the largest prehistoric camp in the county, enclosed by a massive wall of rubble along the shoulders of the hill. Discovered objects on the site suggest that it was inhabited from the Iron Age through to the fourth century AD.

Secondly, from the summits of Yeavering Bell, one has splendid views over the flood plain of the River Glen where in 1949 aerial surveys revealed (via cropmarks) the plan of the seventh-century summer palace of King Edwin, Ad Gefrin. There is a small memorial by the roadside marking this. It was here that Edwin's priest described human life to be "as brief as a sparrow's flight", as he watched a bird make its journey through the great hall and out of the opposite window. Here too, Paulinus is said to have baptized hundreds of people in the nearby River Glen. The ubiquitous Alnwick–Coldstream railway runs close by.

GLOSSARY

Words within entries set in bold type are themselves defined elsewhere.

aisle   in a church, either the areas either side of the **nave**, separated from it by pillars, or a passage running between the rows of seats

ambo   raised stand or lectern for proclamation of the Gospel in a church

ambulatory   usually at the far east end of a church enabling people to walk around the **retro-choir**

apse   a rounded recess with a domed roof, often situated at the end of the **choir**, **aisles** or **chancel** of a church

apsidal   semi-circular termination to a building, often of a **chancel** or **presbytery**

arcading   decoration by means of a series of arches

Augustinian   monks following the Rule of St Augustine of Hippo

baptistry   separate building or area within a church containing the font

barbican   an outer defence or fortified gatehouse

barrel vault   a vault with a semi-cylindrical roof

basilica   a rectangular hall with two rows of columns and an **apse** at the end, based on the Roman hall for the Prefect

Benedictine   monks following the Rule of St Benedict

boss   ornament at intersection of arches of a **rib vault**

buttress   a structure built against a wall to support it; a **flying buttress** is a later development with an arm resting upon a half arch

Carmelite   friars following the Rule of Our Lady of Mount Carmel

cartouche   ornamentation in scroll form

chancel   the part of a church used by clergy and choir, to the east of the **nave** and **transepts**

chantry   a small chapel and originally endowed to pay a priest to pray for departed relatives

chapter house   a building, often separate, used for meetings of a cathedral or monastic chapter

choir or **quire**   that part of a church where the church choir and clergy sit

Cistercian   monks following a reformed development of the Benedictine order, founded at Cîteaux in France in the late eleventh century

clerestory   the upper part of a large church, above the level of the roofs of the aisles, where windows let light into the central parts of the church

cloisters   covered passages connecting the church to other parts of a monastery

close   the enclosed area around a cathedral

Cluniac   monks of that branch of the Benedictine order founded at Cluny in France in the early tenth century

crenellation/crenellating   addition of defensive features to architecture viz. battlement, turrets etc.

crossing   the part of a cathedral where the **nave** intersects with the **transepts**

crenellated (crenelated)   decorated with battlementing or similar defensive structures

crypt   a subterranean cell, chapel or chamber that is usually vaulted

curtilage   area of land attached to a building

Curvilinear   style of window design of the late **Decorated** period featuring flowing patterns of **tracery**

Decorated   architectural period (1307–77) which was characterized by the use of wider windows, projecting **buttresses**, tall pinnacles, and the rapid development of window **tracery** through the **Geometric** and **Curvilinear** styles

dogtooth   ornamenting on **Romanesque** arches

Dominican   friars of the Order of Preachers following the Rule of St Dominic

dorter   a monastic dormitory

downdraft kiln   kiln designed to be of same heat throughout

Early English (EE)   architecture of the earliest phase of the **Gothic** period

erratics   rock formations from very different strata scattered within the landscape

fan-vaulting   a highly decorative and complex type of vaulting of the later **Gothic** period

feretory   a shrine for relics used in procession

flèche   a slim spire that rises from the point at which the **nave** and **transepts** intersect

flying buttress   a prop built out from a pier or other support

and supporting the main structure—see also **buttress**

Franciscan   friars following the Rule of St Francis of Assisi

front   in architecture, any side of a building, usually the one where the entrance is sited

Geometric   a style of window design used in the early **Decorated** period centring on geometric shapes used mainly in the fourteenth century. It later developed into the more flowing **Curvilinear** style

Gothic   architectural style prevalent in Western Europe from the twelfth to fifteenth centuries. It is characterized by the use of pointed windows and arcading.

Gothick   often used of Strawberry Hill Gothick— eighteenth and early nineteenth century early "dainty" **Gothic** revival

grisaille   a particular method of decorative painting on walls or ceilings or plain grey windows

hostry   equivalent to "hostelry" and related to "hospital" and "hotel", the word basically signifies a place where guests could stay or be welcomed

lancet window   high, narrow window with a pointed apex

lierne   rib vaulting of the **Gothic** period in which the ribs cross each other

locutory   part of a monastery set apart for meeting and conversation

misericord   a tip-up seat in a church with a projecting shelf on the underside, designed to support those standing at prayer for long periods

narthex   a vestibule between the cathedral entrance and the **nave**

nave   the main part of a church, running from the main door to the **choir** in a west–east direction

niche   a shallow recess in a wall for displaying a statue or other ornament

pant   drinking fountain

pantile   curved orange earthenware roof tile

pele   small fortified keep or tower house

Perpendicular   architectural style (1377–1485), the latest phase of **Gothic**, when the designs of the **Decorated** period developed into longer, taller and more linear forms

pier   in architecture, a solid masonry support which sustains vertical pressure

porte-cochère   open coach porch

Premonstratensian   monastic order of regular canons, named after Prémontré in France

presbytery   the part of a church beyond the **choir** at the east end, where only the clergy would enter

pulpitum   a large stone or wooden screen or gallery between the **nave** and the **choir**

quatrefoil   in architecture, an ornament in the form of a ring of four leaves or petals

quire   *see* **choir**

quoin   substantial stone often marking the external corner of a building

recusant   Roman Catholic who, following the Reformation, refused to worship with the Church of England

refectory   the dining-room of a monastery

reliquary   a small box or shrine for holy relics (the mortal remains of saints)

reredos   a decorative screen or painting behind the altar

retable   either a shelf for ornaments or a frame for decorative panels, found behind the altar of a church

retro-choir or **retro-quire**   within a church, the area behind the high altar

rib vault   a vault built with "ribs" or arches which support the roof

rococo   highly ornamental baroque architecture

Romanesque   prevalent style of buildings erected in Europe between Roman times and the rise of **Gothic** style in the twelfth century

staithe   port or port jetty for loading of heavy commodities, frequently for coal

Telford road   new direct route, often metalled and built by Thomas Telford or a contemporary in the late eighteenth/early nineteenth century

tracery   ornamental stonework in **Gothic** windows

transept   the part of a cruciform church which crosses the **nave** in a north–south direction; also each of its two arms (i.e. the north and south **transepts**)

Transitional   architecture of the period c.1145–c.1190 when there was a gradual transition from **Romanesque** to Early **Gothick**

tribune gallery   a raised gallery, sometimes styled **triforium** as below

triforium   a gallery or arcade in the wall situated over the arches at the sides of the **nave** and **choir**

turret   a small tower which forms part of the structure of a larger building

tympanum   the space between door lintel and arch

undercroft   a crypt or vault below the floor of a church

wagonway   early trackway, often running on stone paving or cast-iron brackets, forerunner of railways

↑ **ALNWICK** Castle, Ducal Coach

↓ **ALNWICK** Castle, Keep

↑ **BERWICK** aerial view

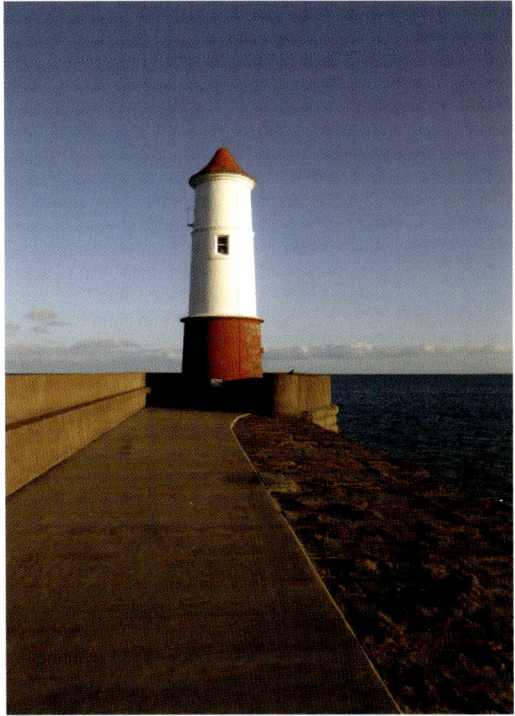

↓ **BERWICK** Barracks, Riding the Bounds

↓ **BERWICK** Lighthouse at the end of the pier

↑ **BERWICK** hay harvest

← **BEWICK** Old Bewick Church
↓ **BLANCHLAND** Post Office
→ Breamish Valley

← **BYKER** Wall

→ **BYRNESS** Church, Memorial Window To
Those Lost In Building Catcleugh Dam

↓ **FORD** Lady Waterford Hall, mural by Lady Waterford

↑ **HALTWHISTLE** water tank at the station

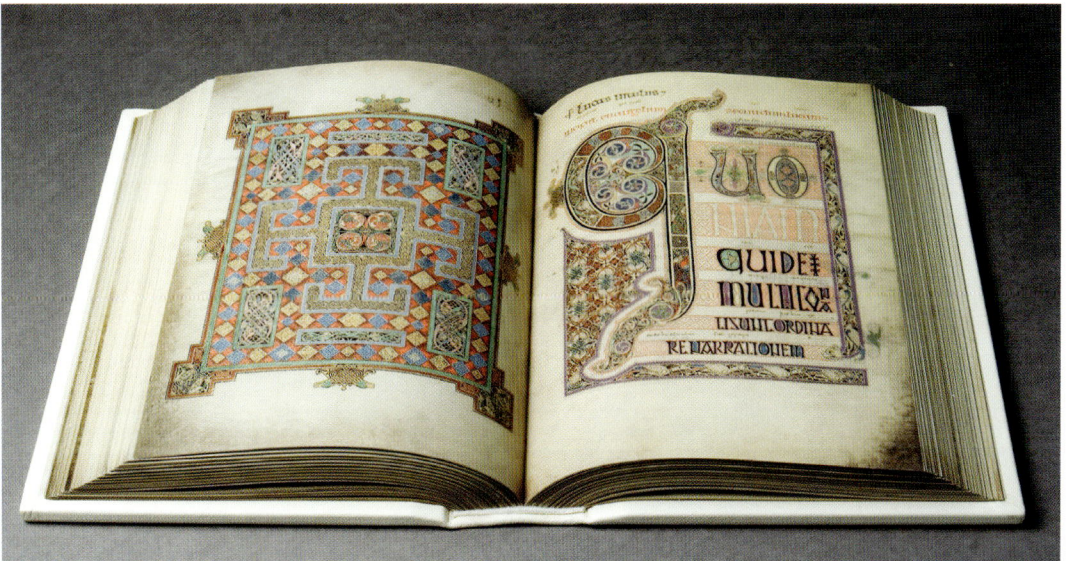

↓ **LINDISFARNE** St Aidan Statue

↓ **LINDISFARNE** Castle

↓ **LINDISFARNE** Priory, The Rainbow Arch

↓ **NEWCASTLE** Cathedral, spire and cityscape

↓ **NEWCASTLE** Crown Spire

↑ J. W. M. Turner, **NORHAM** Castle

→ **SCREMERSTON** harvesting

← Tyne Estuary, light tower at the end of South Pier
↓ **WALLINGTON** Hall, mural in the central atrium
→ Mineworkers' banner for **WEST SLEEKBURN**
↘ Model of Stephenson's Rocket

↑ **WYLAM** Gantry and signal box

↑ Hadrian's Wall, Sycamore Gap

BIBLIOGRAPHY

General Background

Beckensall, Stan, *Northumberland: The Power of Place* (Stroud: Tempos, 2001).

Bede, *Ecclesiastical History of the English People* (Harmondsworth: Penguin Classics, 1990).

Bowden, Charles, *The Last Shepherds* (London: Granada, 2005).

Dixon, David Dippie, *Upper Coquetdale* (Newcastle: Frank Graham, 1974).

Graham, Frank, *Northumbria's Lordly Strand* (Newcastle: Frank Graham, 1974).

Grant, Hester, *The Good Sharps* (London: Chatto and Windus, 2020).

Jackson, Dan, *The Northumbrians* (London: Hurst, 2019).

Jones, David and Coquetdale Community Archaeology, *The Old Tracks through the Cheviots* (Newcastle: Northern Heritage, 2017).

Moffat, Alistair, *The Reivers* (Edinburgh: Birlinn, 2017).

Moffat, Alistair, *The Wall* (Edinburgh: Birlinn, 2017).

Moffat, Alistair, *To the Island of Tides* (Edinburgh: Canongate, 2019).

Percy, Ralph, Duke of Northumberland, *Lions of the North* (London: Scala, 2019).

Pevsner, Nikolaus and Richmond, Ian, *The Buildings of England: Northumberland* (New Haven and London: Yale University Press. 2002).

Ridley, Nancy, *Portrait of Northumberland* (London: Robert Hale, 1973).

Sharp, Thomas, *The Shell Guide to Northumberland* (London: Faber, 1969).

Art and literature

Chaplin, Sid, *The Watchers and the Watched* (Newcastle: Flambard Press, [1962] 2004).

Chronin, A. J., *The Stars Look Down* (London: Gollancz, [1937] 2013).

Feaver, William, *The Pitmen Painters* (London: Chatto and Windus, 1988).

Fox, Barbara, *Is the Vicar in, Pet?* (London: Sphere, 2014).

Hall, Marshall, *The Artists of Northumbria* (Bristol: Art Dictionaries, 2005).

McCullough-Thew, Linda, *A Tune for Bears to Dance to: A Childhood* (Bridge Studios, 1992).

McManners, Robert and Wales, Gillian, *Shafts of Light: Mining Art in the Great Northern Coalfield* (Newcastle: Gemini, 2002).

Scott, Walter, *Minstrelsy of the Borders*, and novels.

Tiernan, Katharine, *Cuthbert of Farne* (Durham: Sacristy Press, 2019).

Tiernan, Katharine, *Place of Repose* (Durham: Sacristy Press, 2020).

Tiernan, Katharine, *A New Heaven and a New Earth* (Durham: Sacristy Press, 2020).

Uglow, Jenny, *Nature's Engraver: A Life of Thomas Bewick* (London: Faber, 2007).

Villar, Diana, *John Wilson Carmichael 1799–1868* (London: Carmichael and Sweet, 1995).

Wilson, James Mackay, *Tales of the Borders*, see <https://www.wilsonstales.co.uk/>.

INDEX OF PLACES

INDEX OF PEOPLE AND OTHER SUBJECTS

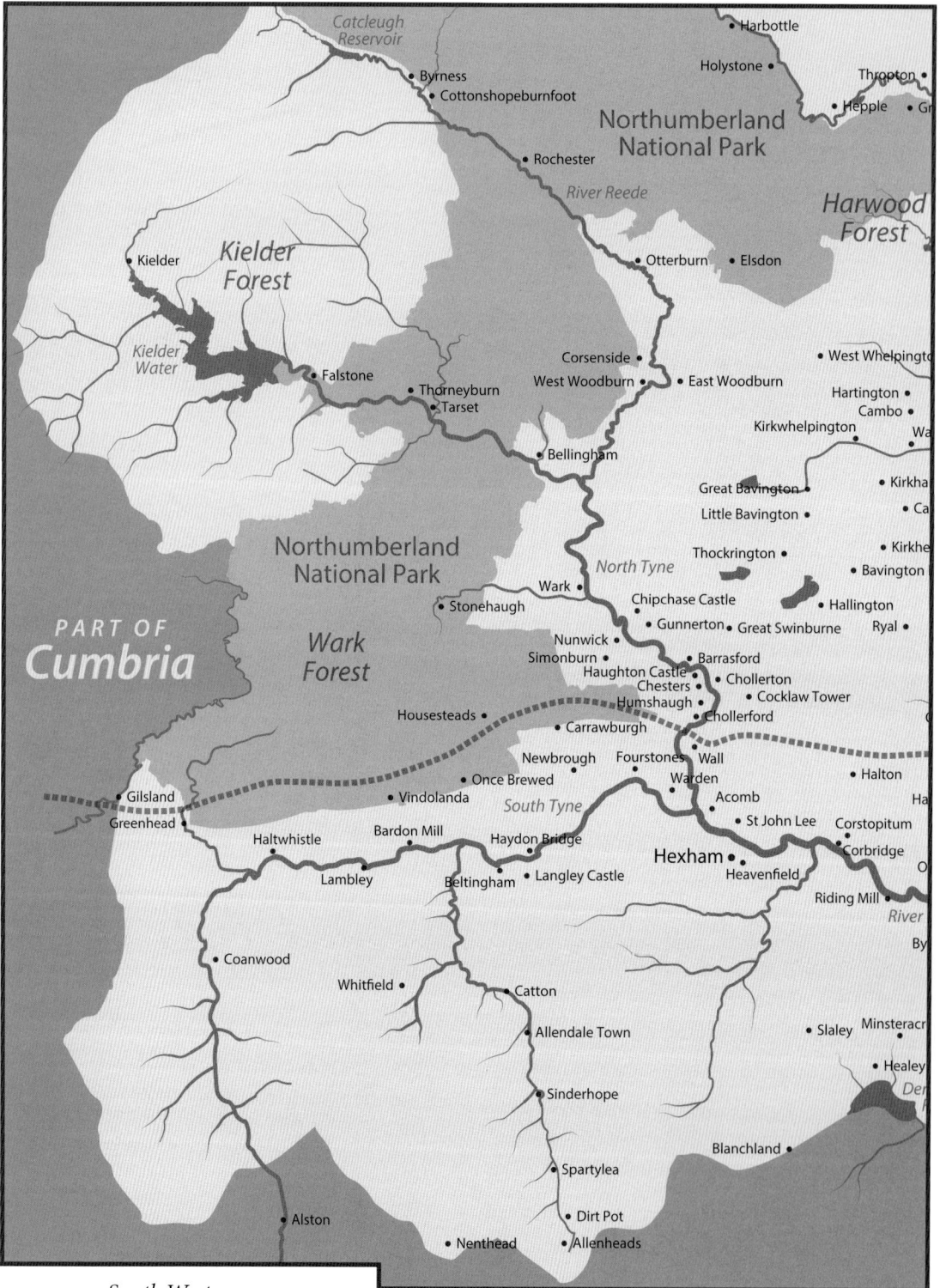

Catcleugh
Reservoir

• Harbottle

Holystone •

Thropton
• Byrness
• Hepple
• Cottonshopeburnfoot
• Gr

Northumberland
National Park

Harwood
Forest

• Rochester

River Reede

Kielder
Forest

• Kielder

Otterburn • Elsdon •

Kielder
Water
• West Whelpingto

Corsenside •

Hartington •

• Falstone
West Woodburn • • East Woodburn
Cambo •

• Thorneyburn
Kirkwhelpington

• Tarset

Great Bavington •
• Kirkha

• Bellingham
Little Bavington •
• Ca

Northumberland
National Park
Thockrington •
• Kirkhe
• Bavington

North Tyne
• Hallington

Wark •
Ryal •

• Stonehaugh
Chipchase Castle •

Wark
Forest
• Gunnerton Great Swinburne

Nunwick •
Barrasford •

Simonburn •
• Chollerton

PART OF
Haughton Castle
Cumbria
Chesters • Cocklaw Tower

Humshaugh •
• Chollerford

Housesteads •
• Carrawburgh
Wall

Newbrough • Fourstones •
• Halton

Once Brewed •
Warden •

• Gilsland
• Vindolanda
South Tyne
Acomb •

Greenhead
• St John Lee Corstopitum

Haltwhistle •
Bardon Mill • Haydon Bridge •
• Corbridge

Hexham •
O

Heavenfield •

Lambley •
Beltingham • • Langley Castle
Riding Mill •

River

By

• Coanwood

Whitfield •
• Catton
Slaley • Minsteracr

Allendale Town •
• Healey

Der

• Sinderhope

• Spartylea
Blanchland •

• Dirt Pot

• Alston
• Nenthead • Allenheads

South West
NORTHUMBERLAND

NOT TO SCALE

Cartington •   Swarland •   Guyzance •   **Amble**   Coquet Island

Thropton •   Rothbury •   Whitton   Brainshaugh •   Hauxley •

Hepple •   Great Tosson •   Longframlington   Felton •   Acklington •   North Togston •

Brinkburn Priory   Eshott •

Harwood Forest

Longhorsley •   Druridge Bay •

Nunnykirk •   Tritlington •   Widdrington •

Netherwitton •   Ulgham •   Cresswell •

Cockle Park   Ellington •

Hebron •   Longhirst •

West Whelpington •   Pegswood •   Woodhorn •

Hartington •   Hartburn •   Mitford •   *River Wansbeck*   Ashington •   Newbiggin-by-the-Sea

Cambo •   West Sleekburn •

...ington •   Wallington •   **Morpeth**   Stakeford •

Bothal •   Sheepwash •

Meldon •   *North Sea*

Kirkharle •   Whalton •   Hepscott •

Capheaton •   Bedlington •

Kirkheaton •   Belsay •   Ogle •   Stannington •   *River Blyth*   **Blyth** •

Bavington Hall •   Cramlington •   Northumberlandia •

Hallington •   Ingoe •   Blagdon •   New Hartley •   Seaton Sluice •

...urne   Ryal •   Seaton Delaval •

Matfen •   Stamfordham •   Seaton Burn •   West Backworth •

Dinnington •   Seghill •   **Whitley Bay** •

...Tower   Hawkwell •   Wide Open •   Backworth •   Earsdon •   Monkseaton •

Ouston Airfield •   Ponteland •   Killingworth •   Cullercoats •

Darras Hall •   Woolsington •   **Tynemouth** •

Halton •   Horsley •   Heddon-on-the-Wall •   Gosforth •   **Newcastle**   North Shields •

Jesmond •   Willington •

Harlow Hill •   Rudchester •   Houghton •   Denton •   Wallsend •   Segedunum •   **South Shields**

Corstopitum •   Wylam •   Newburn •   Condercum •   Byker •

Ovington •   Lemington •   Walker •

Corbridge •   Ovingham •   Prudhoe •   Scotswood •   Elswick •   Stockbridge •

Cherryburn •   Benwell •

Riding Mill •   Eltingham •   Gateshead

River Tyne   Bellasis •

Bywell •   Stocksfield

PART OF Tyne and Wear

Hedley-on-the-Hill •

Slaley   Minsteracres •

Shotley •   Whittonstall •

Healey •   Snod's Edge •

Derwent Reservoir

PART OF County Durham

NOT TO SCALE

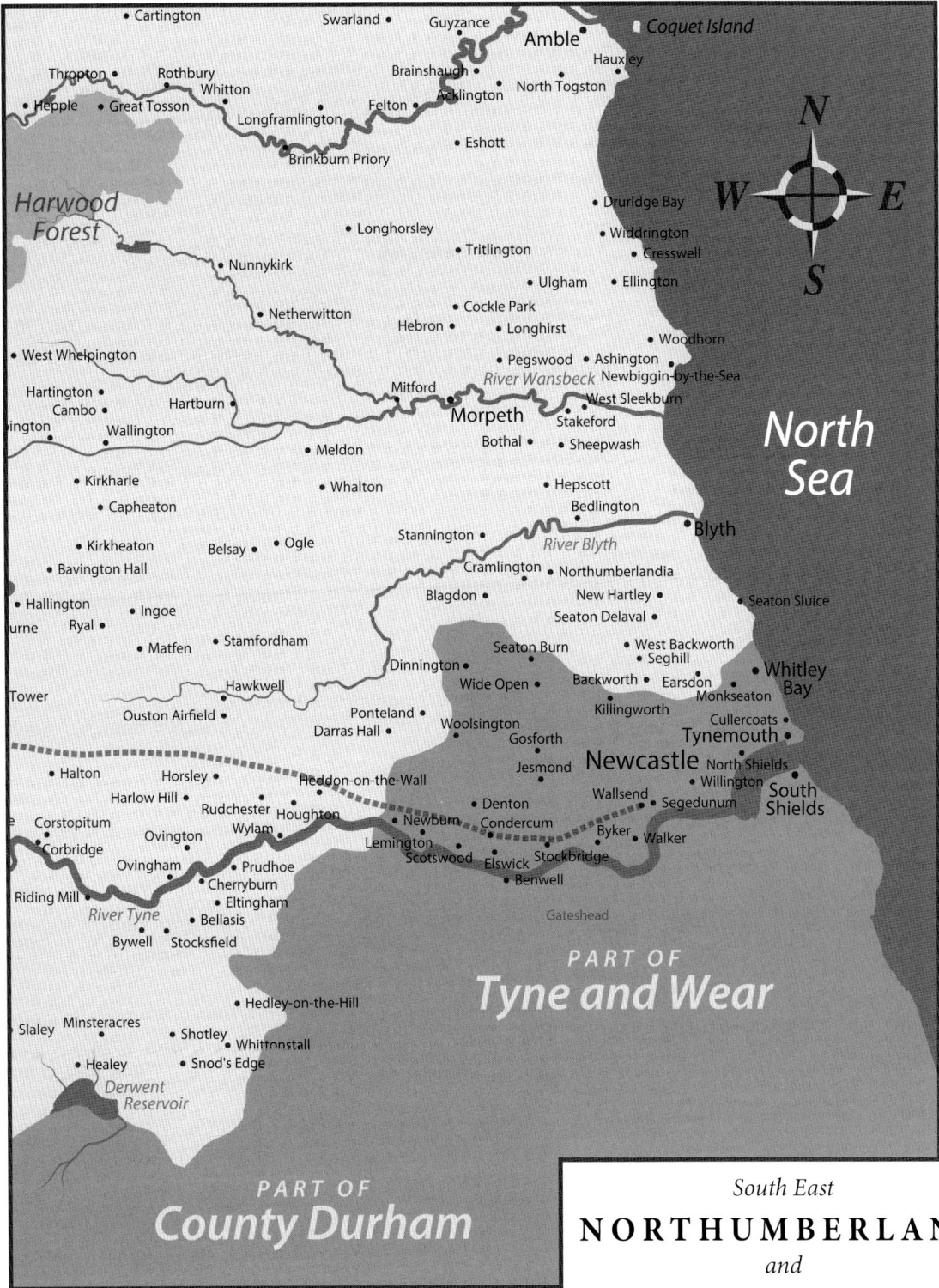

South East
NORTHUMBERLAND
and
NEWCASTLE
UPON-TYNE

North & Mid-
NORTHUMBERLAND

NOT TO SCALE

PART OF
Scotland

Berwick-upon-Tweed

Spittal
Ord
Tweedmouth

Horncliffe

Scremerston

River Tweed

Norham

Cheswick

Goswick

Allerdean
Duddo
Ancroft

Haggerston

Lindisfarne

Holy Island

Beal

Tilmouth
Heaton

Lowick

Coldstream

Cornhill-on-Tweed
Etal

Wark-on-Tweed
Branxton

Crookham
Ford

Carham
Sunilaws

Budle
Bamburgh

Belford
Spindlestone

Howtel
Ewart

Outchester

Thornington
Milfield

Seahouses

Mindrum
Pawston
Kilham

Doddington

Lucker

North Sunderland

Kirknewton
Coupland

Yeavering

Beadnell

wn Yetholm

Hethpool

Wooler
Chatton

Twizell
Warenford

Tughall

Northumberland
National Park

Chillingham

Ellingham

Low Newton

Middleton
Lilburn

Embleton

Ilderton

Old Bewick

North Charlton

Dunstanburgh

Roddam

Wooperton

Rock
Craster

Brandon

Eglingham

Rennington
Howick

Powburn
Hedgeley
Shipley

Longhoughton

Ingram
Branton

Heiferlaw Tower
Denwick
Boulmer

Glanton

Alnwick
River Aln

Whittingham

Lemmington

Lesbury

Alnham

Callaly
Edlingham

Alnmouth

Chew Green

Biddlestone

Netherton

Shilbottle

River Coquet

Alwinton

Lorbottle

Newton-on-the-Moor
Swarland

Warkworth

Harbottle

Cartington

Guyzance

Coquet Islan

Holystone

Amble

Byrness
Cottonshopeburnfoot

Thropton
Rothbury
Whitton

Brainshaugh
Acklington

Hauxley
North Togston

Rochester

Hepple
Great Tosson

Felton

Longframlington

Eshott

Brinkburn Priory

River Reede

Harwood
Forest

Druridge Bay

Longhorsley

Widdrington

Tritlington

Cresswe

Otterburn
Elsdon

Nunnykirk

Ulgham
Ellington

Netherwitton

Cockle Park

Hebron
Longhirst

Woodhorn

Corsenside
West Whelpington

Pegswood
Ashington

West Woodburn
East Woodburn

Hartington
Cambo
Hartburn

Mitford
River Wansbeck
Newbiggin-by-the-Sea

Thorneyburn
Tarset

Kirkwhelpington
Wallington

Morpeth
West Sleekburn

Stakeford

Bellingham

Meldon

Bothal
Sheepwash

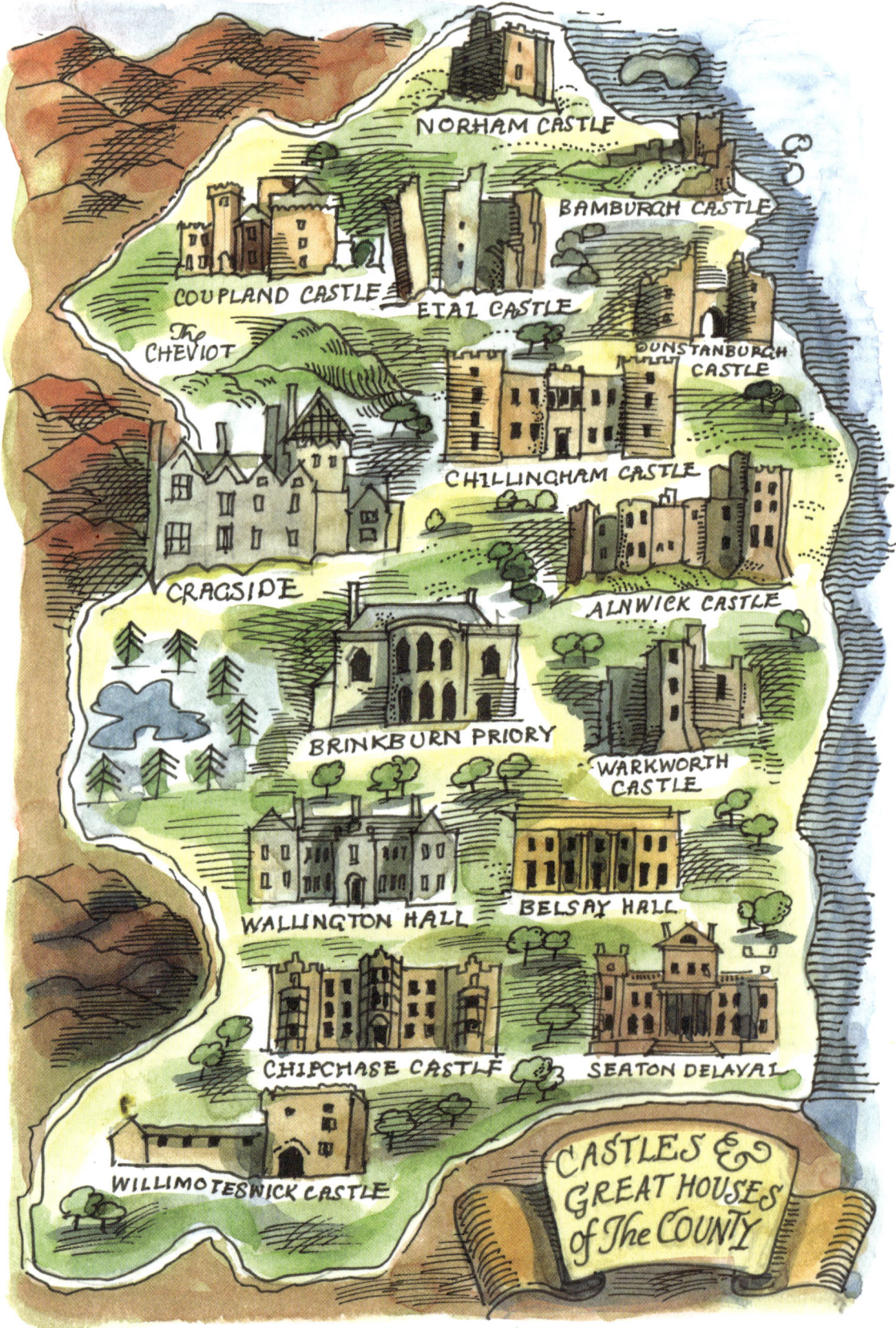

NORHAM CASTLE

BAMBURGH CASTLE

COUPLAND CASTLE

ETAL CASTLE

The CHEVIOT

DUNSTANBURGH CASTLE

CHILLINGHAM CASTLE

CRAGSIDE

ALNWICK CASTLE

BRINKBURN PRIORY

WARKWORTH CASTLE

WALLINGTON HALL

BELSAY HALL

CHIPCHASE CASTLE

SEATON DELAVAL

WILLIMOTESWICK CASTLE

CASTLES & GREAT HOUSES of The COUNTY